Sounds and society

Music and society
Series editors   Pete Martin and Tia DeNora

Music and Society aims to bridge the gap between music scholarship and
the human sciences. A deliberately eclectic series, its authors are nevertheless united by the contention that music is a social product, social
resource, and social practice. As such it is not autonomous but is created
and performed by real people in particular times and places; in doing so
they reveal much about themselves and their societies.

In contrast to the established academic discourse, Music and Society is
concerned with all forms of music, and seeks to encourage the scholarly
analysis of both 'popular' styles and those which have for too long been
marginalised by that discourse – folk and ethnic traditions, music by and
for women, jazz, rock, rap, reggae, muzak and so on. These sounds are
vital ingredients in the contemporary cultural mix, and their neglect by
serious scholars itself tells us much about the social and cultural stratification of our society.

The time is right to take a fresh look at music and its effects, as today's
music resonates with the consequences of cultural globalisation and the
transformations wrought by new electronic media, and as past styles are
reinvented in the light of present concerns. There is, too, a tremendous
upsurge of interest in cultural analysis. Music and Society does not promote a particular school of thought, but aims to provide a forum for
debate; in doing so, the titles in the series bring music back into the heart
of socio-cultural analysis.

Further titles are in preparation

Peter J. Martin

Sounds and society
Themes in the sociology of music

Manchester University Press

Manchester and New York

Distributed exclusively in the USA and Canada by St. Martin's Press

Copyright © Peter J. Martin 1995

Published by Manchester University Press
Oxford Road, Manchester M13 9NR, UK
and Room 400, 175 Fifth Avenue,
New York, NY 10010, USA

Distributed exclusively in the USA and Canada
by St. Martin's Press, Inc.,
175 Fifth Avenue, New York, NY 10010, USA

British Library cataloguing in publication data
A catalogue record for this book is available from the British Library

Library of Congress cataloging in publication data
Martin, Peter J. 1947–
    Sounds and society: themes in the sociology of music/Peter J.
Martin.
        p. cm. — (Music and society)
    ISBN 0–7190–3223–7 (hardback)
    1. Music and society. I. Title. II > Series.
    ML3795.M188 1995
    306,4'84—dc20 94–37797

ISBN 0 7190 3224 5 paperback

Reprinted in paperback in 1996

Typeset in Great Britain
by Northern Phototypesetting Co Ltd, Bolton
Printed in Great Britain
by Biddles Ltd, Guildford and King's Lynn

Contents

All music is folk music – I ain't never heard no horse singin'.

attributed to Louis Armstrong (among others)

Preface

The subtitle of this book should be taken seriously, for in it I am concerned to explore just some of the ways in which, I believe, distinctively sociological ideas can make a useful contribution to our understanding of music. In other words, this is not intended as a comprehensive sociology of music; given the present, rather inchoate, state of the field such an attempt would be both premature and unduly didactic. This may seem a somewhat perverse position, given the long availability to the English-speaking reader of such texts as Adorno's *Introduction to the Sociology of Music* (1962), Silbermann's *Sociology of Music* (1963) and Supicic's more recent *Music in Society: A Guide to the Sociology of Music* (1987). However, despite the undoubted value of each of these rather disparate texts, it is my contention that none of them can stand as an authoritative basis for the sociologically informed study of music.

Silbermann's approach, for example, derives from a position which would nowadays be widely rejected as empiricist, or even as an example of 'naive' positivism. His concern, he writes, is with the 'structural elements of the musical world', and he holds that the sociology of music must adhere to the same 'fundamental propositions' as general sociology: 'observation of facts, generalizations based on the examination of these facts, and the construction of explanatory theories on that basis' (1963: 14, 48). As is well known, it was precisely this sort of analysis that Adorno – among many others – was determined to attack as pseudo-science, as ideology masquerading as objectivity. Yet, as I argue in Chapter 3, Adorno's own contribution must ultimately be regarded as grounded on certain philosophical, or aesthetic, presuppositions rather than recognisably sociological ones. Moreover, and in my view equally disabling, all three authors,

steeped in the European intellectual tradition, are concerned overwhelmingly with European 'art' music; that is, far from being concerned with music in societies, they limit their scope to what is in
fact *one* of the traditions of music-making in the western world,
which, for all its prestige and cultural authority, is not and never has
been the music of the majority of the people. Moreover, the very
uniqueness of western 'classical' music, which these authors both
acknowledge and celebrate, means that their analyses, however
insightful, have little to tell us about other cultures, times, and places
– in other words, about most music in most societies.

For Supicic, indeed, the 'lack of education or disposition toward
a highly cultured music in the masses' were 'problems' to be resolved
through the work of sociologists, psychologists, and the formulation
of a 'proper cultural and educational policy' (1987: 231). Adorno, as
is well known, subscribed to Schoenberg's dictum that 'If it is art it
is not for all, and if it is for all, it is not art' and – in so far as he
paid any attention to it – was dismissive of 'popular music', regarding it as above all a commodity which functioned to adjust people
to the 'mechanisms of present-day life' (1990: 311–12). In the present
context, and, I suggest, for sociologists generally, the point is not to
join the partisans on one or other side of the 'mass culture' debate,
nor to attempt to formulate yet another definition of 'art', but to
regard such debates and aesthetic conflicts as themselves the topic
for investigation. Adorno's work, therefore, is to be seen not as neutral or detached in a scholarly way but as a polemic which has served
to add authority and intellectual respectability to one tradition of
musical modernism, and which has contributed to the lowly status
of other forms of musical expression. For the sociologists, terms such
as 'art' and the 'masses' are not concepts whose validity must go
unquestioned but are rather to be understood as rhetorical devices,
inviting us to see the world in particular ways (and not others). So,
despite the sophistication and erudition of Adorno's aesthetic theory,
his claim that it is the business of the sociology of music to make
aesthetic judgements must be disputed. The implication, of course,
is that neither the defenders of the musical hierarchy nor those who
challenge them by championing popular forms are to be regarded as
having access to the truth of the matter. From a sociological point
of view they are all contenders in a perpetual contest for cultural
legitimacy, all making claims on behalf of, or against, particular
ways of doing things. This sort of approach has lately been discussed

by some of those seeking to develop the theory of culture, especially since the renewal of interest in the works of Antonio Gramsci; in this as in other matters, however, the cultural theorists have arrived rather late in the day, often unfamiliar with basic sociological texts. There is, for example, a wealth of insight into the politics of cultural forms in the work of Max Weber, who was himself adamant that aesthetic value-judgements and sociological analysis must be clearly separated (Freund, 1968: 267).

Nevertheless, it is the rise of interest in cultural studies generally which has allowed the serious analysis of popular music, long overdue, to flourish. Not that the hegemony of western classical music has been subverted: even in Christopher Norris's collection of essays on *Music and the Politics of Culture*, which sets out to view music as a 'field of competing social forces' (1989: 10), ten out of thirteen contributors are concerned with composed music of the western art-music tradition. And, perhaps most remarkably, Edward Said – who has done as much as any modern writer to put the parameters of western thought back into a broader cultural context – is exclusively concerned with this tradition in *Musical Elaborations* (1992). But at least figures like Norris and Said are aware, as some of their predecessors were not, that western 'classical' music is neither the sonic form of natural forces, nor a universal language, nor the epitome of human creativity, nor the music to which all cultures aspire. It is indeed a rich and elaborately developed tradition, but that development owes much to a number of significant social processes, not least the gradual release of music from the requirement that it should be functional in some way or another, thus establishing the conditions under which it could become, as Adorno put it, an 'autonomous art'. It is through social processes, too, that the 'classical' tradition has become established as dominant in the hierarchy of musical styles – the economic, political and cultural power of its patrons and prose-lytisers investing it with authority and legitimacy.

Given the cultural predominance – one is tempted to call it hege-mony – of the 'classical' tradition, the neglect of 'popular' forms by scholars is understandable, if not excusable from a sociological point of view. Moreover, to the orthodox musicologist just as to the devo-tee of Beethoven, Mahler, or Stravinsky, much popular music does indeed sound simple, predictable and repetitive. However, as Adorno himself insisted, 'the difference and between the spheres cannot be adequately expressed in terms of complexity and simplicity' (1990:

305) The textures, timbres and rhythms and devices of some of the 'popular' styles, as John Shepherd (1991) has emphasised, simply cannot be reconciled with the conventions of 'classical' music. Moreover, some performers in the non-classical spheres, notably jazz, play music of a complexity approached only by the serious avant-garde, and which 'makes sense' only when heard in different ways, using different criteria of evaluation. Even when music is simple and banal, however, it is not therefore devoid of interest or importance; indeed, such music, and the social practices in which it is embedded, may be of greater interest to the sociologist than to the musicologist.

So one reason for the unsatisfactory state of the sociology of music is the virtual hegemony of the 'classical' music tradition. Another, although related, reason is the somewhat partial views of those often quite eminent sociologists and social theorists who have written about music. In fact there are quite a few distinguished contributors to the field: Herbert Spencer, Georg Simmel, Ernst Bloch, T. W. Adorno, Norbert Elias, Max Weber and Alfred Schütz, among others. Despite their efforts, however, no very coherent sociological perspective on music has emerged, partly owing to their preoccupation with the 'classical' tradition, but perhaps more importantly because each has tended to see music in the light of his own particular theoretical concerns, which are not easily reconciled. Thus, for example, Elias's discussion of Mozart (1993) places him in the context of the general 'civilising process', while Weber (1958) looks at music as an aspect of 'rationalisation' in the western world, and Schütz (1971) argues that it can reveal the fundamental processes of human communication. Both Spencer and Simmel were participants in a somewhat futile debate about the origins of music (initiated by Darwin's view that musical communication preceded speech in humans, being a development of mating calls) (Etzkorn, 1964), while Bloch's remarks give little encouragement to sociological thinking, emphasising the independence of music from 'external factors' and arguing that the work of each 'great master' is autonomous. 'Beethoven', declared Bloch, 'evolves solely from within himself' (1985: 9).

By contrast, the position adopted in this book is that many of the ideas and concepts which have been developed in general sociological discourse can be employed in ways which enhance our understanding of music and of the social contexts in which it is created, performed and heard. Some of these ideas, and their relevance for music, are discussed in general terms in Chapter 1, followed by a consideration in Chapter 2 of the question of musical meaning; it is argued that a sociological perspective not only avoids some of the difficulties of established approaches to this topic but can reformulate the issues in fruitful ways, moving away from a concern with the deciphering of texts and concentrating on the social processes through which meanings are constituted and sustained. Another fundamental matter is taken up in Chapters 3 and 4, where we examine the idea that the form and character of music somehow reflect – or echo – the nature of the society in which it is produced. This is done first through a discussion of Adorno's views on the relationship between music and society, and then (in Chapter 4) by considering certain more recent attempts to demonstrate correspondences between musical and social structures.

Despite the widespread acceptance of the idea that there is some sort of link between forms of music and forms of society – and the fact that this notion is itself a fundamentally 'sociological' one – I argue that efforts to specify the connection in a theoretically adequate way have been largely unsuccessful. Indeed, the difficulties which are encountered in this context – notably an ambivalence over the nature of musical meaning and a tendency to reify social structures – are characteristic of 'structural' sociological perspectives in general; thus in Chapter 5 an alternative approach, drawing on the 'interpretive' tradition and in particular Howard Becker's view of social organisation as collective action, is outlined. This perspective serves also to reorient the field, switching attention away from hypothetical 'structures' and focusing on the processes through which real people, in real situations, both make music and make use of music. Among other things, this way of approaching musical life leads us to see it less as 'Art' and more as work: some studies of music- making and of musicians as an occupational group are considered, but it should be evident that this is an area where further research would pay dividends.

The idea of music as work leads fairly directly to the notion of music itself as a commodity, one which has generated a quite large industry in modern capitalist societies. It would take another book, or a whole series of books, to consider the theme of music and the rise of capitalism in any adequate way; accordingly, some of the topics of particular interest to sociologists are briefly outlined at the start of Chapter 6, followed by a more extended discussion of the music business, its social organisation, and its fundamental problem of reconciling the rationalised formal business procedures of advanced capitalism with volatile artists, on the one hand, and a hugely unpredictable market, on the other. (Accountants cannot feel entirely comfortable with the knowledge that the fortunes of a multi-million dollar business may depend on the mood swings of thousands of sullen adolescents or the antics of a handful of zany disc jockeys.) Thus the industry faces the perpetual problem of trying to work out what 'the kids' will buy. For the sociologist, however, the fascination lies in the fact that – until now, at any rate – they have bought music, and have continued to buy it as they have grown older. This persistent demand, and a sequence of remarkable technological innovations, have given people unprecedented access to, and control over, music; it is arguable that music is now a more central element in the culture of advanced industrial societies than it has been in any earlier time or place, and thus that it is worth trying to remedy the rather undeveloped state of the sociology of music.

As I have already said, however, this is in no respect intended as a comprehensive treatment. Given space, and time, it would have been useful to have said more about the work of a whole range of European scholars (there is a helpful bibliography in Supicic, 1987) and about music in non-western societies (Manuel, 1988, provides an excellent introduction). It has taken some time to assemble this book, during which the field itself has changed, particularly with the substantial growth of popular music studies (see Frith and Goodwin, 1990, and Bennett *et al.*, 1993) and the welcome emergence of critical perspectives emanating from recent feminist thought (see McClary, 1991, and Solie, 1993). Some of these developments are considered in this text; it is a safe bet, however, that their full effects are yet to be felt.

I am grateful to a very large number of people who have helped this project in various ways. My colleague David Morgan and the students on our 'Sociology of Literature, Art & Music' course provided the encouragement and the opportunity to develop some of the ideas which follow; over the years when we ran it, the topics raised in SLAM moved from the margins to the centre of sociological concerns, stimulated by the growth of interest in cultural and media studies. I am particularly grateful, too, for conversations with Tia DeNora, Ian Kemp, David Horn, John Shepherd, and – a very long time ago – Howard Becker. Parts of the manuscript were read by

David Horn, Tia DeNora, Anita Roy and my colleague Rod Watson; to them I offer thanks, and the hope that they will not be blamed for the outcome. Successive editors at Manchester University Press – John Banks, who got the whole thing going, Anita Roy and Vicki Whittaker – have been not only patient but invariably supportive. My colleagues in the Department of Sociology at the University of Manchester allowed me a period of study leave in which some of the initial work was done, and two of them – John Lee and Wes Sharrock – have for many years managed to combine the roles of teacher, colleague and friend.

I am immensely grateful to them all, but above all to Yvonne, Tom, and Claire, who made it possible.

1

Introduction: sociology and music

the spread of a realistic, social view of music would be dangerous to those for whom the confusion and mysticism of the present viewpoint is valuable.

Elie Siegmeister (quoted in Chanan, 1981: 222)

Sociology's misfortune is that it discovers the arbitrary and the contingent where we like to see necessity, or nature ... and that it discovers necessity, social constraints, where we would like to see choice and free will.

Pierre Bourdieu (1990: 14)

Sociology has often been seen, not without reason, as a somewhat perverse sort of enterprise, apparently generating problems where none exist, and persistently enquiring into matters which, to most sensible people, seem perfectly straightforward. The sociologist who applies the theoretical perspectives of the discipline to music must expect, therefore, that the effort will be met with a degree of suspicion. What's the problem? For most of us, to a greater or lesser extent, music is part of our lives. It is, as the economists say, a 'good'. We can do things, all sorts of things, to it. We can buy it in various recorded forms, or play it ourselves. We hear it on radio, television and in films and go to performances at which it is the main attraction. In short, in advanced industrial societies music is all around us, a major element in our culture, in contrast to the situation in pre-electronic times when it was a much less pervasive medium, and a much smaller part of most people's experience. It is this contrast, though, that may serve to arouse our sociological

curiosity: instead of just taking music for granted, we might begin to
ask *why* it has come to occupy such a prominent place in our world.

After all, it is generally accepted that the culture of modern industrial societies, particularly capitalist societies, is formed above all by
the impersonal ethos of scientific rationality, on the one hand, and
by the cold imperative of economic calculation, on the other. The
religious ceremonies of earlier times, in which music was central,
have dwindled in importance, as have the communal festivities and
social events at which music was played. So why has music – deeply
personal, emotional, even ephemeral – not only survived but flourished in such an apparently inhospitable culture? Seen from this
angle, it is not at all obtuse for the sociologist to ask who listens to
music and who plays it, or when and why they do so, especially in
view of the importance which people so often attach to their music.
These initial questions can lead us on to consider a range of wider
issues concerned with music, culture and society, some of which are
explored in this book. There are many people, of course, who react
with suspicion to the very idea of a sociology of music, and some
who will flatly reject the contention that sociological analysis can
add anything useful to either the study or the enjoyment of music.
So another aim of the book is simply to suggest that such views are
mistaken.

Sociological perspectives

However, before discussing the contributions that sociological work
can make to our understanding of music, it may be helpful to make
some preliminary remarks about the nature of sociological ideas
themselves. This is important, mainly because some of these ideas
will emerge in various guises throughout the book, but also because
– in my experience at least – such ideas and their profound implications are not always well understood. Indeed, there is a strong current of opinion which regards as 'sociology' virtually anything which
happens to be said or written about society. All sorts of self-proclaimed pundits and do-gooders are routinely described in the media
as sociologists, despite their lack of qualifications in the subject and
their evident unfamiliarity with it. Sadly, too, it must be said that
some sociologists themselves have from time to time displayed a
somewhat cavalier attitude to the aims and boundaries of the discipline. The activities of all these people have done much to reinforce

the widespread view of sociology as a less than coherent subject in which 'anything goes'.

The reader may be reassured (or perhaps disappointed) that I do not share such a view. On the contrary, my initial supposition is that if sociology, no less than any other area of enquiry, is to be entitled to the status of an academic discipline, then both its aims and the specific nature of its contribution must be clearly defined. This can best be done, I believe, by considering the position of sociology amongst the other human sciences.

Unlike economics, or political science or law, for example, sociology is not concerned with a certain subset of social activities: rather it provides a particular perspective on all such activities, with a view to increasing our understanding of them. Thus there is a sociology *of* economic activity, *of* politics, *of* law and so on, just as there can be a sociology of music. So the crucial question concerns the nature of this perspective: what is distinctive about the way in which the sociologist examines the activities of human beings and the societies in which they live? At first sight it may seem impossible to give a simple or straightforward answer, since one of the things for which sociologists are notorious is their inability to agree on such basic matters as the proper aims of the discipline, the theories which should inform social research and the methods with which such studies should be carried out. Such disagreements, it should be said, are not peculiar to sociology, being apparent to the practitioners of every science, though seldom to the wider public. (Moreover, it may be argued that far from being an indication of sociology's immaturity, the intensity of such disputes may reflect a degree of theoretical sophistication not always encountered in, say, economics or psychology.) Despite the widespread and profound disagreements, however, it is possible – and necessary – to identify a common thread running through the work of even the most apparently disparate of sociologists. All such work, from the apocalyptic macro-theories of structural Marxism to the detailed investigations of conversational analysis, is guided by the perception that the words, thoughts and deeds of individual human beings are profoundly influenced by the nature of the social circumstances in which they occur. It follows that in order to understand the former we must investigate the latter.

As we shall see presently, such a perspective does not entail the idea that human beings are no more than puppets whose strings are manipulated by the greater forces of society, or that as individuals

we simply mirror the characteristics of our cultural context. None
the less, it has been the specific contribution of sociological thinkers
to emphasise the extent to which we do absorb, or 'internalise', elements of our cultures, and that the ways of thinking, acting and feeling which we assume are normal and natural are in fact the results
of a lengthy and complex process through which we *learn* to operate in accordance with prevailing conventions – the process of
'socialisation.'

The works of the classic sociological thinkers are permeated by
such ideas. In challenging the political economists of his day, for
example, Karl Marx rejected their assumption that 'economic man',
acting rationally in pursuit of self-interest, could serve as a model of
the natural qualities of human beings. On the contrary, Marx
argued, capitalist society does not reflect the basic or innate qualities
of people; rather, such characteristics as calculated self-interest, com-
petitiveness, pursuit of wealth and acquisitiveness are engendered by
such a society. These are the qualities which you need to have in
order to make out in this kind of society, and they may, as in modern
western societies, come to be regarded as 'human nature'; in other
cultures, however, and in other historical periods they may be absent
or regarded as aberrant. So economic man did not create capitalism
as the ultimate stage of human progress: capitalism created economic
man, and in Marx's view this was not so much the realisation of
human potential as its perversion. The whole thrust of Marx's thinking on this point is conveyed in one of his most celebrated aphorisms: 'It is not the consciousness of men that determines their being,
but on the contrary it is their social being that determines their consciousness' (1976: 3).

For all the sociological insight of Marx's writings, however, it was
not at all his intention to contribute towards the establishment of an
academic discipline. But such an aim was explicit in the work of
another of sociology's classic theorists, Emile Durkheim. Running
through all of Durkheim's studies is an unremitting criticism of those
who have sought to explain society, which he held to be a collective
phenomenon, in terms of the characteristics of individuals. Logically
and historically, Durkheim argued, society is prior to the individual.
Indeed, the evolution of human societies has involved a gradual transition from original conditions in which human consciousness was
primarily collective, in the sense that people were aware of themselves primarily as members of a tribe or clan, to more modern, dif-

ferentiated, forms in which we think of ourselves as unique, distinctive and autonomous persons. In Durkheim's view then, our modern concept of 'the individual' is itself a historically specific, and comparatively recent, phenomenon.

Durkheim's arguments thus provide a powerful critique of 'individualistic' theories of society, whether political (as in the idea of the 'social contract') or economic (as in the assumption of 'economic man'). They also brought him directly into conflict with psychology in so far as that discipline attempted to account for human action in terms of either some supposed fundamental structures of the mind, or if individuals' particular mental make-up, as in the modern concept of personality. In general, sociological thinkers have been dubious about the idea of universal or innate structures of the mind, since (a) no one has satisfactorily demonstrated what these are, and (b) the idea is hard to reconcile with the sheer variety of modes of thought which have been found empirically. In other cultures, and at earlier historical periods in our own culture, people whose brains are almost identical to ours have perceived their world in fundamentally different ways – even such apparently basic notions as our concepts of space and time seem to be culturally variable, as is, to anticipate a later point, our idea of music. Moreover, sociologists have followed Durkheim in insisting on the idea that individual personalities are not the irreducible elements of social life but are formed in an already existing cultural environment. Through the ubiquitous process of socialisation we learn to accept the validity of conventions, customs and beliefs which, however weird or arbitrary they may seem to the cultural outsider, have acquired the status of binding moral rules. Thus in his teaching on education, for example, Durkheim was concerned to stress that it is not so much a process in which our inherent capacities are brought out as one in which the values, beliefs and behavioural norms of society are instilled into us. Whatever our individual desires, urges and abilities may be, we are none the less shaped in the image of our societies.

Above all, in learning a language we are not only developing a technical ability to communicate with others, we are simultaneously absorbing the concepts, categories and cognitive style of the culture which envelops us. The ability to communicate symbolically through language is what distinguishes us as humans from other animals, and ultimately allows us to control the natural environment to which they are still subject. It should be clear from what has been said already that the very process which makes us distinctively human is a social process. We do not, as infants, create our own individual language, but must learn the ones we hear around us, and so implicitly accept the patterns of thought that they convey. Moreover, as we learn to interact with others, their reactions to us lead us to understand prevailing notions of right and wrong, correct and incorrect and so on. It is from the responses of others, too, that we develop the very idea of our 'selves' (Mead, 1934). And even in that mysterious realm of awareness that we call 'subjective' there are limits to our autonomy. 'The social world and its organisation of social activities is *basic* to any understanding we might derive about mental life. Real intentions, real motives, real thoughts and real understandings are social phenomena through and through (Coulter, 1979: 6). The point is of considerable importance in the present context, as Vulliamy and Shepherd make clear: 'If the significance of music is irrevocably linked to the patternings of individual minds, then it must likewise be linked to the fluid, dynamic and abstract patterning of the social world that lies behind the creation and construction of those minds' (1984: 60).

It is in such ways that culture may be said to mould the personality, and society to penetrate the individual; these considerations also suggest the contrast between sociological and psychological approaches to phenomena such as music, and indicate why sociologists tend to regard the latter as, at best, only part of the story. In *The Psychology of Music* John Davies argues that 'the psychological study of music involves examination of the relationships between the rules of music and the laws of perception and cognition, in so far as these latter are understood (1978: 19). But, as I have suggested above, the thrust of sociological thinking is to question whether there are in fact 'laws of perception and cognition' in the sense that such laws could be said to govern *all* human thinking. How could such laws be reconciled with the amazing heterogeneity of cognitive modes which have been observed in different cultures? However, what initially seems like a basic conflict between sociological and psychological perspectives can, I think, be reconciled. Firstly, whereas psychologists have been much concerned with what might be described as the mechanisms of perception and cognition – with our sensory apparatus, the anatomy of the brain and so on – sociologists have been interested in *what* people perceive and think: with the consequences of the remarkable fact that human beings whose brains are virtually identical can nevertheless come to think in fundamentally different, and often irreconcilable, ways. Secondly, as John Davies himself points out, musical rules 'are not laws in the physical sense (e.g. the law of gravity) but are conventions which musicians have simply agreed upon' (1978: 15). As we shall see, it is such conventions which constitute the reality of the social world, and the processes by which they are established and 'agreed upon' are of great importance for our understanding of it. Indeed, another psychologist, John Sloboda, has emphasised that 'we *learn* the structures that we use to represent music', both informally, through 'everyday social experience', and through formal training (1985: 6–7).

The rules and conventions of social life, then, are determined neither by the physical environment (though obviously it limits them) nor by the fundamental structures of the mind. Rather, they are socially constructed, maintained and from time to time challenged. Thus they are constantly, often imperceptibly, changing, though overt challenges are relatively rare. Mostly, we do conform to conventional modes of, for example, dress, appearance or demeanour, and innovators in all spheres of activity are often treated with suspicion or hostility. To modern western ears, the diatonic scale (do, re, mi, etc.) is not only normal but the 'natural' basis of musical organisation: music based on other principles is hard to make sense of, and we experience difficulty in singing or playing intervals of less than a semitone, even though these are possible and practicable. Similarly, the 'laws of harmony' to which Davies refers seem right and inevitable to westerners – yet such laws have been accepted only in the relatively recent past, and only in the so-called 'classical' music tradition. Indeed, some highly developed musical cultures lack any formal harmony. What seems to the westerner an essential element of music turns out to be a socially constructed convention, and a powerfully established one.

When the implications of these ideas are considered, some familiar distinctions begin to look distinctly shaky. If individuals are so deeply imbued with the values and beliefs of society, can we make a clear distinction between the individual and society? Where does culture stop and personality begin? The issue, though fascinating, cannot be pursued here. What we must acknowledge, though, is that if the commonsense distinction between the individual and the social is problematic, so too are explanations of social life which rest wholly on *either* individualistic or sociologistic premises. Just as sociologists have, rightly, been scathing about the claims of many individualistic theories, so it must be accepted that an equally one-sided sociologism will be just as unsatisfactory. As many of Durkheim's critics, both inside and outside the sociological community, have argued, human action cannot be satisfactorily explained in terms of collective forces (Blumer, 1969: 65; Weber, 1978: 13, 15), nor can we ignore the evident differences between individuals who have been socialised in the same culture.

Yet the inevitability of individual differences, and the possibility of free will, serve only to emphasise the point that human life is, essentially, social life. For despite the uniqueness of every person's character, interests and experience, our encounters with others are, mostly, routine and unproblematic. How is this orderliness achieved in the face of such manifest diversity? Despite our undoubted ability to say or do new things, to reject established conventions and to change the habits of a lifetime, we do accept the orthodox procedures and routines, most of the time. Stability in social relations is normally achieved, despite the constant potential for chaos. The sociologist wants to know how this comes about. It may well be that Marx and Durkheim, intent on demonstrating the inadequacies of successive versions of nineteenth-century individualism, exaggerated the dependence of the individual on the collectivity, reducing the former to a puppet and reifying the latter. But if some of their solutions may be found wanting, it was a great achievement of the classic theorists to have formulated the fundamental issue: the problem of social order. It is a problem to which we will return.

Culture and conflict

The discussion above, though necessarily limited, may at least serve to provide an initial orientation to the task of applying sociological ideas to the analysis of music. As a routine part of the process of socialisation, we absorb the music of our cultural environment, just as we learn its language. The music which we thus 'internalise' comes to sound right and natural, even though we may subsequently realise that the conventions which organise it are arbitrary, in the sense that they are not shared by other cultures, and represent only a fraction of the possible ways in which melody, harmony and rhythm may be combined. And however hard we try, we may find it difficult to appreciate the music of other cultures as we can our own. The point serves, once again, to emphasise the power of the socialisation process: we learn to think, and to hear, in certain specific ways, and it is extremely hard to escape them. Moreover, music illustrates well what theorists such as Durkheim mean by describing society as a *moral* order: established rules and conventions, however arbitrary, come to seem right and proper, not to be tampered with or lightly disregarded. People who know nothing of formal music theory can instantly identify a 'wrong' note, and they often react to one just as they would as if some other sort of social rule had been violated. The rules themselves are simply taken for granted, known but not noticed, and often they only become objects of our attention when they are violated (Garfinkel, 1967: Chapter 2; Heritage, 1984: Chapter 4).

Durkheim's ideas about the nature of social change are also helpful in the present context, since the process outlined above, in which members of a society are effectively socialised into accepting its culture, seems more applicable to simple, relatively unchanging societies than to complex modern ones where rapid change is normal. While socialisation processes are equally effective in the latter situation, it is hard to accept the idea that the norms, values and beliefs which are being transmitted belong to a single cultural system. On the contrary, one of the most striking aspects of modern societies is their heterogeneity. There is no single musical tradition, for example, which is absorbed by all members of such a society; rather, there are various distinct styles and genres, which often reflect other important divisions in society – those of class, age, ethnicity and geography, for example. Nor can it be said that all individuals are equally imbued with musical awareness; though they may find it hard to escape altogether, people can choose not to listen to music should they so wish. The whole process seems to exemplify Durkheim's view of the gradual transition from simple, undifferentiated societies to complex, differentiated ones, and parallels the evolution of religious activities. In the earlier phase all members of a society were imbued with the same religious beliefs, and deviation from them was not tolerated; in the latter period we are familiar with a plurality of religious faiths which coexist (though not always peacefully), and as individuals we are not obliged to join any of them. Through the process of differentiation, then, cultures move from homogeneity to heterogeneity, and social organisation from simple to complex forms. This idea is characteristic of much nineteenth-century thought, which viewed all natural organisms as evolving in the direction of greater specialisation and greater structural complexity. For Durkheim and many others, society could be treated also as a sort of natural organism. Moreover, the idea of differentiation was closely linked, as in the works of Darwin and Spencer, to that of progress: organisms not only became more complex but moved from lower to higher stages of development.

The idea of progressive differentiation, however, returns us to the problem of social order. If there is no common tradition, and if the interests of individuals and groups are diverse and divergent, how are social stability and orderliness achieved? In terms of general sociological theory, Durkheim's own position has been regarded as unsatisfactory, and later answers to the question have emphasised the processes of conflict and competition in various ways. In particular, the ideas of Marx and Max Weber have been influential, suggesting that social order need not rest on either consensus or interdependence but may simply reflect the ability of some people, classes or nations to impose their will on others. In this view, coercion replaces shared values as the cement which holds society together. In the Marxist tradition, the fundamental conflict is between the dominant economic class and all those who are exploited and subordinated by it: such a class will attempt to present its own interests and values as those of the whole society. Thus, for example, it has been argued that the dominant musical tradition in western industrial societies – generally, if misleadingly, called 'classical' music – reflects the cultural preferences of the social class which came to dominate such societies from the eighteenth century onwards, the bourgeoisie of Marxist theory. This class includes only a tiny proportion of the population, but, because it controls economic production and dominates politics, is in a position to lay down the 'rules of the game' for all members of society and in the same way to impose its authority on the process of artistic production. Thus, to this day, 'classical' music is legitimised as 'serious' or 'art' music, to the evident disadvantage of all other styles. It is protected, though never as much as its practitioners would like, from the economic discipline of the market by grants and sponsorship far in excess of those awarded to other genres. It retains privileged positions in broadcasting schedules and, above all, educational curricula: the result is that even if people don't learn to love classical music,

they are none the less imbued with a sense of its greatness and superiority over other forms (Green, 1988: Small, 1980; Shepherd and
Vulliamy, 1994).

The validity of such an analysis will be considered further below.
For the moment, though, it may serve to illustrate how cultures need
not be understood simply as monolithic, coherent bodies of fact and
value, which we all absorb, but rather as the *outcome* of a perpetual
process of competition, in which individuals and groups pursue what
they believe to be their interests. The process of differentiation, as
described by Durkheim, ensures that in modern societies people are
socialised into a vast range of divergent and often conflicting cultural
patterns. As noted above, the emergence of order out of this endless
and endemic conflict is of central importance to the sociological theorist (Collins 1975: 56–61 and *passim*). There are many different contenders, and the resources available to them vary considerably, so
that outcomes may be very unequal, as the example of music suggests. Dominant groups, too, will attempt to persuade others,
perhaps through formal education and the mass media, that such
inequalities are right and proper, in other words will create an ideology which sustains their position of advantage. Thus, for example,
the belief that classical music deserves support and respect because
it is 'great' music can be said to have an ideological function in the
sense that it provides a legitimation of the music's privileged status.
The values and interests of the dominant group may be presented as
those of the whole society: 'British music' is generally taken to mean
the network of orchestras, chamber groups, opera companies and
music societies which perform within the classical tradition, even
though that tradition is not culturally indigenous, its repertoire
almost entirely foreign, and the fact that – despite the advantages
mentioned above – it still appeals to only a minority of the population. In a survey conducted for the Arts Council of Great Britain in
1991, it was found that 11.7 per cent of all adults attend performances of classical music (though only 4.8 per cent go more than
once per year). Moreover the proportion attending jazz concerts (5.9
per cent) was the same as that for opera (Arts Council of Great
Britain, 1991: 4). In other words, despite its privileged place in the
school curriculum and in the 'quality' press, as well as having a state-
sponsored national radio channel dedicated to it, nearly nine out of
ten adults in Britain choose not to attend concerts of classical music.
On the other hand, jazz attracts as many people as opera – without

the favoured cultural status of the latter, and its protected public subsidies.

By now, readers who are themselves deeply attached to classical music may be somewhat irritated. Indeed, the remarks above might even have prompted the thought that the sole contribution of the sociologist seems to be the denigration of a worthy tradition, one of the great achievements of western civilisation. This is not the intention, which is simply to illustrate one sociological perspective on the process by which cultural forms become established, and stratified. Moreover, it seems appropriate at this point to emphasise that the proper role of sociological analysis is neither to attack nor to defend any particular style of musical expression. On the contrary, the only defensible position for the sociological analyst is that of the detached observer, in so far as this is possible: we must remain indifferent to the arguments of musicians, critics and so on in their various debates and disputes. It is no business of the sociologist to take sides, or to arbitrate the validity of their claims, but rather to examine the perpetual processes of conflict and negotiation in their own right. Put more concretely, it is not for the sociologist to decide whether classical music is really the embodiment of the highest strivings of the human soul, or whether blues is really the cry of pain of an oppressed race, though such questions are the crucial matters for many musicians and listeners. What is central for the sociologist are such matters as when and where such forms crystallise, who plays them, who listens to them, and who pays for them; how they develop and become culturally dominant forces (as in the case of classical music) or remain inchoate and marginal (as with the blues) (Collins, 1975: 21).

In short, what people say about music and the claims they make for it must be treated by the sociologist not as objective descriptions of it but as data which are an indication of their beliefs about it. Such beliefs, clearly, are important elements in any culture; they are also the bases on which people formulate courses of action. 'Human beings act toward things on the basis of the meanings that the things have for them', wrote Herbert Blumer (1969: 2), and another influential theorist, W. I. Thomas, made the general point in what has become a sociological commonplace: 'If men define situations as real, then they are real in their consequences'. The implication of these ideas is that, if we wish to understand human action, we must first grasp the nature of the ideas and beliefs which motivate that action, regardless of how bizarre, or wrong or immoral such ideas may seem to be.

The sociological position outlined above – albeit briefly – may strike some people as unduly limiting, in that it excludes from consideration many of the topics and issues which have often been considered 'sociological'. I make no apology for this, believing, as I indicated above, that sociology like any other discipline must display a distinct, coherent and circumscribed perspective if it is to make any worthwhile contribution to knowledge. There may be those, too, who will judge the position to be evasive, in the sense that it appears to free the researcher from the onerous tasks of deciding what the 'real' nature of music is, and of evaluating music in an aesthetic sense. These are after all, as I readily acknowledge, vital matters for those who create music and those who listen to it. They are also, respectively, the concerns of the philosopher and the aesthetician, and again I make no apology for excluding such speculations from the sociological agenda. On the contrary, there are compelling reasons why they should not be there. For one thing, such concerns presuppose that there is an essential meaning in music, or that an aesthetic hierarchy of styles and works is ultimately demonstrable; in general, these things have been assumed rather than established. For another, though the ideal of scientific objectivity may be ultimately unattainable, it is more likely to be approached through the adoption of a detached position rather than the espousal of a particular cause.

For Max Weber, the purpose of the sociology of art was not the production of aesthetic value judgements. Rather, '[the] sociologist starts with the fact that art works exist. His task, therefore, is to understand why and how men orient their conduct meaningfully in relation to the existence of these works. In short, he accepts the premise that aesthetics are meaningful to man' (Freund, 1968: 26). Or in Weber's own terms,

> it is one thing to state facts, to determine logical or mathematical relations or the internal structure of cultural values, while it is another thing to answer questions of the *value* of culture and its individual contents, and the question of how one should act in the cultural community and in political associations. (Gerth and Mills, 1946: 146).

For Weber, then, the proper concern of the social scientist is with the former set of issues; the aim is to establish what is, rather than what ought to be. In general, science can provide us with the means to realise our ends, but cannot – and should not – determine what these ends may be.

The emergence of music

Music is a social activity, and as such is a proper object of socio-logical scrutiny. Inevitably, the initial result is to cast as problematic much of what we ordinarily take for granted. This is not because sociologists take a perverse delight in creating problems where none exist but because, as I suggested earlier, the social order rests on countless shared meanings concerning what is right, proper and nat-ural (and what is not), and on the processes by which some inter-pretations become established as authoritative at the expense of others. To pursue our sociological enquiries, therefore, we must first attempt to suspend some of our habitual assumptions about the world we experience. Soon, a different and fascinating order of things may emerge, as we see when we consider the concept of music itself.

To members of modern western societies, the concept is normally unproblematic, as is the distinction between music and non-music. Music is generally defined as some sort of pattern of organised sounds, deliberately created in order to produce certain effects. Thus it is distinguished from naturally or randomly occurring sound, or noise, even though the latter may sometimes be similar to the ele-ments of music. And apart from some avant-garde composers and 'free' improvisers who deliberately set out to challenge the conven-tions, this sort of commonsense definition is good enough for most people, most of the time. It would seem, then, that the sociologist of music could usefully start by regarding the production of organised sound as the basic subject matter, and so proceed to examine the social circumstances of such production.

But while such an approach might be adequate in western societies, it may well not be universally applicable, since the definition of music on which it is based is specific to these societies. The point has been made forcefully by Charles Keil:

> Tiv, Yoruba, Igbo, Efik, Birom, Hausa, assorted Jarawa dialects, Idoma, Eggon, and a dozen other languages from the Nigeria–Cameroons area do not yield a word for music gracefully. It is easy to

talk about song and dance, singers and drummers, blowing a flute, beating a bell, but the general terms 'music' and 'musician' require long and awkward circumlocutions that still fall short, usually for lack of abstraction. (1979: 27)

The concept of 'music', then, so simple and fundamental to westerners, does not necessarily translate into other cultures. Nor is this because western concepts are more abstract, as Keil points out:

A large number of important Western abstractions can be subsumed under the heading of or translated into Tiv as *inja*, for example: character, custom, culture, color, habit, nature, behaviour, reason, meaning, sort, type, kind, method, style, utility, correctness.

The example serves to emphasise that even such an apparently straightforward concept as music cannot be assumed to be 'natural', in the sense that all cultures will have a term for it, and to illustrate the idea that the process of socialisation can lead human beings, whose brains are fundamentally similar, to think in different and often irreconcilable ways. It is as hard for me as a Westerner to grasp the usage of the Tiv notion of *inja* as it is for Tiv people to understand our concept of music, and Keil is critical of attempts to recover or construct the latter in cultural contexts where it is not normally found (ibid: 28–9).

So it is likely that the western concept of music as a distinct activity, performed on specific occasions by particular people, is itself a product of the process of differentiation discussed above. In a relatively undifferentiated society the organisation of, and participation in, activities which westerners might describe as 'musical' was and is an integral part of the experience of every member of the society: most obviously, ceremonial and ritual occasions would have musical elements, but so too would hunting, child-minding, tilling the soil, going to war and all sorts of other pursuits. It makes little sense, therefore, for the researcher to wrench the 'musical' elements out of such contexts, and analyse them in terms appropriate to western 'art' music. The conclusion seems inescapable: we must learn to see the world in ways which are consistent with other people's categories, and think with their concepts, so far as this is possible. Above all, we cannot presuppose the universality of even such an apparently innocuous concept as music.

If we accept Durkheim's contention about the relative modernity of the concept of the individual, however, a similar conclusion about

music should not surprise us. Indeed, other analyses lend support to
the idea that music has gradually but inexorably come to be seen as
a specific and specialised activity in the West. 'Primitive music',
writes Ivo Supicic, 'is an expression of a collective experience. It is
not the well-defined work of a single individual (1987: 91). By the
nineteenth century, however, Romantic composers had come to
regard music as a medium for the expression of their own personal
feelings, rather than those of the collectivity. Then again, we must
remind ourselves that such individual inspiration is itself nurtured
within a certain social context, and, to find acceptance, must be
channelled in ways which reflect, or at least acknowledge, existing
conventions (Supicic, 1987: 59). There is thus a sort of ironic dialectic inherent in the belief that music can express the subjectivity of
individuals, as Dahlhaus points out: 'Expression ... is paradoxically
yoked to convention, the particular to the general ... expression,
being subjective, is unrepeatable, yet at the same time, in order to
make itself clear, it yields to a compulsion of being established'
(1982: 23). We can glimpse here the two contrasting forces from
which social order emerges: the active and creative impulse of individuals, and the limitations and constraints which the existing order
imposes on them.

The general historical process, then, involves the differentiation of
music from other activities and the gradual emergence of specialised
social roles. Through time the composer, the musician and the listener become separated, with the latter – particularly in the western
'art-music' tradition – becoming increasingly passive (Supicic 1987:
91). In the West, the now normal procedure of attributing pieces to
individual composers seems to date from the fourteenth century
(Supicic, 1987: 202–3); by the beginning of the nineteenth, music –
which began as an inextricable part of everyday social experience –
was coming to be seen as an autonomous and intrinsically worthwhile activity, in short as an 'art' in its own right. Thus Supicic talks
of the 'disfunctionalisation' of music, that is, its liberation from the
requirements of particular social events and performers and its establishment as a pursuit in its own right (1987: 174). Increasingly, in a
struggle which continues to this day, composers and performers have
sought to free themselves from the demands of church, state, patrons
and the public, increasingly seeing themselves as 'artists'. Bourdieu
viewed this development as

correlated with the establishment of a distinct social category of pro-fessional artists, who are more and more inclined to follow no rules other than those of their own artistic tradition (rules passed down from their predecessors which furnish a point of departure or rupture), and more and more able to free their production and products from all social servitude. (Quoted in Supicic, 1987: 175).

Just as music became perceived as an autonomous sphere of social activity, so it in turn became increasingly fragmented. Medieval church music acquired its own traditions and conventions, which may be distinguished from the indigenous 'folk' music of various parts of Europe, and which prepared the way for the later emergence of 'art' music, not least by the establishment of an internationally recognised system of notation and rules of correct procedure. (Weber, 1958: 83). It was the development of conventions to indicate the time values of notes, by twelfth-century monks at Notre Dame and Cologne cathedrals, which completed the fundamental system of notation which is still in use, and which, in Max Weber's view, was decisive for the establishment of polyphonic composed music in medieval Europe. In a characteristic argument, Weber suggests that the necessary preconditions for such music were 'of at least equal intensity in other regions of the world and notably so in Hellenic antiquity and in Japan' (1958: 83). But only in the West did polyphony and the modern tonal system become established, and it was the system of notation which was crucial, as it made 'planned written compositions' possible: 'Only the elevation of many-voiced music under notational art created the composer proper and guar-anteed the polyphonic creations of the Western world, in contrast to those of all other peoples, permanence, after-effect, and continuing development' 1958: 88).

Just as there was an early separation between sacred and secular music traditions in Europe, so sacred music itself generated the pre-conditions for 'art' music. Indeed, the potential tension between the devotional and the purely aesthetic effects had long been recognised: Pope Gregory (590–604) made a great contribution by organising the plainchant which still bears his name, but was determined that music 'was to be the servant of worship, but not more than this. His cele-brated interest in the art of music may have been due to real enthusiasm, but was also surely at least in part a cautious watch lest it should get out of hand' (Headington, 1977: 32).

Music and modernity

In the modern period, the fragmentation of musical genres has accelerated. Though it may seem surprising to twentieth-century minds, purely instrumental music was regarded with suspicion and hostility as late as the eighteenth century. 'Instrumental music,' writes Dahlhaus, 'unless provided by a programme note with some intelligible meaning, was regarded not as eloquent but simply as having nothing to say' (1982: 24). As we shall see in the next chapter, the gradual acceptance of instrumental music was accompanied by disputes, which have continued unabated, concerning its meaning. 'It is at the opposite pole from painting tone-pictures or delineating characters and thus from the methods of composition that provided the only justification for despised wordless music discernible to the aesthetics of the early and middle eighteenth century' (Dahlhaus, 1982: 28). (Though the validity and independence of instrumental music was established by the nineteenth century, it is interesting to reflect that the general public, as opposed to composers and musicians, continues to display a marked preference for vocal over instrumental pieces, in so far as mass tastes are reflected by purchases of records and tapes (Frith, 1987b: 97).)

Further familiar distinctions were established in the early nineteenth century. By the 1830s 'serious' was being distinguished from 'light' music (Supicic, 1987: 176), and increasingly through the century music, like most other human products, was coming to be regarded as a commodity to be bought and sold on the market. The rising tide of Victorian capitalism brought first a swelling demand for sheet music and instruments, particularly pianos. Ehrlich has estimated, though cautiously, that between fifteen thousand and twenty thousand pianos were being produced annually in England by the mid nineteenth century (1976: 37). And the 'extraordinary piano mania of late Victorian society' was remarkably enduring: 'by 1910 there were some two to four million pianos in Britain – say one instrument for every ten to twenty people', which was a far higher proportion than in other industrial countries (1976: 91). It is interesting to note, too, that by this time English manufacturers were already beginning to lose out to German firms producing higher-quality instruments. This sort of demand not only stimulated the proliferation of instrument-makers but in turn created work for composers, engravers, repairers, music teachers, retailers and so on; the activities of these people sowed the seeds of the modern music business. By the latter part of the century, some of the benefits of industrial capitalism were at last beginning to filter through to the mass of people who had created them, generating a huge and sustained demand for music as entertainment. This was the period when the music halls proliferated in the burgeoning urban centres of Britain, and the development of the modern music business was further stimulated. 'The first stars of mass entertainment, complete with agents on 10 per cent, made their appearance with the Great Macdermott, whose rendering of G. W. Hunt's "We don't want to fight" gave the word "jingoism" to the language in 1878'; there followed a galaxy of other entertainers whose names are still revered in the business (Fraser, 1981: 218).

The power of the consumer, then, was added to that of patrons, the church and the state to call forth different kinds of music for different purposes; nor was it long before the consumer was sovereign, reducing the others to relative insignificance. Moreover, two other factors were intensifying the process of musical differentiation. One was the 'discovery' of different musical traditions. In the period of imperialism prior to the First World War the music of other cultures was brought to western ears: 'an international range of musical innovations appeared towards the end of the century, which spread across frontiers and oceans partly through tourism and the medium of the musical stage, mainly through the new practice of social dancing in public' (Hobsbawm, 1987: 237). This was, too, the period in which the academic study of non-western cultures became established; for present purposes the most significant event in this process was the delivery of a paper 'On the musical scales of various nations' by A. J. Ellis to the meeting of the Royal Society of Arts in London on 27 March 1885. Indeed, Ellis's conclusion may serve to introduce the whole tradition of work in the sociology of music: 'the Musical Scale is not one, not "natural", nor even founded necessarily on the laws of the constitution of musical sound ... but very diverse, very artificial, and very capricious' (Ellis, 1885: 526). In other words, the ways in which patterns of sound are organised in the music of different societies is the outcome of cultural processes rather than determination by nature.

Other factors contributed to the proliferation of musical styles in this period. The neo-Romantic reaction against industrialisation led to the rediscovery – some would say invention (Hobsbawm and

Ranger, 1983) – of the music of the 'folk'; though, as Harker (1985) and Boyes (1993) have shown, what was presented as the indigenous music of the people was 'mediated' by self-proclaimed authorities whose commitments reflected the ideology of the bourgeoisie rather than the actual musical practices of the 'folk'. Others, pursuing a rather different sort of national identity, saw music as an important accompaniment to nationalistic aspirations. The outcome of all these various trends and movements was the simultaneous availability of an unprecedented range and variety of musical styles and traditions.

Above all, however, it was the invention and development of recording technology which gradually but explosively accelerated the differentiation of musical styles. It would be difficult to exaggerate the importance of this for the cultural history of the twentieth century.

> Three aural technologies – the telephone, the phonograph, and the radio – were about to bombard the ear with more aural information than had ever been experienced in the history of man. A shift in the technological base was constructing a whole new environment of structured and meaningful sound ... Most noticeable to many was the sudden omnipresence of music. (Biocca, 1988: 61–2)

In the 1920's, it has been claimed, more music of all kinds was heard than 'throughout all the previous history of mankind' (Pearsall, 1976: 103). For the first time, music did not depend on the physical presence of performers in specific settings, or the simultaneous presence of an audience. Music was freed, so to speak, from the social context of its production (Schafer, 1977: 89), which meant – among many other things – that an enormous and unprecedented variety of sounds could be experienced by one individual. It is instructive to contrast the situation in the late twentieth century with that which confronted the young Hector Berlioz in Le Côte Saint-André, near Grenoble, in the early part of the nineteenth: the *only* music which Berlioz heard as a child was in church, sung by women at work or peasants in the fields, or provided on occasion by the town band (Cairns, 1990: 77). And it was the same Berlioz who, as an established composer, was forced in 1847 to travel from Paris to Russia overland, for the latter part of the journey in a box-like sledge, carrying all his orchestra parts with him. How else could his music have been heard? (Berlioz, 1970: 517–19).

Just as spatial restraints have been removed, so have temporal ones. In the 1990s we are able to select music recorded over nearly a whole century: the sound of Caruso in 1907, Louis Armstrong in 1927, Toscanini in 1940 or the Beatles in the 1960s can all be reproduced at home by millions of people, and relatively cheaply. Thus although music has become a more specialised activity in modern times, technological innovations have meant that it is now experienced by more people, for more of the time, than ever before. What's more, the mass availability of radios and disc or tape players has given people unprecedented *control* over their own sound-environment. Given the simultaneous availability of countless styles of music, and indeed the capacity to record one's own, it can now be used, like clothes, to establish or proclaim a whole range of possible lifestyles or identities.

A remarkable diversity of music, then, is simultaneously available in modern societies, and, as we shall see in Chapter 6, its production and consumption constitutes a major industry. This cultural heterogeneity, however, is not simply a matter of the fragmentation of distinct styles, or the combination of their elements to form new ones. Like any other aspect of culture, music reflects the hierarchical divisions of a society – its pattern of social stratification. I have already mentioned the argument that the dominant musical tradition in modern western societies is that which was institutionalised by the nineteenth-century bourgeoisie, and some of the links between music and social class will be considered more fully later. For the moment, though, it is important to note how the study of music has, overwhelmingly, presupposed the validity of the conventional hierarchy of musical taste. The commonsense distinction between 'art' and 'popular' music, between 'serious' and 'light', between 'elite' and 'mass' has gone virtually unquestioned by the vast majority of scholars as they have investigated the great music and great composers of the 'classical' tradition.

There is a comprehensive catalogue of doctoral and masters' dissertations and theses on music submitted to North American universities between 1861 and 1983. As you would expect, it is a substantial list, running to 255 closely packed pages. Yet the section devoted to 'Jazz and Popular Music' takes up just *one and a quarter* pages (UMI, 1983). This is, moreover, the historical period in which African-American styles became arguably the most profound influence in global music-making, and in which the American music industry came close to world hegemony. Overwhelmingly, and the point applies *a fortiori* to European studies, the only music which has been considered a legitimate object of study is that of the 'classical' tradition; other forms and styles have implicitly or explicitly been treated as inadequate or inferior. Moreover, its procedures and conventions, which as we have already seen are of relatively recent origin, have been held to be typical of music in general. Typically, it is assumed, even by the most broad-minded of scholars, that music consists of notated 'pieces', created by a single 'composer' (usually a man, of exceptional gifts or inspiration), performed by specialist 'musicians' (sometimes under the direction of a 'conductor') before an 'audience' of passive, indeed silent, listeners.

What is sociologically interesting about this list is that it describes no more than a small fraction of all the occasions on which music is created, even in modern western societies. To concentrate on just those activities would not only yield a restricted and distorted view of music in society but would involve granting a privileged status to the words and activities of some people we may be studying at the expense of others: to take for granted their assumptions about music, for example, and to ignore the claims of others, who are likely to be in the majority. This seems neither very sociological nor very scientific. Once again, we are led to the conclusion that what people say or write about music cannot be regarded as a factual description of it; from a sociological perspective such views must be treated as data, however strange or muddled or persuasive we may find them, which will help us to understand why people create music, use it and respond to it in the ways that they do. Thus the sociologist may not start with the opposed concepts of, for example, 'serious' and 'light' music as a resource with which to categorise pieces or performances: rather, the concepts *themselves* are the topics for investigation, as is the use to which they are put. Whose interests are served by the institutionalisation of such a distinction? How did it come about? Is it being challenged, and to what effect? The example serves to illustrate how the concepts and ideas which people employ in order to describe their world tell us as much about their own particular interests and values as about a presumed 'objective' state of affairs.

Scannell (1981) has discussed, in fascinating detail, the ways in which categories of music were established for the purposes of British radio broadcasting, and how the BBC's Music Department successfully manoeuvred so as to free itself from the obligation to cater for a mass audience. The story is an excellent example of the way in which economic interests, aesthetic judgements and institutional commitments are all defined and articulated in terms of a basic conflict over resources, and of how one particular interest, which could mobilise both cultural and organisational support, came to predominate (1981: 260). The example serves also to illustrate the diversity of perspectives which are likely to be encountered in any specific historical situation, as producers, administrators, various shades of audience opinion, regional and national interests, musicians, politicians, trades unions and music societies all attempted to define the situation in terms favourable to themselves. 'Where,' as Carl Dahlhaus has asked, 'in the muddle of competing and often incompatible opinions of an age, is the "real" spirit of the times to be found?' The problem seems intractable, yet it is reassuring that Dahlhaus's conclusion, derived from the study of music history, is consistent with the sociological perspective to be developed here: 'The problems, it would seem, are labyrinthine and virtually inextricable. There is little an historian can do to avoid falling victim to them other than take them up as topic' (Dahlhaus, 1983: 85; Zimmerman and Pollner, 1971).

The scope of the sociology of music, then, cannot be confined to western classical composers and their works, however impressive and well established, but must encompass all the sounds that people describe as music and all the things they say and write about such sounds. In some interesting respects, the situation resembles that which Berger and Luckmann observed in their account of the development of the sociology of knowledge. Most studies in that field, they suggested, had been concerned with 'intellectual history, in the sense of the history of ideas' (1971: 26): with great ideas or theories, with religious belief systems or political ideologies, for example. But such systems of ideas, however attractive to intellectuals, are only a part, and a small part, of the knowledge of a society. Accordingly, 'the sociology of knowledge must concern itself with whatever passes for "knowledge" in a society, regardless of the ultimate validity or invalidity (by whatever criteria) of such "knowledge" ' (1971: 15). Moreover, such a perspective involves a recognition that this 'commonsense' knowledge is culturally relative and can be shown to be socially constructed.

Berger and Luckmann's remarks are apposite for a number of reasons. In the following chapter I shall consider the specific contribu-

tion that sociologists can make to the debate concerning the nature
of musical meaning, by arguing that such meanings are not inherent
or self-evident but are socially constructed. Berger and Luckmann's
approach also emphasises the theme that ideas and beliefs must be
the objects of sociological investigation, irrespective of their 'ultimate validity or invalidity': in the same way that the sociologist of
religion is unlikely to share the zealot's belief in the one true faith,
so the thoughtful sociologist of music will be sceptical of the notion
that only one tradition of music has any value. But such beliefs, their
origins and effects, must be studied carefully, for they are what motivate real people. Above all, though, Berger and Luckmann's account
of the sociology of knowledge is a powerful reminder that the sociology of music must take as its subject *all* sorts of music, and the
relations between them.

Boehmer has put the matter succinctly, and in terms which echo
Max Weber:

> Unlike traditional musicology the sociology of music does not recognise
> 'aesthetic' differences between art music, folk music and the more
> recent phenomenon of light or popular music; it sees these categories
> from the viewpoint of social history, and investigates the conditions
> under which certain social classes and strata ... produce and consume
> different musical idioms and forms....
>
> A further difference between traditional musicology and the sociol-
> ogy of music is that the latter proceeds from the social relevance of
> musical consumption and not from the alleged aesthetic or formal
> qualities of the musical product. For instance, even if musicologists
> avoid light music because of its high degree of uniformity, this sector
> of music production commands the music sociologist's attention for the
> very reason that it constitutes more than 90% of all music production
> and consumption. (1980: 433)

In this chapter I have outlined some very basic sociological ideas, and
suggested that these have significant implications for our understanding of music. It is time to put the ideas to work.

2

The social construction of musical meaning

You cannot prescribe to a symbol what it *may* be used to express. All that a symbol CAN express, it MAY express.

Ludwig Wittgenstein (quoted in Monk, 1991: 165)

The problem

The debate about the nature of musical meaning has a long history. While it seems obvious that music does convey some sort of meanings, it has proved extraordinarily difficult to specify what these are, or how they are communicated to people. There are few who have never felt that music has stirred some intense feeling in them, and the vast demand for recorded music in the twentieth century is convincing evidence that millions of people find the experience of music pleasurable. But how does it produce its effect?

Finding an answer to this question is complicated by the very nature of music. Organised patterns of sound, like any other noises, are evanescent – no sooner have the notes sounded than they are gone. In contrast to the situation in the visual arts, or literature, there seems to be no material 'text' which can be subject to analytical scrutiny. Indeed the question of what the musical text actually is has generated the sort of academic dispute which is as intriguing for its participants as it is infuriating for the general public. The idea that the essence of music exists in sheets of notation is less than convincing – quite apart from the fact that such pages generate no sounds at all, most of the world's music has never been transcribed. Moreover, even in the western classical tradition, musical scores can never be a completely accurate guide to composers' intentions.

'Bach's own performance on the clavichord, as his contemporaries
testify, made such a difference in the effectiveness of his sonatas and
fantasies that their notation transmitted mere abstract schemes'
(Dahlhaus, 1982: 22). So perhaps the essential core of music is lodged
in the heads of composers. Again, though, the suggestion leads to
problems: a great deal of music cannot be ascribed to a single composer, and in many cultural settings the concept of 'composer' is
itself alien. And how are we to establish precisely what composers'
intentions are? Whereas some will have a very precise idea of what
they are tryig to 'say' in thier music, others – like Stravinsky – will
deny the proposition that music can express anything at all. Moreover, the whole question of the extent to which we can obtain valid
knowledge of other people's ideas or intentions is a vexed issue in
both philosophy and social science methodology.

It seems plausible, then, that we must seek the musical 'text' in
performances themselves. But this only returns us to our original
difficulty – the ephemeral nature of the medium. In this chapter I will
suggest that some specifically sociological ideas which we have
already touched on can help us towards a fuller understanding of
musical meaning. Firstly, though, it will be useful to place this discussion in the context of the more general debate about the nature
of meaning.

In the simplest terms, two general positions have dominated this
debate. On the one hand are those who hold that we are able to
grasp the meaning of things because, through the operation of our
senses, we are able to perceive their properties and qualities, rather
as a camera allows patterns of light to be fixed on a film, or recording equipment can 'fix' patterns of sound on magnetic tape. In both
cases we are able to produce a representation of aspects of the external world; for present purposes, it is important to note the direction
of this process – *from* the external world *to* the representation of it.
In a similar way, it has been argued that all our ideas and concepts
are ultimately derived from our experience: through our senses we
receive impressions of external reality. To take a famous example,
once we have seen, heard and touched a horse, we have built up an
impression of a particular horse which allows us to form an idea of
horses in general. Thus although the notion of 'horses' is an abstraction divorced from any particular beast, it has meaning for us
because of our initial sensory impression of an actual horse. On this
view, then, the objective characteristics of the world impress them-

selves on our minds. It is worth noting, too, that this empiricist theory of meaning is in some respects similar to our everyday, commonsense assumption that objects in the world are independent of us and have properties that we cannot normally alter: it seems self-evident that a horse is a horse and must be treated as such.

The empiricist theory of meaning has had wide application, including the analysis of music: it has been argued that we understand music because its meaning is inherent in it, and so through our aural perception it is communicated to us. We shall consider such a claim presently. Before that, however, we must mention the opposing point of view — that the meaning of objects resides not in their ability to excite our senses but in the nature of the means which we have to perceive them. We have already touched on this perspective in considering the suggestion that there are innate or fundamental structures of the mind: such an idea implies that, far from objects imposing their qualities on us, we impose meaning on them. In other words, we understand the world as we do because of our unique and distinctive human capacity to engage in reasoning. Through our rational faculties, the argument goes, human beings can work out the true relations between things and so arrive at valid knowledge of them. 'Our intellect does not not derive its laws from nature', wrote Kant, 'but imposes its laws upon nature.'

Rationalists have always doubted empiricist theories of meaning since they rest on what Descartes called 'the fluctuating assurance of the senses' (Korner, 1971: 260). Appearances may be deceptive, and the simple evidence of our senses can lead us into error. A stick appears to bend when pushed below the surface of a pond, but we know that it is not 'really' bent. How do we know this, other than by applying our reason? And, to take another example, our commonsense experience of the earth suggests that it must be more or less flat, but we now know that it is not. And lest it should be objected that this knowledge was obtained as a result of Columbus's empirical observations, it is worth recalling that he did not discover the roundness of the earth so much as confirm what scholars already knew. 'All the European princes had globes in their libraries', writes Granzotto, 'and Christian, Jewish and Arab scientists all believed that the earth was round. But such ideas were theoretical; they remained achievements of the intellect' (1986: 49). Rational deduction, then, rather than empirical evidence, provided this particular scientific breakthrough, just as, four hundred years later, Einstein's ideas were formulated many years before experimental evidence was available to support them.

Descartes was the founding father of modern rationalism. Dismissing intuition and metaphysical speculation as sources of valid knowledge (still a radical step in the seventeenth century), his view was that 'the truth about the natural world is hidden, but it is not occult, nor are occult powers needed to uncover it. It is hidden in the form of a mathematical structure which underlies sensible appearances. It is uncovered by systematic scientific enquiry and the use of the rational intellect' (B. Williams, 1978: 28). This 'rational intellect', moreover, 'was to be found in everyone, in such a way that anyone ... given help in clear thinking and free from prejudice, could pursue reasonings which would lead to truth in philosophy, science, or mathematics' (1978: 28). The presumption of the 'rational intellect', however, entails the view that, *ceteris paribus*, human minds work in basically similar ways. And as I have already suggested, it is precisely this notion which has been cast into doubt by studies of diverse cultures. Moreover, if there are fundamental structures of the mind, these have not yet been satisfactorily demonstrated, despite Kant's claim that 'the organising principles of the mind are fixed and given' (Anderson *et al.* 1986: 23–4).

Clearly there are serious difficulties confronting both the empiricist and rationalist theories of meaning, and further discussion of them would lead us far from our main concern, the analysis of musical meaning. In order to progress, though, what we can do is examine certain modern sociological ideas which, it has been suggested, overcome some of the problems of both empiricism and rationalism, and indeed transcend the dichotomy that they seem to present. Significantly, given the argument of the preceding chapter, both these approaches rest on individualistic assumptions, as Manicas has pointed out:

> the alternative sciences of the mind of 'rationalists' and 'empiricists' were all instances of *epistemological* individualisms, of the idea that nothing *social* needs to enter into questions regarding the truth of belief, that truth is a relation determined by a solitary subject standing in relation to an independent reality. (1987: 11–12)

Once again, the sociological critique of individualism is evident, and no one has drawn out the implications more clearly than Herbert

Blumer in his outline of the symbolic interactionist perspective, which

> does not regard meaning as emanating from the intrinsic makeup of the thing that has meaning, nor does it see meaning as arising through a coalescence of psychological elements in the person. Instead it sees meaning as arising in the process of interaction between people. ... Thus, symbolic interactionism sees meanings as social products, as creations that are formed in and through the defining activities of people as they interact. (1969: 4–5)

As Blumer argues, such an approach to the understanding of meaning generates a distinctive and powerful perspective which regards the human being not as an isolated individual but as a social actor, inevitably and inextricably part of a particular culture. Such an approach, though, is not unique to those who call themselves symbolic interactionists. The central thrust of the 'interpretive' sociology which was developed on the foundations largely laid by Max Weber is to demonstrate, firstly, that human action is not simply a response to external stimuli, since it is formulated on the basis of the actor's meanings, and, secondly, that such meanings must be understood as collective rather than individual. As we have already seen, this does not mean that individuals are simply conditioned by the culture of their society: as Blumer argues, the process of social interaction is one in which meanings are constantly being affirmed, modified, abandoned, negotiated and so on.

Weber, too, was insistent that while the social world normally seems orderly, with people simply accepting prevailing definitions and meanings, there is always the possibility of change – social relationships must be understood in terms of probabilities rather than certainties. As Freund put it:

> This does not mean that social structures themselves are necessarily precarious, but merely that their meaning may alter with time, if men in their relevant conduct should assign another meaning to them under the pressures of necessity, or because of new interests or of technical and rational progress; and if men divest them of all meaning, they will vanish altogether. (Freund, 1968: 117)

The commonsense meanings with which we make sense of the world, then, are to be understood as the result of a perpetual process of collaborative definition (rather than a passive acceptance of received wisdom) and as such they are created, sustained and transformed through human interaction.

Some of the implications of the sociological perspective emerge when it is compared to the two traditional theories of meaning. In contrast to varieties of empiricism, sociology must remain agnostic about the possibility of our ever knowing the true or ultimate meaning of anything. As human beings, what we perceive is not the essential quality of a phenomenon but what Kant called the 'world of appearances'. It follows that the social sciences are therefore concerned with understanding people's beliefs about the world, rather than the world as it 'really' is. 'It is this,' says Weber, 'which distinguishes the empirical sciences of action, such as sociology and history, from the dogmatic disciplines in that area, such as jurisprudence, logic, ethics, and aesthetics, which seek to ascertain the 'true' and 'valid' meanings associated with the objects of their investigation' (1978: 4). The sociologist of music, then, will not be concerned to establish the 'true' meaning of a piece, but will be interested in what people believe it to mean, for it is these meanings that will influence their responses to it.

Like the rationalists, then, sociology accepts that human beings bestow meaning on the world. But whereas traditional rationalism (and, as we shall see, some more modern varieties) rested on the notion that this process reflects fundamental categories or qualities of mind, the sociological view emphasises its active, creative and above all *collective* nature. One evident implication of such a view, which can serve to return the discussion to the analysis of music, is the inadequacy of aesthetic theories which claim that the essence of art consists of some quality which is common to all art objects or artistic activities. A persistent problem for such theories is that no one has been able to produce a satisfactory definition of such a quality, or show what it is that all artworks have in common (Sheppard, 1987: 55). The sociological approach overcomes this difficulty by suggesting that 'artistic' activities and objects may be anything that is collectively defined as such, thus accounting for the remarkable heterogeneity of artworks and the constantly changing definitions of what they are. It also helps us to see how there comes to be an aesthetic hierarchy *within* the realm of works defined as artistic − as critics, patrons, audiences and artists themselves endlessly debate the nature of true artistic value. Thus works that were once considered the epitome of sophistication − like virtuoso piano recitals – are now seen as rather vulgar, while whole new areas of activity, like jazz, may seek to become redefined in such a way that they receive 'artistic' status. But as these examples suggest, such matters are always contentious, always a matter for negotiation, never settled in a final way acceptable to all. The commonsense reality, then, at any given moment simply reflects a temporary balance of opinions and interests.

To avoid possible misunderstandings, two points should be clarified at this stage. Firstly, it should be clear that the process by which collective definitions are established – the social construction of reality – is in principle independent of the intrinsic properties of the activities and objects being defined. Mahler's scores have presumably remained basically unchanged since his death, for example, but public perception of them has been transformed. As a musical style, jazz has changed very rapidly, yet there remains little awareness of this within the arts 'world' or the general public. Musicologists and aestheticians can demonstrate to their own satisfaction that Schoenberg is a 'better' composer than Andrew Lloyd Webber; the public remains unmoved. To repeat: for the sociologist it is the perception or definition of objects and activities which is of fundamental concern, rather than speculation, however fascinating, about their essential qualities or aesthetic merits.

Secondly, it would be wrong to give the impression that the social construction of reality is like some sort of vast democratic forum, where everyone has an equal chance to have his or her voice heard. The establishment and sustaining of meanings, like that of the social order generally, involves the active pursuit of interests by individuals and groups whose resources are significantly different. Established and entrenched positions may resist challenges simply because they are established and entrenched, being legitimated as the repositories of the cultural tradition of the whole society (even when, as in the case of 'classical' music, they manifestly are not). Economic interests, too, play a significant part either in maintaining the status quo when it is profitable to do so or in abandoning it when new sources of profit seem more attractive. Record companies, promoters, agents, critics, patrons, arts organisations and so on are not disinterested groups who simply respond to changes in the climate of the musical world; rather, they seek to control it, or at least to impose some sort of order on the areas in which they operate. To the extent that the players in this game can command the necessary resources – money,

time, access to the media, political contacts and so on – they may be
successful in promoting their interests and thus securing a favourable
environment for their activities. Without such resources, their claims,
however profound or artistically compelling, are unlikely to prevail.
To anticipate a later argument, there is nothing automatic or
inevitable about the emergence of an individual performer or a musical style – if Wagner, for example, had not secured the patronage of
King Ludwig II of Bavaria in 1864, both he and his works *might* now
be obscure as many of his contemporaries are (Taylor, 1983: 266ff.).
Certainly, the course of modern western music would have been different. And we may be equally sure that, in every age, there are
figures as gifted as Wagner whose talent is never discovered, perhaps
never even recognised. A sociological perspective, then, may lead us
to be sceptical of the old adage that 'talent will out': sheer talent may
be regarded as a necessary, but not sufficient, condition for artistic
success and recognition. Moreover, there are plenty of examples of
people of relatively modest talents who have been successful in music
because they have been 'in the right place at the right time', or been
aggressively ambitious, or been promoted by powerful backers.
Inevitably, talent and reputations are moulded, nurtured, channelled
and managed successfully before they are recognised as such, and the
processes through which this occurs are social ones (Long and Long,
1988). As we shall see when we come to consider the operation of
the modern music business, it should not be assumed that those who
seek to promote certain musicians or styles at the expense of others
are motivated purely by artistic considerations.

The idea of the social construction of reality also allows us to conceive of the social order in a rather more sophisticated way than
simply as a transmission of culture from one generation to the next.
While such a process is fundamental, we also need to account for the
ways in which culture changes, and, as we have already seen, for the
heterogeneity of cultural patterns and traditions which are such a
conspicuous feature of modern societies. In the Marxist tradition,
attention has been focused on the ways in which, it is held, dominant economic classes attempt to impose their views of the world –
their meanings – on the mass of the population: whereas in the
Middle Ages the populace was subordinated through the teachings
of the church, argued Louis Althusser, under modern capitalism it is
the educational system which imbues people with respect for the
social order which ensures their exploitation (1972: 242–80). Simi-

larly, Gramsci's concept of hegemony refers to the process by which a ruling class seeks to defend its position by maintaining a 'cultural ascendancy' (Merquior, 1986: 101). There are echoes of such views in Lucy Green's discussion of music within the 'dominant ideology' of capitalist societies:

> classical music has in fact maintained a hegemonic position of cultural superiority ever since the Enlightenment. Ideology immanently ratifies and maintains the dominance of an elite musical institution that, along with its reified products, is made to seem superior: and it does so by propagating the appearance that there is a musical mass which, along with its profane products, is not really very musical. Hence a complex and multifarious division is created and maintained between elite and mass productive and receptive musical modes, and between the elite and mass musical styles to which these modes correspond. (1988: 11)

In Green's view, music teaching in schools and colleges doesn't simply pass on information about music. Implicitly, the existing stylistic hierarchy is legitimated, as is the myth that most people are 'not really very musical' in comparison with a tiny minority who are. This is the message which is conveyed by the 'hidden curriculum', or, as Althusser put it, 'the school ... teaches "know-how", but in forms which ensure *subjection to the ruling ideology* or the mastery of its "practice" ' (1972: 246).

Although influential within the Marxist tradition, however, versions of the 'dominant ideology' thesis have not been universally accepted. Abercrombie, Hill and Turner have argued forcefully that the thesis has all too often been accepted *a priori*, and is both vague and empirically falsifiable at crucial points. Rather, they suggest, 'the importance of ideology has been greatly exaggerated' (1980: 3); in conditions of modern capitalism, where the vast majority of workers are completely separated from the means of production, they are compelled by sheer economic necessity to submit to the authority of the employers, irrespective of their own beliefs and values (1980: 165). Moreover, such a state of affairs is generally accepted not through some widely disseminated 'false consciousness' but because it *is* the existing state of affairs: 'pragmatic acceptance is the result of the coercive quality of everyday life and of the routines that sustain it (1980: 166), as Berger and Luckmann, too, have argued. Once again, then, we are led to a view of the social order which emphasises both the socially constructed nature of reality and the idea that

such reality is the outcome of a perpetual struggle among contrasting and conflicting beliefs. Thus workers and other groups may seek
to resist or change the conditions which confront them through political action, and such conditions themselves are constantly being
altered as a consequence of the inherent dynamics of capitalist production. In general, then, the meanings which allow us to make sense
of our environments arise out of, and are sustained (and changed) by
the active pursuit of interests by individuals and groups. We take
them to be solid and incontrovertible, yet they rest ultimately on the
actions and interactions of other individuals. Just as a complex pattern of countervailing forces gives stability and coherence to a physical object, so the social order emerges out of millions of routine
transactions, but appears to us as objective. As individuals, members
of groups or organisations, we seek to achieve what we define as our
ends, within circumstances which we must take as 'given'.

It has been suggested that a sociological perspective can help to
overcome some of the difficulties encountered by traditional theories
of meaning. Meanings are held to be inherent neither in objects nor
in the human mind, rather they are generated in the process of communicative interaction between people, but are no less real for that.
In the remainder of this chapter, my aim will be to argue that such
an approach can help us to understand the nature of musical meanings. Firstly, though, it will be useful to consider certain established
positions on this topic. It would be wrong to categorise these as
either 'empiricist' or 'rationalist' in too rigid a manner – such
abstractions are useful in general discussions, but always fail to do
justice to the complexities (and contradictions) in the work of individual thinkers. Nevertheless, it will be seen that the works considered below do reflect the traditional dilemma: is the meaning of
music inherent in it, or is it generated by our basic mental equipment?

The language of music

The arguments of Deryck Cooke may usefully be considered here,
since they add up to a clear and coherent statement of the view that
the meaning of music is inherent in it. 'Notes, like words, have emotional connotations', writes Cooke (1959: 33), and his basic thesis is
that music is a language which expresses our unconscious emotions.

Thus in his book Cooke 'tries to pinpoint the inherent emotional characteristics of the various notes of the major, minor and chromatic scales, and of certain basic melodic patterns which have been used persistently throughout our musical history' (1959: xii). A two-note phrase, for example, falling from the minor sixth to the fifth of the diatonic scale, has been used to express 'anguish' by composers from Josquin in the fifteenth century to Schoenberg in the twentieth (1959: 14). And, a point to which we will return, 'tragic subjects' have forced composers into the minor, while 'brighter subjects ... turned them inevitably towards the major'(1959: 14). By judicious combinations of notes, harmonies and melodic devices, then, composers knowingly or otherwise create works which have an inherent meaning: musical notes are 'sounds which have clear but not rationally intelligible associations, rather inherent associations, with the basic emotions of mankind' (1959: 26). As in a language, all such elements combine with others to produce an overall pattern which is perceived as meaningful (1959: 113); ultimately, 'the fundamental (i.e. psychological) "content" of ... musical masterpieces' will be revealed (1959: 273).

It is in this musical language, then, that composers are able to convey their subjective feelings. This, for Cooke, is the great significance of music, not its 'purely aural beauty' or the intricacies of its 'technical construction' (1959: 33). It follows that the 'great artists' who can use this language are special people: 'an artist has two separate selves, the everyday, conscious self, which is a prey to many passing trivial emotions, and a deep, unconscious, creative self which is always there to return to, "inspiration" permitting' (1959: 16).

Most of Cooke's analysis is, appropriately enough, of a detailed and technical nature, as he outlines the 'elements of musical expression' and the sixteen 'basic terms of musical vocabulary'. But implicit in the discussion is a general theory of musical development and its social aspects. Cooke makes it clear that he is concerned with tonal European music in its 'harmonic' period (1959: 47), which he dates as 'roughly between 1400 and the present day' (1959: 50). This musical system is based on the rational elaboration of properties of the harmonic series, so far as this is possible; it is the music that sounds normal, even natural, to western ears. Indeed, for Cooke it *is* natural:

That the major third should be found to express pleasure should surprise no one, since it is present ... early on in the harmonic series: it is
nature's own basic harmony, and by using it we feel ourselves to be at
one with nature. (1959: 51)

More generally, says Cooke, there are 'close natural correspondences
between the emotional effects of certain notes of the scale and their
positions in ... the harmonic series' and he speaks of 'the "strength"
of the fifth and the "joy" of the major third' (1959: 25). Cooke's
empiricism is displayed clearly here – the simple consonances of
major thirds and fifths are indubitable properties of the natural
world, and their inherent meaning is held to be impressed on us
through our aural sense. This, however commonsensical it may
sound, is a bold claim: even Kant struggled to demonstrate correspondences between properties of the natural world and our
experience of them.

Gradually, through the late medieval period, modern tonality
came to supplant the set of modes which were the organising principles of church music. The church authorities fought a determined
but ultimately futile campaign against the major third, but, once it
was allowed, 'all the different modes began to transform themselves
into the more "human" Ionian and Aeolian (major and minor)
modes' (1959: 52). This suggests, says Cooke, that there was already
an established secular tradition of music utilising the major third, as
exemplified by the celebrated round 'Summer is icumen in', dating
from about 1240. Thus the opposition to 'major' music on the part
of the church involved more than just a reluctance to accept the corruption of the ancient and sacred modes: the major scales conveyed
feelings of joy and earthly well-being, in contrast to the severe and
spiritual messages of the modes, and so what was ultimately at stake
was the authority of the church itself. Eventually, though, the papal
authorities had to bow to the inevitable: 'in music, as in life, the natural tendency was towards secularity' (1959: 52). It is worth noting
that Cooke provides here an excellent example of the process by
which musical conventions, like social norms generally, may be
regarded as the outcome of a struggle between contending forces.

The two opposed forces, however, displayed significantly different
characteristics. On the one hand were the church authorities, deliberately trying to protect the status quo and fighting a losing battle
against the encroachments of the major third. On the other hand was

the tradition of secular music – not a consciously organised, formal body like the church, but a gradual, informal but none the less irresistible movement which represented in musical terms the world-view of modern humanism, with its rejection of the old absolutism of church and state, and its celebration of 'the individual's right to progress towards personal material happiness' (1959:54). For Cooke, then, the language of tonal music not only is 'natural', in the sense discussed above, but expresses the values of the great social current which brought forth the Renaissance and the Enlightenment; indeed, Cooke's analysis also provides a good example of the idea that musical systems can and do express the ideology of social collectivities, a topic which will be discussed in the following chapters.

For the present, though, it will be useful to consider some of the consequences of Cooke's argument. The idea that western tonal music bears the ideological message of humanism does indeed seem plausible from a historical point of view: as we have seen, the system became established only after a protracted struggle with the authority of the church, and appears to have flourished most strongly during the eighteenth and early nineteenth centuries, which was also the high tide of liberal humanism. Cooke's analysis also helps to explain the evident decline of tonal music from the mid-nineteenth century to the 'crisis' of tonality by the start of the twentieth, and various 'modernist' responses to this crisis: this was precisely the period in which, increasingly, confidence in the great ideas of the Enlightenment – notably the belief that social progress would be brought about through the rational application of scientific knowledge and the individual's pursuit of happiness – were eroded (Hobsbawm, 1987: Chapters 10–11). Moreover, Cooke makes some interesting suggestions concerning the differentiation of musical taste in the twentieth century: 'Only those who still believe strongly in the concept of happiness cling to the major triad' (1959: 54). This observation recognises that the perception of a crisis of confidence is, as ever, an intellectual movement rather than a popular one. The 'pleasure-biased population at large' (1959: 54), therefore, happily sing and dance their way into the encircling gloom: pop music still exploits the major triad relentlessly, most concert-goers prefer works from the 'Bach to Brahms' period, and, when the political authorities in the former USSR wished to inculcate confidence and optimism among the population, non-tonal music was banned (1959: 55).

Cooke's argument, then, contains an implicit theory of the relationship between social change and musical development, and one which, as we shall see, is in many respects similar to the analyses offered by other influential writers on this topic. What is distinctive about Cooke's discussion, however, is his explicit claim that the meaning of music is both inherent and naturally given. Clearly, such a claim is not compatible with a sociological perspective which emphasises the social construction of reality.

Cooke himself takes up the issue directly, if briefly:

> Is the traditional language of music ... a genuine emotional language, whose terms actually possess the inherent power to awaken certain definite emotions in the listener, or is it a collection of *formulae* attached by habit over a long period to certain verbally explicit emotions in masses, operas, and songs, which produce in the listener a series of conditioned reflexes?
>
> It seems most likely that the answer is 'both'. (1959: 24)

We do, Cooke acknowledges, come to accept certain conventions and forms of expression through sheer custom and habit. 'But', he continues, 'it is difficult to believe that there is no more to it than that' (1959: 25), since, in his view, the correspondences between tonal patterns (natural) and emotional reactions (experiential) could not have been established if it had not been inherent in the first place. In what follows I wish to suggest that this fundamental claim, far from being established by Cooke's arguments, is in fact undermined by them.

Before taking up some specifically musical issues, though, it is worth noting that Cooke's argument rests on certain general assumptions which have themselves received substantial, and in my view damaging, criticism. Among these, three are of particular importance in the present context. In the first place there is Cooke's assertion, at the start and at the end of his book, that music expresses our 'unconscious' emotions. It is clear from the discussion that Cooke's notion of these involves such experiences as 'joy', 'grief', and so on, so we see immediately that his conception of 'the unconscious' is rather at odds with that of Freud, who was concerned primarily with matters such as sex and repression. More troubling is the simple assumption that there *is* an inaccessible realm of mental activity which we can call 'the unconscious', since the very existence of such a realm is open to question (MacIntyre, 1958: 71–2; Coulter, 1979: 3–4).

The second general assumption links the 'unconscious' with the idea of the 'artist'; 'an artist has two separate selves', the second of which is 'deep, unconscious, creative' (Cooke, 1959: 16). Again, however familiar such assertions are, they remain pure speculation – reflecting Romantic ideology – rather than accepted fact. And just as we may question the ontological status of 'the unconscious', we must ask what evidence there is to support the myth of the 'artist' as some sort of extraordinary person, endowed with special creativity. Obviously, certain people *claim* such a status, but that is another matter.

The third preliminary problem arises from Cooke's view of music as a language, in which patterns of notes, like patterns of words, have inherent meanings. The difficulty here is that words do not have inherent meanings. The same sounds, uttered in the context of different languages, can mean quite different things; indeed the same sounds regularly mean different things *within* a language (Is the Sea Symphony in C? Let me see...). As the experience of listening to speakers of a foreign language makes clear, we must *learn* how to hear the words and how to use them in order, literally, to make sense: their meaning is not inherent, though we can come to understand it. Such elementary considerations, I suggest, cast some doubt on Cooke's claim that music is to be understood as a language, in that they reveal his own understanding of the nature of language to be unsatisfactory.

This conclusion is supported by his suggestion that notes and phrases are the elementary units of the musical language, with which the composer creates large-scale structures, each with its own inherent meaning, in the same way that a child can construct houses and castles with simple building blocks. Again, it can be objected that ordinary language simply does not work in this way. The meaning of words, phrases, whole sentences even, depends on the ways in which they are *used* (Wittgenstein, 158: 20); it is not inherent in them. For present purposes, we may simply note two consequences of this – firstly that the perception and attribution of 'correct' meanings is a social process in which we learn the rules of conventional usage, and secondly that it is an active process. The meanings of sounds or words does not simply impress itself on us – as the example of the foreign language suggests; instead we are constantly engaged in an active process of defining and interpreting the relevant aspects of our cultural environment according to rules, preconceptions, expectations, etc., which past experience has provided us with. As Tia DeNora has argued, neither ordinary language nor musical communication can be understood as a system by which an unambiguous message passes from a transmitter to a receiver. Rather, DeNora stresses the active role of the hearer in making sense of sounds which are organised according to linguistic or musical conventions, pointing out that the meaning of music depends on the 'interpretive procedures' of the listener as well as the work of the composer (1986: 90). Indeed, DeNora argues, it is the very indeterminacy of musical meaning which affords ample opportunity for listeners to do the 'work' of imputing meaning to it, and for powerful groups to seek to impose authoritative meanings on it (1986: 93). Inevitably, we will return to this topic; for the moment, enough has been said, I hope, to suggest the inadequacy of Cooke's assumptions about the nature of language and communication, about the 'artist', and about the 'unconscious'. We may now return to his specifically musical argument.

As we have seen, Cooke restricts his analysis to the tonal music of the West since the fifteenth century, yet he persistently generalises his claims to encompass all of humanity (e.g. 1959: 26). Two things follow from this. Firstly, all other patterns of musical expression must be judged in terms drawn from those of western tonality and its conventions. Cooke implicitly assumes that 'music' is produced by an individual (male) composer, and played by specialist musicians before a passive audience. I have already suggested that these conditions simply do not obtain in most of the cultural contexts where music is performed; from a sociological viewpoint, therefore, there are reasons to doubt that Cooke's assumptions reflect 'natural' conditions. Secondly, Cooke's position seems defensible only if it is accepted that western tonal music is a higher, or more developed, form than other musical systems. There are many who would agree with this, arguing – as Max Weber did – that its elaborate and rational harmonic system is a unique achievement of western civilisation. What is at stake, however, is not the aesthetic or technical merit of this achievement, but the claim that it is based on nature rather than culture. And it is here, at the heart of the matter, that Cooke's thesis seems flawed. He concedes, as he must, that the joyful emotions which he regards as inherent in music based on the major triad are in fact expressed in quite different ways in other cultural traditions. (Indeed, there are plenty of exceptions to his 'rule' *within* the western system, but let that pass.) This, I believe, is the crucial passage:

> it is only natural that, outside of the orbit of Western European civili-
> sation, and outside the period of its belief in the individual's right to
> progress through material happiness, people whose lives have not been
> based on this attitude have not insisted on the major third, but have
> expressed their own assertion of vitality in different ways. (1959: 55)

So they have, and so they do, and so much for the notion that the
musical meanings encoded in western tonality are 'natural'. But still
Cooke will not give in, arguing that wherever western culture and its
values have penetrated other cultures, tonal music 'has begun to oust
the music of that culture from the people's affections' (1959: 55), thus
demonstrating, presumably, that their own traditions are inadequate.
Quite part from the fact that Cooke's claim is untrue, this is either
a naive or a disingenuous argument, lacking any appreciation of the
massive economic and political forces that bear on traditional cultures once they are penetrated by the agents and ideology of rational Western capitalism. If European classical music was established
in, say, Nigeria in the nineteenth century (Collins and Richards,
1989) and, rather more successfully, in Japan in the twentieth, this
does not mean that the music is therefore to be regarded as the natural expression of human aspirations. Rather, it suggests that the
lifestyles and ideals of competitive capitalism have been legitimated
as those to which progressive individuals ought to aspire, instead of
the established traditions of their culture; an important part of this
legitimation consists in casting the old ways in an unfavourable light,
as 'primitive' in comparison which the sophistication of the West –
just as Cooke's analysis does.

   In sum, I suggest that Cooke's view of western music is open to
exactly those sorts of criticisms which Marx made of the early political economists when they argued that capitalism was both the natural condition of economic relations and the highest stage in the
development of society. The conventions and institutions of western
music are not natural, in the sense that they correspond to the fundamental laws of nature: plenty of societies have developed sophisticated musical cultures quite unlike those of the West. But all such
cultures come to seem natural and normal to those who have been
socialised in them. Just as the diatonic scale sounds natural to western ears, so there is a belief in western societies that human beings
are naturally competitive and acquisitive. This is held to be 'human

nature'. But, as we have seen, the sociological and anthropological evidence does not support such a belief; what it does suggest is that human beings do not 'naturally' conform to any particular type of character. What we are naturally born with is the capacity to *become* all sorts of different people through our learning abilities (Gould, 1984: 331–3). Significantly, Cooke seems to concede as much in trying to deal with what is, for his position, a thorny problem – the fact that people often fail to perceive the 'natural' meaning of a piece of music, and indeed offer highly varied interpretations of it. To extricate himself from his difficulties, Cooke resorts to further psychological assumptions: some listeners 'are just plainly unmusical' (1959: 22); those who don't accept the conventional (i.e. his) interpretation of the *Eroica* are 'emotionally undeveloped' (1959: 22). Eventually, those who still find it hard to agree with him are simply abused: 'One is bound to regard anyone who reacts in this way as either superficial, unmusical, or unsympathetic to Beethoven' (1959: 23).

Plainly, this is not good enough. Yet in considering his own deepening appreciation of Mozart, Cooke himself suggests the way out of the tangle. Our understanding of music does not involve the direct appreciation of inherent meaning but the process through which, both informally and via direct instruction, we *learn* the culturally appropriate ways to hear it. Once again, we are led to consider the power of socialisation, the way in which elements of our culture penetrate deeply into our thinking, to the point where we find it hard to conceive of things in any other way. In other words, we become so committed to our established interpretive procedures that we believe they must be natural. This is, I believe, why authors such as Cooke feel it so important to establish that their own view is 'natural', and why, as in many other contexts, they betray a certain irritation with those who cannot or will not see things their way. But the stubborn fact is that there are other ways, and the evidence does not support Cooke's belief that his interpretation of tonal music describes its inherent meanings. On the contrary, what his arguments lucidly display are the ways in which, in the western tradition, certain meanings have been conferred on certain patterns of sound. We shall consider the process in more detail below.

The forms of music

I have considered certain aspects of Cooke's discussion in some detail in order to emphasise the ways in which a sociological perspective on musical meaning differs from one which presupposes that meanings can be inherent in the objects, or in this case the patterns of sound, that we perceive. But what of the second traditional approach to the analysis of meaning, the rationalist idea that the way we perceive the world is determined by the fundamental processes of the human mind?

Eduard Hanslick's essay *The Beautiful in Music* was first published in 1854, more than a century before Cooke's work. But in that time it has become recognised as a classic statement of a position exactly opposite to that of Cooke: the view that music cannot represent things in general, or express emotions in particular. The same music, Hanslick argues, may be subject to a wide range of interpretations, and he provides a celebrated example, from Gluck's *Orfeo*, of a melody which 'would accord equally well, if not better, with words conveying exactly the reverse' of their meaning in the opera (Hanslick, 1891: 48). Hanslick's main aim was to emancipate the appreciation of music from what he considered its primitive, vague and subjective condition, and – much in accordance with the spirit of his time – to establish it on a proper scientific basis. Only by employing the methods of 'natural science', he suggested, can we 'determine what is permanent and objective in [things], when dissociated from the ever-varying impressions which they produce' (1891: 16), a view which echoes Descartes' rational argument against 'the fluctuating assurance of the senses'. Above all, says Hanslick, aesthetic investigations must 'consider the beautiful *object*, and not the perceiving *subject*' (1891: 17), and he scornfully dismisses those who hold that we can understand music by the effects it produces: 'We might as well study the properties of wine by getting drunk' (1891: 24).

So what, for Hanslick, are the objective properties of music? Essentially, these are the relationships between tones which constitute its form, the 'sound and motion' (1891: 67) which the composer creates in order to express ideas which are 'specifically musical. By this we mean that the beautiful is not contingent upon, or in need of, any subject introduced from without but that it consists wholly of sounds artificially combined' (1891: 66). Both the meaning and the beauty of music, then, are inherent in the formal properties which, in contrast to the array of subjective impressions which may be engendered, can be objectively identified and analysed.

At first sight, it might seem as if Hanslick had produced another version of the empiricist position, in that he holds formal properties to be objective, and meaning to be inherent in them. But beautiful and meaningful forms, he says, are not given by nature, nor by God: they are the creations of the human intellect. It is in this sense that Hanslick's work echoes many of the themes of Enlightenment rationalism. The fundamental elements of modern western music, he emphasises, have not been learnt 'from surrounding nature' (1891: 146); on the contrary, they are 'slowly gained triumphs of the human mind' (1891: 147) The sounds which envelop us – the infant's cry, the babbling brook, the howling wind and so on – must be regarded as 'mere noise – i.e. an irregular succession of sonorous pulses' (1891: 149) By contrast, the great tradition of western music is a specifically intellectual achievement (1891: 151), founded on the measurable tone, which does not occur naturally. Hanslick sums up his position with characteristic vigour: 'Not the voices of animals, but their gut is of importance to us; and the animal to which music is most indebted is not the nightingale but the sheep' (1891: 152).

Time and again in his essay, Hanslick emphasises the idea that both the composition and interpretation of music are specifically intellectual achievements, in which meaning is *imposed* on our physical environment, rather than being received from it. He compares the work of composition to that of a sculptor carving a fine form out of an amorphous yet obdurate material; in doing such work both composer and sculptor are guided by their 'imagination' (1891: 80), as each seeks to give 'an objective existence to his ... ideal' (1891: 100–1). Similarly, the pleasure to be derived from listening to music is primarily an intellectual one: 'the intellectual satisfaction which the listener derives from continually following and anticipating the composer's intentions' (1891: 135). It is here, too, that Hanslick is most dismissive of the school of thought which holds that music expresses emotions. He does not deny that music produces emotional reactions, but holds that these are secondary effects, caused by the physical effects of sound on our nervous system (1891: 122). To suggest that the main aim of music is the production of such effects is thus to degrade it to the level of a mere physical stimulus, something subhuman or, at best, characteristic of less developed civilisations.

For this reason, Hanslick describes such a response to music as 'pathological' (1891: 124).

We can now identify some of the assumptions on which Hanslick's argument rests. Human progress has, above all, involved the gradual development of our rational, that is intellectual, capacities. It is the power of our ideas that has liberated us from subjection to the material environment, and enabled us to change and dominate it. The great achievements of modern western civilisation, such as its musical system, are above all intellectual achievements and must be appreciated as such: even the Greeks, who sought to identify specific feelings and states of mind with each of their musical modes, were still experiencing music in an emotional manner, and thus had not yet achieved true 'art' 1891: 134). However, 'creations of the human intellect demand a different attitude of mind, unless we would drag them down to the level of mere physical stimulants ... it is precisely the "specifically-musical" element of the creation of inventive genius which the contemplating mind apprehends and assimilates' (1891: 126, 127).

In the present context, it is significant that in attacking the widely held ideas that music represents things or expresses emotions, Hanslick was led to emphasise the theme of music as essentially a creation of the human mind. Whereas, as we have seen, Cooke argued that the basic elements of the western musical system reflected fundamental properties of the natural world, Hanslick is adamant that the system is, on the contrary, a *construction* which, while obviously limited by the laws of physics, owes its substance to the creative work of the human intellect. Sounds do not impose meaning on us; we impose it on them. And despite the claims and assertions which strike the modern reader as outdated, even offensive, there is considerable force in Hanslick's critique of the idea that music can 'represent feelings' (1891: 11). The idea that the creation of music is above all an intellectual activity, and hence the view that it is only in the relatively recent past that music has acquired the status of 'art', remains influential: 'the phenomenon of music', said Stravinsky, 'is nothing other than a phenomenon of speculation' (1942: 27).

Yet from a sociological point of view one further assumption, which serves to confirm Hanslick as a child of his times, is of central importance.

> Though music possesses beauty of form without any extrinsic subject, this does not deprive it of the quality of *individuality*. The act of inventing a certain theme, and the mode of working it out, are always so unique and specific as to defy their inclusion in a wider generality. These processes are distinctly and unequivocally *individual* in nature. (1891: 173)

The musical work, then, is the realisation of the composer's unique consciousness: 'the subjectively-producing mind is essentially individual' (1891: 173). Clearly, it is just such a claim, so characteristic of much nineteenth-century thought, that was disputed by the classic sociological thinkers. As we have seen, both Durkheim and Marx were concerned to demonstrate the extent to which individual consciousness is dependent on social context, and the concept of socialisation alerts us to the ways in which, inevitably, we 'internalise' elements of the culture which surrounds us. Moreover, composers do not simply express their individuality in idiosyncratic ways, but typically must attend to established forms and conventions, even when they seek to transcend them. Before they create so much as a semiquaver, composers are already imbued with the habits of thought of particular cultural contexts, and for their music to be experienced as meaningful such habits of thought must be shared by a community of listeners (see chapter 5).

A similar point has been made in relation to the concept of form as it is used by authors such as Hanslick. 'These forms satisfy us', writes Scruton, 'because we have an understanding of the structural relations which they exemplify' (1983: 39). What is problematic is where such an understanding comes from. It has already been argued that the comprehension of music cannot be intuitive: the music of other cultures may mean nothing to us, and even when we do derive pleasure from its sounds it is doubtful whether we can be said to 'understand' it until we have learned to participate in the intellectual and social system that produced it. So once again we are led back to the fundamental importance of the concepts of culture and socialisation in accounting for the nature of our understanding of music. This, too, is the implication of Scruton's discussion of 'absolute' music:

> The relations are grasped by the ear in an intuitive act of apprehension, but the satisfaction that springs therefrom is akin to the satisfaction derived from the pursuit of mathematics. It is not a satisfaction that is

open to everyone. Like mathematics, it depends on understanding, and understanding can be induced only by the establishment of a proper musical culture. (1983: 39)

The implication seems clear. The meaning of music is not inherent in it, but neither is it understood by direct intuition. Whether by direct instruction or informal experience, we *learn* to hear music as meaningful and coherent patterns of sound, just as we learn to 'make sense' of everything else in our social world. It must be said, however, that most of those who have considered the question of musical meaning have emphasised psychological processes at the expense of social ones. For Suzanne Langer, authors such as Hanslick fail to confront the central difficulty: if music does not carry some sort of emotive content, in other words if it is not 'significant', then it is 'meaningless' (1969: 27). Langer's own account rests squarely on claims and speculations about the operation of the human mind: 'there are certain aspects of the so-called 'inner life' – physical or mental – which have formal properties similar to those of music – patterns of motion and rest, of tension and release, of agreement and disagreement, preparation, fulfilment, excitation, sudden change, etc' (1969: 228). For Langer the form and character of music reflect 'the morphology of feeling' (1969: 238), but no particular feelings or emotions. So, she argues, we can now explain why the same music, as in the example from Gluck used by Hanslick, is capable of conveying quite different meanings: emotions which we experience as different may be similar in their underlying form (1969: 238). Thus, 'music conveys general forms of feeling related to specific ones as algebraic expressions are related to arithmetic' (1969: 238). It follows that the power of music is seen as its capacity to represent the 'life of feeling' in a way that language cannot (1969: 243), and Langer is led to endorse Wagner's claim that music can express 'what is unspeakable in verbal language; (1969: 235).

We are not at present primarily concerned with the validity or otherwise of Langer's interpretation, although it is worth remarking that, contrary to her assertions, the similarity between musical structures and patterns of human experience is not a 'well-established fact' (1969: 226). What is of central importance in the present context is the way in which her arguments rest on certain assumptions about the universal properties of the human mind. The forms of music are held to follow 'inherent psychological laws of "rightness" '

(1969: 240), and its structures and conventions to reflect deep, ineffable mental processes. If this is the case, it becomes difficult to account for the range and diversity of musical forms; however, once again it is evident that by 'music' Langer means the art-music tradition of western Europe. (And her arguments implicitly serve to legitimise this tradition as the apex of human musical creativity – it is held to reflect, after all, the fundamental structures of the mind.)

The idea that the underlying forms of music are in some ways consistent with the fundamental structures of the human mind has been expressed in a variety of ways, from Schopenhauer, who held that music was 'the most direct and immediate expression of man's self-consciousness' to the musicologist John Blacking, who suggested that 'at the level of deep structures in music there are elements that are common to the human psyche, although they may not appear in the surface structures' (1976: 109). In recent years such ideas have flourished under the widespread influence of Noam Chomsky's work in linguistics, and, as Chomsky himself points out, such thinking is a modern version of traditional rationalism: 'if we take the essence of this view to be that the general character of knowledge, the categories in which it is expressed or internally represented, and the basic principles that underlie it, are determined by the nature of the mind' (1971: 27). In short, 'the basic properties of the output are a consequence of the design of the device' (1971: 125–6). This position has been elaborated in respect of music by Lerdahl and Jackendoff in their *Generative Theory of Tonal Music*; for present purposes, the central issue arises from their claim that 'much of the complexity of musical intuition is not learned, but is given by the inherent organisation of the mind, itself determined by the human genetic inheritance' (1983: 281).

As with the works discussed above, a detailed consideration of Lerdahl and Jackendoff's analysis is beyond the scope of this chapter; it is already apparent, however, that the assumptions on which it is based amount to a powerful claim that the nature of music is governed by the fundamental properties of the human mind. Our ability to make sense of music, according to Lerdahl and Jackendoff, is just one aspect of our more general capacity to impose an order, an organised pattern, on the infinite variety of sense-data with which we are constantly bombarded. Musical intuition is thus held to consist of 'largely unconscious knowledge ... that the listener brings to his hearing'; such knowledge enables us to form a coherent mental representation of the music's 'surface patterns' (1983: 63). The whole process depends on our possession of a sort of 'grammar' of music, in the same way that linguists such as Chomsky claim that we have an 'innate universal grammar' (1972: 87), which allows us to create and use languages.

Yet it should be clear that an approach which rests on the assumption of an 'innate universal grammar' must be open to the same kind of sociological objections as traditional rationalist perspectives. It would be naive to assume that the structure of the human brain had no effect on our cognitive processes; it is quite another matter to claim that the latter are *determined* by the former. Such claims, as Coulter has argued, implicitly rest on a reification of the concept of mind as a 'measurable and objectified' property of persons (1979: 68). In so far as this involves treating a concept, mind, as if it were a tangible object, it is a metaphysical speculation which is hard to reconcile with the requirements of scientific discourse. By contrast, interpretive sociologists, following G. H. Mead in particular, have developed the idea that thinking is an activity and mind a *process*, rather than a thing (Mead, 1934).

Another influential theorist, Leonard Meyer, also emphasised the psychological processes involved in producing our responses to music although, as we shall see, his arguments lead to a very different perspective from that of Lerdahl and Jackendoff. Meyer's point of departure is the 'psychological theory of emotions' which suggests that 'Emotion or affect is aroused when a tendency to respond is arrested or inhibited' (1970: 14). According to this theory, the source of an emotional response should be sought neither in the object which acts as a stimulus nor in the 'responding individual', but in the relationship between them (1970: 13). When an event is followed by another in a normal, routine way, or when we bring about a desired state of affairs according to our expectations, we experience little emotional arousal. But if something unexpected happens, or our expectations are frustrated, we are likely to feel some sort of increase in emotional tension. Related to music, says Meyer, this idea explains why we can have an emotional response although the stimulus – the music – does not represent or refer to anything specific. The clever composer, for example, can lead us into suspense and uncertainty by frustrating our harmonic or melodic expectations: 'The greater the buildup of suspense, of tension, the greater the emotional release upon resolution' (1970: 28). And, we might add, the

greater the challenge to the creative ingenuity of the composer. For
Meyer, then, sequences of tension and resolution, engendered by the
manipulation of musical conventions, are the basis of our emotional
response to music.

Such a perspective, says Meyer, also helps to account for the
tremendous power of music:

> Musical experiences of suspense are very similar to those experienced
> in real life. Both in life and in music the emotions thus arising have
> essentially the same stimulus situation: the situation of ignorance, the
> awareness of the individual's impotence and inability to act where the
> future course of events is unknown. Because the musical experiences are
> so very similar to those existing in the drama and in life itself, they are
> often felt to be particularly powerful and effective.
>
>   Musical suspense seems to have direct analogies in experience in
> general: it makes us feel something of the insignificance and powerless-
> ness of man in the face of the inscrutable workings of destiny. (1970:
> 28)

No one could accuse Meyer of understating his case: musical
experience may lead us to confront the ultimate uncertainties of the
human condition, and, although he does not discuss the point, this
interpretation of the emotional power of music might also be used
to explain a rather different experience, the positive sense of well-
being produced by various forms of popular music. In much of the
latter there is little in the way of departure from established conventions, melodies are generally simple and unadventurous, and –
above all – rhythm is rudimentary and repetitive. Such tensions as
do arise are soon resolved, again and again. It is no surprise then that
from Meyer's point of view such music is likely to be experienced as
positive and affirmative.

My present concern, though, is neither to develop nor criticise
Meyer's arguments, but, as in the case of the other authors who have
considered these topics, to examine the assumptions on which his
claims are based. It is evident, as we have seen, that Meyer regards
the 'psychological theory of the emotions' as an important principle;
he also holds that the theory (which, incidentally, soon becomes a
'law') has universal application, and describes the 'law of affect' as
'a general proposition relevant to human psychology in all realms of
experience' (1970: 62). It would be quite misleading, however, to
leave the impression that Meyer's ideas rest only on an unredeemed

psychologism. On the contrary, what is of particular significance in the present context is the extent to which Meyer recognises the *cultural* preconditions of the processes with which he is concerned.

Despite his claim that the 'law of affect' has universal applicability, Meyer is critical of those psychologists who believe that 'the responses obtained by experiment or otherwise are universal, natural, and necessary' (1970: 5). Reactions of pleasure and displeasure to experimental stimuli, far from being universals, are in fact 'products of learning and experience' (1970: 5). Similarly, the system of western music is neither a reflection of the properties of the physical world nor an expression of the deep structures of the human mind: 'the particular organisation developed in Western music is not universal, natural, or God-given' (1970: 66). So how is this insistence on the culture-specific nature of both general experience and the forms of music reconciled with the general psychological principle outlined above? The clue lies in his discussion of the effects of tension and resolution. For the arousal of affect, as we have seen, expectations must be frustrated in some way; but for this to occur we must have some prior notion of what a normal or desirable outcome would be. Thus in music we must have some sort of general expectations about harmonic progressions, tonality, melodic contours, rhythm and so on before we can make sense of it, and before it can arouse an emotional response in us. (Meyer does not deny that it is possible to derive pleasure from hearing the music of a culture with which we are unfamiliar; what is doubtful in such a case is whether we can experience the music in the way that its performers and indigenous audience do. Whereas their experience is a shared one, ours will be private and idiosyncratic. As Meyer put it, we can hear the sound but not the music.)

Again and again, Meyer insists that the process of socialisation is a precondition of our ability to make sense of music. Culture, not nature or intuition, is what makes music meaningful. If, purely for heuristic purposes, we make a distinction between 'expectations that arise out of the nature of human mental processes' in general, and those that 'are based upon learning in the broadest sense of the term', it emerges that the latter have a considerable influence on the former. 'Paradoxical as it may seem, the expectations based upon learning are, in a sense, prior to the natural modes of thought' (1970: 43). Here Meyer relies on the arguments of Edward Sapir, whose ideas were a formative influence on the modern study of sociolinguistics. The forms of the language that we acquire, said Sapir, is the fundamental influence on the ways that we learn to think – providing us with the concepts and categories we habitually employ, the distinctions and discriminations we are able to make, and pre-selecting the intellectual operations that we learn to perform. Ferdinand de Saussure made the point graphically: 'In itself thought is like a swirling cloud, where no shape is intrinsically determinate. No ideas are established in advance, and nothing is distinct, before the introduction of linguistic structure' (quoted in Sturrock, 1986: 18). It is in such ways that a *social* institution, language, comes to shape the consciousness of individuals. Similarly, Meyer suggests, 'the expectations which result from the nature of human mental processes are always conditioned by the possibilities and probabilities inherent in the materials and their organisation as presented in a *particular* musical style' (1970: 43, emphasis added). It is for this reason that the conventions of a musical system come to sound normal, and indeed natural, to those who have absorbed them through the process of socialisation, and other systems may seem strange, incomprehensible or simply wrong.

To repeat, I am not primarily concerned here with Meyer's own account of the nature of musical meaning, or the validity of the psychological 'law of affect' on which it is based. For present purposes, however, Meyer's work is of considerable interest in that it gives explicit recognition to the vital process which both empiricist and rationalist approaches have tended to neglect – the social construction of meaning. Indeed, Meyer draws on the work of one of the most influential of modern sociological theorists, G. H. Mead, in rejecting the beliefs that meaning is either inherent in objects or generated intuitively by the observer; it arises, rather, out of the triadic *relationship* between the object, the thing indicated or designated by the object, and the observer. Such a relationship is simply a formal way of describing the basic process of cultural learning, as in language acquisition, for example, when a person (the observer) learns that an arbitrary sound (the object) represents another object or idea (the thing designated). The example also serves as a reminder that while the particular sounds, in the form of words, which come to represent things are arbitrary (i.e., the same sounds can mean different things in different languages, and different things in different usages within the same language), the practical connection between words and their meanings is not an arbitrary one. On the contrary, the whole process of symbolic communication through language depends on our acceptance of normal, proper and conventional usages which are neither subjective nor self-evident but are created, maintained, and changed in the course of collaborative social inter-action. The very existence of a language implies a community of – literally – like-minded people.

In recognising that socially derived knowledge is prior to indivi-dual experience, Meyer is inevitably led towards some of the themes which are central to a sociologically informed perspective on musi-cal meaning. It will be useful to emphasise these before considering the perspective as a whole.

Above all, and following directly from what has been said above, it should be clear that the possibility of shared musical meanings, and the communication of such meanings, presupposes a community of people who, as a result of socialisation, share a more-or-less common frame of reference which provides them with the 'taken for granted' knowledge (Schütz 1972: 74), or in Meyer's terms the appro-priate expectations, with which to interpret what they hear in a cul-turally competent way. Such knowledge and expectations can range from the vague general assumptions about what would be an appropriate course of events at, say, a formal concert, or a disco, or a rain dance, to highly precise ideas about style which enable the expert to distinguish Brahms from Schubert, John Coltrane from Sonny Rollins, or The Clash from The Damned. Meyer also draws on G. H. Mead's work in his discussion of the communication of musical meanings. In order to communicate, said Mead, we must first make the assumption that our acts and utterances mean the same to others as they do to us; to the extent that we share the same culture, and so have a 'reciprocity' of perspectives, the assumption is reasonable and thus a good basis for practical action. It is because they can make the assumption of a shared musical culture, says Meyer, that composers are able to predict the effects that their sound patterns will have on audiences, and plan their works accordingly (1970: 40–1). In Mead's terms, the composer does what we all do in everyday communication – that is, 'take the role of the other'. (It is worth remarking in passing that the point applies just as much to those who seek to challenge existing conventions as to those whose aim is to conform; the idea will be developed in Chapter 5.)

The idea that the communication of musical meanings presup-poses a community of hearers has other significant implications. In

western societies, the typical experience of socialisation gives most
people diffuse and general – though none the less powerful – expectations about the nature of music. But such vague, commonsense
knowledge can be augmented by formal or informal learning, and
the consequent production of groups with specialised knowledge or
expertise – performers, teachers, composers, critics, as well as 'music
lovers' of all kinds. Each of these groups may be further differentiated according to the types and styles of music with which they are
concerned, and each of the groups and subgroups may be regarded
as a 'community of hearers'. Two points, both of which are of considerable theoretical importance, follow from this. Firstly, it is in the
nature of this process of differentiation that such specialised groups
may perceive themselves to have less and less in common with each
other, and indeed may be engaged in conflicts with others over musical principles and, crucially, access to resources. It is the outcomes
of such struggles, however temporary or provisional, which establishes the parameters and constraints of the 'music world' as it is
experienced by participants. Secondly, it is obvious that the process
of differentiation and fragmentation, in principle, may be continued
to the point where we ultimately recognise only the unique
configuration of interests and experience which characterises particular individuals. However, as I have suggested in Chapter 1, sophisticated sociological theory seeks not to deny the uniqueness of
individuals' experience but to illuminate the processes by which
orderly social life emerges in spite of it. In the present context, what
matters above all is not whether people in fact do 'share' meanings
or display a 'reciprocity of perspectives' but that they *believe* themselves to do so (Heritage, 1984: 54).

Communities of hearers may be characterised, by their members
or by outsiders, by the common frame of reference they are believed
to display, as we talk of different 'styles' of music. 'Musical styles',
says Meyer, 'are more or less complex systems of sound relationships
understood and used in common by a group of individuals' (1970:
45). As noted above, such shared understandings are the consequence
of socialisation, and so there is a general, though loose, relationship
between the socio-economic stratification of a society and the hierarchy of musical styles which is reflected in its musical institutions.
'Cultural needs are the product of upbringing and education', writes
Bourdieu, the consequence being that 'To the socially recognised
hierarchy of the arts, and within each of them, of genres, schools and

periods, corresponds a social hierarchy of the consumers' (1984: 1).
We will return to this theme more than once.

Meyer is more concerned with another aspect of stylistic differentiation – the way in which a specific pattern of musical expectations
is engendered in each listener:

> The norms and deviants of a style upon which expectation and conse-
> quently meaning are based are to be found in the habit responses of lis-
> teners who have learned to understand these relationships ... These
> dispositions and habits are learned by constant practice in listening and
> performing, practice which should, and usually does, begin in early
> childhood. (1970: 61)

More particularly, such 'dispositions and habits' lead the listener to
have certain specifically musical expectations: 'what a musical stimulus or series of stimuli indicate and point to are not extramusical
concepts but other musical events which are about to happen' 1970:
35). The meaning of such stimuli, therefore, is the expectation
aroused in the competent listener that some particular events are
about to happen in the music; it is in this sense that Meyer speaks
of meaning as being 'embodied'; that is, both the stimulus and the
consequences it implies 'are of the same kind' (1970: 35). By contrast,
'most of the meanings which arise in human communication are of
the designative type' (1970: 35) – as when words or graphic symbols
are used to designate objects or ideas which are substantially different from themselves. As we shall see, several authors have drawn a
similar distinction between musical meanings which are 'embodied'
or intrinsic and those which are 'designative' or extrinsic.

One further theme in Meyer's work should be mentioned, as it will
be discussed further in the following section. Despite the psychological elements in his theory, and his use of the concepts of stimulus and response, it is clear that Meyer does not imply any simple
behaviourist explanation of human action. On the contrary, through
his emphasis on the prior knowledge which a listener brings to a
musical event (and which, indeed, allows the listener to interpret the
situation correctly as a 'musical' one, with all its attendant expectations), he is alerting us to the fact that objects must be *defined* as
stimuli, and their meanings correctly interpreted, before they can
produce any response. Three aspects of this may be briefly noted.
Firstly, as we have seen, music has meaning for us only to the extent
that our past experiences provide us with the various expectations

which we bring to the listening situation, and which we use to make sense of it. Secondly, more general, non-musical, expectations may also be a powerful influence on our interpretation of such a situation. Of particular interest in this context is the belief, which has proliferated in western societies only in the last two hundred years or so, that there is a realm of 'art' which can provide specifically 'aesthetic' experiences: 'the attention given to a work of art is a direct product of the belief in the significance and vitality of aesthetic experience' (Meyer, 1970: 74). Thirdly, as we have seen, musical styles are 'in the last analysis, artificial constructs developed by musicians within a specific culture' (1970: 60), and are recognised as such only by a community of hearers.

Taken together, the above points serve to remind us that the idea of listeners as passive recipients of unambiguous messages, an idea perhaps encouraged by the conventional passivity of western concert audiences, is highly misleading. Listening to music, just like listening to speech, involves an *active* process of interpretation. The implications of this are profound. Human beings do not 'behave' in predetermined ways, like the fall of apples from trees or the movement of billiard balls after they collide. It follows that human action cannot be explained in terms of simple sequences of cause and effect: we do not just 'respond' to stimuli. Rather, we actively identify significant objects in our environment, interpret them on the basis of our prior knowledge, and decide on an appropriate course of action. This holds good regardless of how swiftly or routinely we perform an action, for there is always the possibility that we may decide to do something different. In short, human beings *act*, they do not 'behave', and listening is an active process.

Socialisation and commonsense knowledge

The constant succession of sounds which constitutes our acoustic environment is, like all the other objects and entities that surround us, literally meaning-less. That is, as we have seen, such things in themselves do not impose their significance upon us; on the contrary, as socialised humans we not only endow things with meaning but indeed constitute them as discrete objects in the first place. The main thrust of sociological thinking on these matters has already been introduced – the idea that this process of reality-construction must be understood as a collective rather than an individual one. The example of language is of paramount importance in this respect: it is an institution which is collectively created and sustained, which we must learn in order to become a competent member of society, and which profoundly if imperceptibly shapes our consciousness even as we acquire it. Moreover, languages are never static: change is constant, the outcome of the activities of countless individuals through time. It is in this sense that language, like other institutions, may be said to be alienated – we create it, yet it appears to us as independent, and can come to dominate us.

It follows that the meanings of music are neither inherent nor intuitively recognised, but emerge and become established (or changed or forgotten) as a consequence of the activities of groups of people in particular cultural contexts. The way that we 'make sense' of music is not innate but depends on our acquisition of commonsense, taken-for-granted ideas about how it *ought* to sound. In every culture, some conventional patterns of organised sound becomes accepted as normal and even natural. The range of sounds within which human beings can reliably distinguish different pitches extends from around 27 cycles per second (very low pitch) to, for practical purposes, about 10,000 cycles per second (many people, especially when they are young, can hear sounds of even greater frequency – i.e. higher – but find it hard to distinguish between their pitches) (Backus, 1970: 111). But according to Backus the highest useful frequency of sounds produced by musical instruments is around the 4186 cycles per second which are generated by the top note on the piano. So 'the working range of fundamental frequencies ... is then approximately 27 to 4200 cycles per second' (1970: 111–12). It is this range that is conventionally divided up, in western tonality, into the eighty-eight 'notes' of the full-sized keyboard, ascending and descending in equal 'semitone' steps.

For present purposes, what is interesting about this arrangement, apparently so reasonable and natural to the western ear, is that it is neither necessary nor inevitable. The pitch of a sound is, after all, a point on a continuum, not a clearly demarcated step: think of the way in which it is possible to slide from a low note to a high one (or vice versa) on a violin or a trombone, or, best of all, using the human voice. The sound comes out as a continuous ascent or descent, not a series of separate notes. Moreover, most people are able to make pitch discriminations much more fine than the semitones which are the smallest conventional steps in western music – in the upper part of the frequency range, we can distinguish sounds which are only 0.04 of a semitone apart (Backus, 1970: 113). Thus, there could, hypothetically, be twenty-five separate 'notes' within every semitone, and we could build a piano with about 2,200 keys. This may seem absurd; the point is to emphasise that there is no *natural* reason why such an instrument could not be created, and that the tonal organisation of western music is the product of culture rather than nature. Out of the greater number of possible pitches 'we select certain discrete frequencies for musical purposes; the array of chosen frequencies is called a scale' (Backus, 1970: 115).

The construction of scales, of course, involves certain practical constraints. Too many notes would result in an unmanageable system. (The advent of the computer and the synthesiser could change all that, although the mass production of portable electronic keyboards seems destined to reinforce, rather than undermine, the hegemony of western tonality.) On the other hand, the physical properties of the harmonic series can be used to construct very simple pentatonic or diatonic scales which can be standardised and which generate elementary harmonies (See Piston, 1978: 535ff.). It would be wrong, though, to assume that such scales are therefore determined by nature rather than human ingenuity. For while the properties of the harmonic series, as supposedly elaborated by Pythagoras (though see Barnes, 1987: 37), are indeed invariant and part of the obdurate natural environment, cultures have varied enormously in the uses to which such properties are put. Octave unison lines, or even the elementary harmonies, are simply not employed in some musical systems, and in fact the development of a comprehensive rational harmonic system is unique to western art-music, as Max Weber pointed out:

> The musical ear of other peoples has probably been even more sensitively developed than our own, certainly not less so. Polyphonic music of various kinds has been widely distributed over the globe. The cooperation of a number of instruments and also the singing of parts have existed elsewhere. All our rational tone intervals have been known and calculated. But rational harmonious music, both counterpoint and harmony; formation of the tone material on the basis of three triads with the harmonic third; our chromatics and enharmonics, not interpreted in terms of space, but (since the Renaissance) in terms of harmony; our orchestra, with its string quartet as a nucleus, and the organisation of ensembles of wind instruments; our bass accompaniment; our system of

notation, which has made possible the composition and production of modern musical works, and thus their very survival; our sonatas, symphonies, operas; and, finally, as means to all these, our fundamental instruments, the organ, violin, piano, and so on; all these things are known only in the Occident, although programme music, tone, poetry, alteration of tones and chromatics have existed in various musical traditions as means of expression (1930: 14–15).

For Weber, as we shall see in Chapter 6, western music was an early and important aspect of the general process of rationalisation which was the decisive and distinctive characteristic of European civilisation; far from being determined by nature, human activities were rationalised precisely in order to render them controllable and subject to the dictates of reason (Weber, in Gerth and Mills, 1948: 139).

Moreover, the actual arrangement of notes in western music is not a direct reflection of the harmonic series: since the time of Bach the system in common use has been a modified, or 'tempered', one, which is intended to eliminate some of the inherent irregularities of naturally sounding harmonics. The conclusion to one of the standard works on western harmony emphasises the significance of this: 'The tempered system, so different from nature, is symbolic of the whole art of music: more than any other, music is the sublime artificial art, the creation of the mind of man' (Piston, 1978: 543). Another authority, Charles Rosen, makes a similar point about our conceptions of 'right' and 'wrong' harmonies:

> Which sounds are to be consonances is determined at a given historical moment by the prevailing historical style, and consonances have varied radically according to the musical system developed in each culture. ... It is not, therefore, the human ear or nervous system that decides what is a dissonance ... A dissonance is defined by its role in the musical 'language' as it makes possible the movement from tension to resolution which is at the heart of what may be generally called expressivity. (1976: 33)

Rosen's remarks serve to bring the sociological considerations back into sharp focus. Certainly, music is the creation of the 'mind of man', but such a mind has been shaped in the process of socialisation before it can create anything, and, as cultures differ, so do the qualities and capacities of human minds. To be sure, the harmony and polyphony which are the great achievements of western music have not developed in other cultures, but many of these have exploited different possibilities – for example rhythmic complexity – in ways unknown to the West. The simple but fundamental point is that what people take for granted as the normal and reasonable organisation of sounds, indeed what they take for granted as 'music', is culturally variable. Moreover, as I have repeatedly suggested, such taken-for-granted notions are deeply ingrained, so much so that we may – just like Deryck Cooke – find it hard to accept that they are not natural and inevitable. (It is surely one of the quirks of our own culture that it seems so important for people to legitimise things as 'natural'. To the sociological mind, what is surprising is that while people are happy to acknowledge the wonders of what they call nature, they are often uninterested in the equally miraculous, and equally natural, process of *cultural* production.)

Nevertheless, the realities of the everyday world of experience are socially constructed and sustained. For westerners the diatonic scale and certain elementary harmonic progressions have become such taken-for-granted realities: virtually everyone can identify a 'wrong' note or a passage that is 'out of tune', and the standard songs of the twentieth century have a pleasing inevitability to millions who have never heard of a harmonic progression. Moreover, while the principles that underlie such conventions can be formulated by anyone with a little technical knowledge, the vast majority of people acquire an understanding of the rules without being able to describe them in any clear or coherent fashion. The situation is similar to the way in which we use ordinary language – normal adults become competent and confident participants in a linguistic community, yet few can even begin to specify the rules of correct and incorrect usage which their speech presupposes. Even amongst the experts, such things are keenly disputed.

Two further points deserve emphasis. Firstly, it should now be apparent why an important strand of social theory, made explicit in Durkheim's work, has placed great emphasis on the idea of human society as a moral order. That is, for two or more people to co-ordinate their activities with any degree of success they must share a common frame of reference, or, more precisely, they must *believe* that they share a common frame of reference which leads them to interpret their environment in basically similar ways (Heritage, 1984: 54). Such a frame of reference consists of a whole stock of 'commonsense' ideas about what is good and bad, right and wrong, true and false, and so on. These ideas, as I have already suggested, should not be regarded as concerned only with matters which we conventionally describe as ethical or theological. On the contrary, *all* our thinking is imbued with such ideas – as when we react to a 'wrong' note.

It follows that challenges to the established conventions, or disregard for them, may be considered – by those who are committed to the status quo – as instances of deviance, deserving punishment. The fact that from a sociological point of view such conventions are culturally relative, and arbitrary, matters not at all to us when we are caught up in the conflicts and entanglements of everyday affairs. Indeed, when customary practices are challenged, we may feel personally threatened – such is the pervasive power of socialisation. Our response is often to denounce the challenger as bad, mad or even a charlatan, and such has been the reaction to countless innovative musicians. Writing of his critics, Arnold Schoenberg remarked that 'I never understood what I had done to them to make them as malicious, as furious, as cursing, as aggressive' (Rosen, 1976: 10–11). And when Charlie Parker and Dizzy Gillespie first played the music that was to become the major influence on jazz in the second half of the twentieth century, 'nearly every established jazz writer ... dismissed Parker and Gillespie as fakes' (G. Sales quoted in Feather, 1986: 299). Why should music that is new and a little bit unfamiliar provoke such violent reactions? Clearly there is more to this than a few experiments with some fresh ideas.

The second point concerns the nature of 'commonsense' knowledge. Given the individualistic assumptions of modern western culture, assumptions which have themselves inhibited the reception of sociological ideas, we tend to regard such knowledge as personal or private, in a word subjective. However, it should be clear by now that patterns of social organisation must be understood as depending in fundamental ways on beliefs and ideas that are held in common, in a word intersubjective (Schütz 1972). It is precisely the intersubjectivity of basic assumptions which enables us to speak theoretically of a 'culture', or empirically of a 'community'. As we have seen, any kind community depends on what G. H. Mead called 'a common social process of experience' (1934: 89). In the present context, the crucial point is that for us to be able to make sense of music, or for it to have meaning for us, we must belong to some sort of community of hearers, in which certain basic assumptions are held in common.

The idea of such a community, of course, no longer implies any kind of geographical separation – the rock fan, the early music specialist, the country and western enthusiast and the opera buff all mingle in modern cities. But each has learned to hear certain sounds in certain ways, and to ascribe to them meanings which are shared by some other people. It is possible, indeed likely, that many individual will belong to more than one such community, having deliberately or fortuitously learned how to participate in them. And, since our capacity to learn can last a lifetime, our perceptions and values can change: most people can think of pieces of music, or whole styles, that they disliked or disregarded at first hearing, but subsequently came to enjoy. As Becker argued in a classic paper, even experiences which we come to perceive as pleasurable do not arise in a direct and unmediated way but depend on socialisation processes which can, in themselves, be difficult and disturbing (1963: 41ff.). The central implications of these ideas is that the kind of people we become is largely dependent on the nature of the socialisation experiences that we have. Thus we can begin to explain such things as why people in one country think and act in different ways from those in another, why the ideas of young people differ from those of their elders, why there are identifiable regularities between social class position and political beliefs and why musical preferences, too, have a great deal to do with social class and education.

Moreover, as Meyer has argued, it is because composers (and performers) believe that they belong to – or can create – a community of like-minded people that they are able to anticipate what the responses of such people to certain patterns of sound will be, and thus can try to influence their responses. The activity of composition involves a conscious process of deliberation; in direct contrast are those performers whose success in communicating with their audiences seems to involve little reflection or planning. But this may well arise when both performer and audience are already imbued with similar values and assumptions, as when artists appear to express and articulate the innermost feelings of their audience. In Mead's terms, such performers, perhaps without realising it, are 'taking the role of the other' (the point will be developed in Chapter 5).

Of course, the apparent spontaneity of many performances usually stems from careful planning and contrivance. But even when music is believed to express the 'inner being' of the composer or performer, the effective communication of such feelings requires them to be presented in ways that the intended listeners can understand. Even the impassioned outpouring of the heart, then, must take account of the ways in which these things are expected to be done, or run the risk of seeming non-musical.

In fact, such a 'breakdown in communication' does tend to arise when composers or performers do not share the same frame of reference as those who hear the music. The most obvious case, as we have seen, occurs when we are confronted with the music of an alien cultural tradition. While we may (or may not) derive some pleasure from the patterns of sound that we hear, 'the music can only legitimately be understood in terms of the analytical categories which are an aspect of a particular group or society's reality' as Vulliamy and Shepherd have put it (1984b: 249). 'The crucial question ... is whether the response is true to the culture and the music' (Vulliamy and Shepherd, 1984: 63). Only through a lengthy process of socialisation, and perhaps not even then, can we learn to 'hear' other people's music in the way that they do. Moreover, when music is created which deliberately ignores the established conventions, it is widely perceived as meaningless: however strong their principles and motivation, 'serialist' and 'aleatory' composers have struggled to win much public recognition for their efforts, as have the exponents of 'free' improvisation. (It is significant, too, that when attempts are made to cast these activities in a positive light, the status of 'art' is usually claimed for them.)

Sounds and meanings

The perspective on musical meaning which has been outlined is based on sociological ideas which are fundamental and well known, although their implications are not always appreciated. It has been argued that the meaning of music is neither inherent in it nor grasped intuitively by 'the' human mind; rather meaning is created in the processes of social interaction which mediate all our experience of the world. It remains, finally, to consider some of the ways in which meanings do become attached to patterns of sound.

In this context it is useful to make a distinction which, although admittedly arbitrary, has been employed by several authors. Essentially this involves distinguishing between instances in which sounds are held to represent, or refer to, or describe, non-musical objects or events, and those in which a sound is held to have meaning purely by virtue of its relationship to other sounds within the same set of musical conventions. Examples of the first kind would include the 'wedding march', the 'theme' of a television series, the belief that music expresses emotions, or the simple attempt to represent non-musical things through patterns of sound – the gathering storm, the peace of the countryside, the bustle of the city, or – as Langer reminds us – 'the inevitable cuckoo'. Examples of the second kind of meaning would be the notes of the diatonic scale, each of which becomes significant as a result of the ways in which it is related to the others, or the way in which a D minor seventh chord followed by a G seventh is said to 'imply' a 'return' to a C major. The first kind of meaning may be called extra-musical, as it relates to things outside the music itself, and the second intra-musical, since it arises as a result of its own internal organisation.

The distinction between extra- and intra-musical meanings has appeared in several different forms: Meyer (1970) distinguished 'designative' from 'embodied' meanings, D. F. Wright, following Coker (1973), contrasts 'extrageneric' and 'congeneric' (1975), and Lucy Green opposes 'delineated' and 'inherent' (1988). Inevitably, there are important differences in the ways in which each author uses the distinction – Green, for example, points out that her use of the term 'delineated' is intended to emphasise 'the social, political, and historical construction of meaning' (1988: 149) in contrast to Meyer's usage of 'designative'. This is an important theme, to which we shall return. In general, though, consideration of the two aspects of musical meaning (which, of course, are separable only in an analytic sense) points towards the conclusion that Wright draws – that *both* must be understood as arising out of social experience (1975: 420).

Given the arguments above, the socially constructed nature of extra-musical meanings should be evident. Socialisation leads us to interpret the music we hear in particular ways, and the ways that we invest it with meaning reflect our cultural conventions, rather than intuition or the decoding of its inherent message. The process is no less profound, or remarkable, for that. Similarly, we may simply learn to associate certain music with particular events, activities or ideas. But it is important in this connection to emphasise the ways in which, once the association between the music and its 'external' referent has been established, it is subsequently likely to be regarded as normal, proper and indeed inevitable. This is but one instance of the phenomenon that Georg Simmel called the 'tragedy of culture'

– the way in which the cultural creations of human beings come to have an apparently objective existence, and so to dominate people, who feel that they are both natural and authoritative (Oakes, 1980: 40).

There are several quite simple ways in which sounds and meanings can become conjoined. The *Leitmotif* was a device much used by Wagner – 'a musical theme that becomes associated with a specific object, personality, situation or idea' (Taylor, 1983: 96). It is, writes Taylor, particularly effective when seeking to convey abstract ideas and emotions: 'it is the association with ideas and with developing states of mind which brings the psychological intensification of the meaning of the action from which Wagner's mature works derive much of their musical depth and power' (1983: 97). The operatic example is significant in the present context, since it is precisely the craft of a composer to produce the anticipated effects (in a suitably socialised audience) while simultaneously concealing the means by which such effects are produced. Similarly, in everyday life we take for granted the realities of the world that confronts us, untroubled by the fact that they are arbitrary, relative and socially constructed.

This deliberate linking of music with specific meanings has become a ubiquitous feature of films and television programmes; indeed there are instruction manuals for writers of music for the movies, indicating which sounds should be used to produce which effects. Television uses brief musical passages to indicate beginnings, breaks, returns and endings, and to establish the appropriate mood for a programme – one five-second 'sound bite', for example, will lead the experienced listener to expect the news, while another heralds Tom and Jerry. Above all, advertisers – to the frequent chagrin of 'serious' music-lovers – attempt to convey a favourable impression of their products by using music they consider suitable. (Parts of Dvořák's *New World* Symphony have been used on British television to promote both brown bread and cat food (among other things), and an extract from Mahler's Seventh regularly accompanies some dripping engine oil. (I rather doubt that these associations are either inherent in the music, or intuitively perceived.) The important point is that the music may become identified with the product, and vice versa, irrespective of the intentions of the composer, or previously accepted understandings of the piece's meaning. Such interpretations will be real, and important, for many people; the music cannot be said to have a true, or ultimate, meaning.

'Programme' music, too, is deliberately intended to convey a message or an idea, or tell a story. This can be done in a straightforward way, with the musical sounds reflecting naturally heard ones – babbling brooks, raging seas, battles and railway trains have all been popular subjects – not to mention the inevitable cuckoo – or more indirectly, as when the composer provides a text which aims to guide the responses of the listener: the intended meaning of each section of Berlioz's *Symphonie Fantastique*, for example, is described in some detail by the composer. The problem here, of course, is that the music may very easily come to mean quite different things, as we have seen in the case of the *New World* symphony. Nor is it obvious just *how* the music is related to the text which accompanies it. This was how Schoenberg 'explained' the sequence of his challenging Piano Concerto:

> Life was so easy
> Suddenly hatred broke out
> A grave situation was created
> But life goes on.   (MacDonald, 1976: 217)

Even the publishers of Christmas cards look for a bit more sophistication than this in their texts. But while the thoughts as written down are banal, even trivial, the music is exactly the opposite, displaying enormous intelligence, complexity and an undeniable sophistication. The link between the original ideas and the musical work is, to say the least, tenuous.

When the music is heard without its 'programme', it may be appreciated perfectly well without suggesting any of the things the composer had in mind, or indeed suggesting anything at all. Potentially, as Silbermann suggests, there are as many 'meanings' of a piece of music as there are listeners to it (1963: 67–8). But in practice, descriptions of music play an important role in fixing its meaning, as Dahlhaus points out: 'Consciousness of music is determined, to no small extent, by literature about music. Even people who scoff at it can hardly escape the effect of what is written. Musical experience almost always involves memory-traces from reading' (1982: 62). The point is worth emphasising, not only because it reminds us of the ways in which extra-musical ideas can influence the ways that we hear music, but because, as Dahlhaus suggests, the interpretations of composers or performers are not privileged, in the sense that they disclose the authentic or final meaning of a piece. Their voice may be influential, but once the music becomes an object, even a commodity, they become only participants in a more general debate, to which other musicians, critics, audiences, promoters, agents, journalists and so on also contribute. Thus the meaning of a piece of music must be regarded simply as the consensus which may emerge from such a debate, if indeed there ever is one. This position allows us to understand why disputes about the 'real' meaning of music, or the relative value of different genres, never seem to reach resolution. We can see too why different and incompatible interpretations may nevertheless coexist, and why accepted meanings change over time.

The establishment of musical meaning, then, may usefully be seen as a *political* process, in the specific sense that interested participants, with varying resources at their disposal, attempt to impose their own preferred interpretation on others, often in the face of resistance. But the fundamentally political nature of the process is most apparent when we consider the ways in which definitions of music are presented in formal education. By the time they reach school age, children are already imbued, through socialisation, with a strong sense of how music ought to sound. Formal education builds on this; gradually but inexorably, the distinction between 'serious' and 'popular' music is etched on to the consciousness of the young, to the general detriment of the latter. And at the highest levels of the education system, approached only by the chosen few, and at great expense, the term 'music' means *only* the composed works of the western 'art' tradition (despite the token recognition of other styles and genres which has recently been presented as evidence of a new broad-mindedness). The curriculum and criteria of evaluation represent a cultural tradition which has become dominant, and they do much to sustain its legitimacy. Moreover, conventional music teaching effectively serves the purpose of grading and classifying the students, a process which, seen from the perspective of the whole society, is of far greater importance than the ostensible one of developing their musical skills (Collins, 1980). Christopher Small explains: 'examinations are by their very nature tools of standardisation ... to permit any considerable manifestation of individuality would destroy strict comparability and thus undermine the very function which they are designed to serve' (1980: 197).

The importance of formal music education, then, derives from the ways in which, through its processes, meanings are attached to music in an *authoritative* manner. The most obvious aspect of this is the way in which conventional explanations of the meaning of particular sounds, or whole pieces or styles, are laid down and reinforced, through both repetition and the weight of established authority. But it has been argued that this 'visible' aspect of the process is only the tip of an ideological iceberg: even more important are the messages conveyed by the 'hidden curriculum', and two particular themes have been elaborated in this context. Firstly, as we have seen, it has been suggested that schools and colleges inculcate the belief, in the general public as much as in their specialist music students, that there *is* a hierarchy of styles and traditions, with Western 'classical' music at the top. This comes about, argues Green, through the 'ideology of autonomy', which

> denies the fact that it is necessary for us to have socially-derived, learnt familiarity with inherent meanings, in order for us to recognise music at all ... In this way, the collective definition of what counts as music appears not to be a social historical development, but a spontaneous result of music's inherent materials themselves, and the latter seem to structure our temporal experiences quite naturally. Great music is made to appear, and required to appear, eternal, natural, and universal: or autonomous. Poor music is rooted in society and allowed nothing but interfering delineations. (1988: 101)

The second message conveyed by the 'hidden curriculum' concerns the nature of musical ability. Western education reflects the assumption that only a small proportion of children are 'musical' in the sense that they possess the particular abilities required of a capable performer. This assumption is not made in other cultures, argues Blacking, nor is it particularly well founded in our own culture. Indeed, the very existence of a professional, or even virtuoso, performer presupposes an audience who participate as listeners in the same musical culture (1976: 9). That is to say, in order to make sense of the music, members of the culture must develop a similar 'capacity for structured listening' to that of the performer (Blacking 1976: 10). In this sense it is clear that they are not at all 'unmusical', which raises the question of what factors promote or inhibit the development of musical ability in a culture. For Blacking, this depends on the functions which music performs in a particular society. For the Venda of southern Africa, with whom he lived for two years, 'the chief function of music is to involve people in shared experiences within the framework of their cultural experience' (1976: 48) and there is no concept of a small group of particularly 'musical' people. In contrast, modern western societies, where the division of labour is advanced and there is an elaborate pattern of social stratification, do have such a concept, reinforcing the belief that music, and certainly music education, may play a significant part in maintaining such hierarchical divisions. Like Pierre Bourdieu, Blacking views conventional assumptions about the distribution of musical abilities, and abilities in general, as myths which serve to sustain and legitimise the existing pattern of inequality (1976: 116). As I have suggested, a recurring theme in Bourdieu's work is the way in which differences which are social in origin are presented, particularly through the ideology of formal education as though they were 'natural'. In this way, the vast majority of people come to believe that they are not 'musical'.

Together, the beliefs that there is an aesthetic hierarchy of musical styles, and that most people are not really 'musical' have a profound effect on the production and consumption of music in modern societies. It is the widespread acceptance of such assumptions that enables a small number of 'authorities' to define, on behalf of the whole society, what is to count as 'serious' music and what is not, and to devalue the experiences of others while claiming public resources for their favoured styles. It is these authorities, too, who claim the right to define the meaning and the value of music, and whose views are disseminated through the mass media (Wright, 1975: 432). So it comes about that most people in western societies, although they have unprecedented choice in respect of the music they want to hear, must nevertheless exercise their preferences while submitting to an aesthetic inferiority complex.

Of course, it would be quite wrong to represent the situation as one in which a coherent musical elite confronted an indifferent mass. On the contrary, like any professional group, the authorities are fragmented and often in dispute with each other (Bucher and Strauss, 1961). Thus specialists in early music, opera, orchestral music, chamber groups, 'new' music and so on may have surprisingly little in common, and even within such specialisms there may be bitter antagonisms arising from such matters as interpretation or aesthetic judgements. Yet each of the protagonists has a similar aim – to pursue an interest, to persuade others of its validity, and to speak authoritatively about music. Moreover, the boundary between the dominant group and those who assert alternative values is never clear-cut. In recent years, for example, some styles of jazz have received the recognition of official bodies in the sense that they are now considered 'serious' and so worthy of grants and sponsorship. (Though this may also stem from the wish of the 'classical' establishment to buy off a vocal and troublesome pressure group.) After all, it should not be assumed that established definitions of music and its meaning are automatically accepted by other sections of society, especially those whose own values and preferences are cast in a negative light. Indeed, alternative forms of music, as in other cultural spheres, may be attractive precisely because they represent a rejection of established views, and, particularly for young people, seem to offer a form of resistance to established authority (Bradley, 1992). In the present context, however, the general point which must be emphasised is the idea that the attachment of meanings to music occurs through the activities of individuals and groups as they seek to further their interests, or defend them, or seek to impose their view on others. Such struggles and negotiations are an inherent part of our everyday lives and, though they may only rarely escalate into overt conflict, they are none the less political. Echoing Bourdieu, DeNora puts it thus: 'culture represents a struggle over the definition of social reality and therefore the issue of the meaning of objects is also an issue of who defines or appropriates them, where, when, how and for what purpose' (1986: 93).

The remarks above have been concerned with a few of the ways in which deliberate efforts may be made – by composers, performers, critics, teachers, enthusiasts and so on – to attach specific meanings to pieces of music. This process, however, may be just as effective when it occurs in informal, unintended and accidental ways. Most people can think of music – often, it seems, 'popular' music – which reminds them of events, places, or other people who may have played a significant part in their own lives. Such associations may be of great salience for us, irrespective of what the music is conventionally supposed to mean – a 'happy' song may bring to mind some great sadness, while a mournful dirge prompts fits of laughter. Similarly, most musicians are familiar with the desperate melancholy that can be induced by having to play the same 'cheerful' music night after night. (The condition is intensified by the requirement that you 'look happy' while you're doing it.) It may be objected that such responses are aberrations produced by unusual circumstances, irrelevant to the 'real' meaning of the music. But who is to decide what the real meaning is? Once again, this issue may be seen to be a political one – whose opinion is to prevail? If a jaunty juke box tune reminds me of some great sorrow, or the supermarket's canned music makes me nauseous, then that is the meaning of the music for me at that place and time, regardless of the intentions of those who composed, performed, recorded and promoted it.

A few of the ways in which extra-musical meaning is socially constructed have been mentioned above. It remains simply to emphasise a fundamental point which has already bee made, the idea that intra-musical meaning, too, is established and maintained through social processes. The scales of notes, the harmonic progressions, melodic shapes, and rhythmic patterns which we take for granted as the basis of music within the western tonal tradition reflect neither the properties of the natural world nor the innate qualities of the human mind. As Orlov puts it:

> The correlation between sound and its meaning are neither fully biologically determined, nor must they depend entirely on the whims of individual experiences. The safest assumption is to see them as cultural patterns learned by individuals in the cultural environment.
> ... relations between the signifier and the significate in music are mediated by a cultural convention rather than based on immediately felt resemblance or shared properties. (1981: 136)

The ways in which patterns of sound are organised in human cultures are highly variable, yet members of each culture are socialised into an acceptance of the right and wrong ways in which sounds may be combined. And, as argued above, for all that this process may be informal and taken for granted, it is a powerful and penetrating one. The very strength of our attachment to familiar musical conventions, and our difficulties in grasping strange ones, is a reminder of the point that through socialisation cultural patterns become part of our consciousness. It is in this sense, as Durkheim put it, that society is prior to the individual.

We have also seen how established cultural conventions, however arbitrary, nevertheless come to appear as though they were inevitable, necessary and objective. The products of human ingenuity and creativity can come to dominate and even enslave future generations: this, for Simmel, was the 'tragedy of culture'. So it is with the musical systems which have become institutionalised in human societies: the diatonic scale and rational tonal organisation are generally believed to be the right, proper and natural basics of music, rather than 'conventions ... which musicians have simply agreed upon' (Davies, 1978: 15).

Perhaps because of the very power of the cultural values which we have internalised, there remain strong objections to the idea that musical meaning must be understood as socially constructed. In particular, there is a marked reluctance to conceive of musical meaning as 'arbitrary', in the sense that the link between a sound and its meaning is sustained only by convention rather than by some supposedly more substantial means. So it is important to be clear about just how the term 'arbitrary' is being used in this context. Musical meanings are arbitrary in the specific sense that, as in language, the same sounds can have different meanings, and that different meanings may be attached to similar sounds. This in no way implies that such associations are weak or haphazard on the occasions of their use; on the contrary, much of the foregoing discussion has emphasised the strength and power, indeed the moral authority, of meanings which are neither inherent nor intuitively perceived, but are transmitted and sustained by the process of socialisation. The taken-for-granted realities of the social world are thus not 'just' or 'merely' or 'only' social constructions – the whole process is at the very heart of human culture and communication. It enables us to be what we are, and it is what makes organised societies possible. Indeed, one implication of the idea that our commonsense reality is socially constructed is that we must reconsider the familiar opposition, which has been echoed in the discussion above, between nature and culture. The creation of culture through symbolic communication is the way in which human beings survive in their natural environment, the way in which normal – that is, social – conditions of existence are established. In this respect, culture is part of nature.

Nor does the use of the term 'arbitrary', in the technical sense above, imply that musical meanings must therefore be random, or that any pattern of sound is likely to represent any object or idea. While this remains possible in principle, in practice there are invariably some important constraints, notably, as we have seen, the properties of the harmonic series. Indeed, an influential school of thought has held that the simpler, larger intervals – octave, fifth and third – when sounded together seem more 'stable' and sound more complete than those which are more remote from the fundamental note and derived from more irregular arithmetic ratios, such as the second and seventh. The latter, it has been argued, are more 'unstable' and in need of 'resolution' (that is, a return to one of the simple consonances). Thus, it is claimed, there is a 'natural' basis for the pattern of tension and release which underlie all sorts of musical composition.

Clearly, such an argument returns us to the proposition that certain sounds have inherent meanings, and it is equally evident that some by-now-familiar difficulties are entailed. As we have seen, the tempered diatonic scale which is presupposed by such an argument is *not* in fact a naturally occurring one but a rationalisation of certain properties of the harmonic series. Nor is it the case that the simplest harmonies are those which are most used, either in the West or elsewhere, as Lerdahl and Jackendoff point out (1983: 291ff.). Moreover the system of tonality itself has been developed in the West only in the relatively recent past; other musical cultures have developed in complex, but quite divergent, ways. In short, it is not self-evident that someone from a different cultural tradition would hear a second or a major seventh as requiring 'resolution' to make them consonant and comfortable. So while it is simple common sense to acknowledge that the properties of the harmonic series act as limiting parameters on musical development, in just the same way that other natural laws restrict human possibilities, it is quite another matter to claim that such properties provide the natural basis for human music-making. After all, the harmonic series is the same for all cultures, despite their manifest diversity; what is sociologically significant is the way in which each cultural tradition elaborates some of the possibilities of harmony, melody and rhythm at the expense of others. Finally, it must be said that claims concerning the supposedly natural basis of human conventions are always suspect from a sociological point of view, since one of the distinctive characteristics of culture is the way in which it enables people to *overcome* naturally occurring obstacles: just as different modes of agriculture and animal husbandry enable humans to survive in a great range of climatic conditions, just as houses, boats and planes help us to overcome our physical limitations, so Western tonality may be not so much a reflection of the natural properties of sound as a system which adapts them for our use.

In short, the harmonic series, while basic to any understanding of music, does not take us very far towards an explanation of the *forms* which music-making may take. But every culture does have some

sort of organising principles which underlie the elaboration of musical systems. Some of these may indeed reflect naturally occurring
rhythms and sounds – waves, the wind, animal and bird sounds –
and of the human body: marching, digging, rocking babies and so
on. In other words there are likely to be 'elective affinities', as Weber
put it, between some sounds and certain aspects of human culture.
This doesn't mean that, for example, sadness *must* be expressed by
slow, ponderous music – after all, sadness need not be expressed in
music at all – but only that in a culture where sadness is already
associated with slow movements and quietness, its musical expression is likely to be in some ways consistent with these, if only to
ensure that it is understood.

    This, in turn, suggests that the organising principles of music may
reflect neither the properties of the natural world nor the universal
structure of the mind, but the fundamental cultural patterns which
are the basis of every human society. It is to this claim that we must
now turn.

3

Adorno: music as representation

A really great creative artist is one who, in freely expressing his own fantasies, needs, aspirations and conflicts, articulates those of a whole society. That is made possible by the fact that, through his earliest relationships, mother tongue, upbringing, and all his first experience of life, the cultural heritage on which he has entered at birth is woven into the whole fabric of his personality.

Bryan Magee (1988: 23)

Rarely has there been a movement in art that showed so clearly as bop the lineaments of the social forces behind it. Not merely was the philosophy of the players a product of the currents in the culture, but the shape of the music itself – the actual length and pitches of the notes – to a large degree was determined by shifts in the structure of society.

J. L. Collier (1981: 341)

the music of a well-ordered age is calm and cheerful, and so is its government. The music of a restive age is excited and fierce, and its government is perverted. The music of a decaying state is sentimental and sad, and its government is imperilled.

Hermann Hesse (1972: 31–2)

In their various ways, each of the above quotations asserts a strong relationship between the nature of music and the society in which it is created. Magee, in discussing Wagner's ideas, suggests that great artists are able to express the ideas and aspirations of a whole people because the experience of early socialisation has caused them to internalise the major elements of their culture. For Collier, the new music created by brilliant young black musicians in New York during the 1940s was shaped, down to its finest details, by their awareness of racial inequalities and their urge to promote an alternative identity: positive, confident and aggressive. And in Hesse's account of musical thought in the legendary China of the Old Kings, there is a general statement of the belief – widely if vaguely held in our own culture – that there is an intimate connection between the nature of music and the condition of society. It is indeed a familiar idea – Elgar's music, for example, is held to be quintessentially English, just as the blues have been regarded as the anguished expression of the oppression of black people in North America. Indeed, concert programme notes have become a notorious source of weird and wonderful ideas about the ways in which particular works express the 'spirit' of a people, or a 'national character', or a *Zeitgeist*, and so on.

In the present context, what is of interest is that these sorts of ideas about the inherent qualities of music are essentially sociological – although they are often voiced by people with little knowledge of, or sympathy for, sociology as a field of study. What is being claimed, as the above examples indicate, is that particular patterns of culture – in this case the rules according to which music is normally organised – are both consistent with and ultimately derived from fundamental characteristics of the society as a whole. For Georg Simmel 'apparently [the style of] music is characteristic for the character of a people' (quoted in Etzkorn, 1964: 105–6); this idea has animated a whole tradition of sociological thought, which can be traced back – through the work of Durkheim in particular – to Montesquieu's monumental *L'Esprit des Lois*, first published in 1748. Montesquieu's aim in this book was nothing less than the description, and explanation, of the laws and institutions which were to be found in different sorts of society. Unlike many theorists of the eighteenth and nineteenth centuries, however, Montesquieu did not seek an explanation of legal forms in 'human nature' – they were much too diverse for that to be convincing – but, as Durkheim later put it, 'he derives the laws from the "nature" not of man but of the social organism" (Durkheim, 1965: 21).

For Montesquieu, the pattern of laws in a society reflected not only the structural nature of its government (republic, monarchy or despotism) but, at a deeper and more fundamental level, the 'principle' which underlies it (virtue, respect for authority, or fear). Today, such a system of classification is of interest only to specialists; nev-

ertheless, as Turner and Beeghley have put it: 'The specifics of Montesquieu's political sociology are less important than the general
insight they illustrate: social structures are held together by a corresponding system of values and beliefs that individuals have internalised' (1981: 313). If this was the case, then it followed that laws,
as reflections of the deep-lying principles of social organisation,
could be used as observable indicators of otherwise invisible systems
of 'values and beliefs'. This was precisely Durkheim's strategy in *The
Division of Labour*, where he argued that the development of
societies from 'mechanical' to 'organic' solidarity is reflected in
changes in their patterns of law, from 'repressive' to 'restitutive': law
is thus an indicator of the nature of social solidarity. As with Montesquieu, the details of the analysis are not our immediate concern
here (although I shall return later to some important implications of
the study of legal codes); what I wish to focus on at present is the
idea that the actual, observable customs and practices of a society
have been held to be consistent with, and derived from, the essential,
or 'core' elements of its culture. It follows from this that as these elements change, so will the pattern of culture.

For Durkheim, the central core of a culture resided in what he
termed the *conscience collective*, a rather vague term covering the
concepts rendered in English as 'consciousness' and 'conscience'; as
ever with Durkheim, though, the point is that such a system of
shared beliefs and values is a collective property of a society: 'the
totality of beliefs and sentiments common to average citizens of the
same society' (1964: 79). There are laws against, for example, murder
or theft because these acts offend against moral feelings which are
generally shared in our society. It follows that different sorts of
society will have different sorts of legal codes, since the definition of
acts as criminal or deviant is essentially a social one: 'we must not
say that an action shocks the common conscience because it is criminal, but rather that it is criminal because it shocks the common conscience' (1964: 81). Durkheim's use of the concept of *conscience
collective* is somewhat problematic – he saw it as declining in power
and generality as societies became more highly differentiated, and his
view of its role in modern, 'organic' societies is not altogether clear,
beyond his contention that it is increasingly concerned with the
rights and dignity of the individual (Lukes, 1975: 166, 407). Despite
all this, Durkheim's arguments do constitute a formidable effort to
comprehend theoretically the widespread idea that there is a core of

shared values and beliefs at the heart of any cultural system, a theme
that was developed in the later work of the American social theorist
Talcott Parsons.

Like Durkheim, Parsons emphasised the ways in which, for
normal social order to be established and maintained, certain cultural patterns had to be both institutionalised – acting as an external constraint on people – and internalised, so that the basic elements
of the culture became part of the personality of the individual (Parsons in Black, ed, 1961: 342). In addition, however, Parsons was concerned to show how the fundamental elements of cultures are
themselves 'structured in a particular way' (Rocher, 1974: 36). Any
'social system', Parsons argued, from a brief two-person encounter
to a whole society, must be based on a more-or-less stable pattern of
shared understandings; the ways in which such patterns may vary,
however, are not unlimited, 'for in every society and every social
relationship, there are only a few basic and elementary options'
(1974: 37). For Parsons, there were four such 'pattern variables', constituting a kind of 'deep' structure which underlay every social
system: the actual patterns of culture observed in any society will be
derived from, and consistent with, the particular configuration of the
'pattern variables'.

Parsons's theoretical scheme is extensive, complex and contentious, and it is not necessary to involve ourselves with its detail,
except to note that, like Durkheim, he was deeply involved in the
effort to create a coherent theoretical framework for the analysis of
societies, which took their orderly patterns to be a consequence of a
fundamental core of established values and beliefs. Returning to our
more immediate concern with the nature of the links between
societies and their musical forms, it is clear that similar ideas are
explored, though in various ways and with differing emphases, in the
work of those who have sought to approach this relationship from
a sociological point of view.

It was a social anthropologist, however, who formulated the claim
in perhaps the most general and uncompromising way. For Alan P.
Merriam 'musical sound is the result of human behavioural processes
that are shaped by the values, attitudes, and beliefs of the people
who comprise a particular culture' (1964: 6). The implication,
clearly, is that the forms which music takes are shaped in important
ways by the nature of the shared, 'core' elements of the culture – the
configuration of the 'pattern variables', in Parsons's terms – or in

other words that the organising principles of music are derived neither from the natural properties of the harmonic series, nor from the universal qualities of the human mind, but from the fundamental cultural patterns of the societies in which the music is created. It is this idea, as we shall see, which has been explored in much of John Shepherd's work, and, in the course of criticising both 'absolutist' and 'psychologistic' theories of music, he makes the point concisely: 'The significance of a piece of music lies in the ways its internal structure both reflects and creatively articulates the structure of the group or society in which it was conceived' (1987: 71)

It should be emphasised that this claim goes some way beyond the conventional concerns of the social history of music. In general, the latter approach seeks to illuminate the various ways in which musical production may be influenced by the social context in which it occurs, and much of this work is both interesting and important. It can be shown, for example, how developments in the general pattern of social stratification contributed to the separation of 'popular' from 'serious' music in the nineteenth century, a distinction which, as we have seen, is firmly established in the twentieth (see Chapter 6). It has been generally accepted, to take another case, that the relative abundance of ex-military-band instruments in the South following the American Civil War was an important stimulus to the development of street parade bands in New Orleans, with momentous consequences for the development of African-American styles. The investigation of such historical links has much to offer; the sort of connection which is the principal focus of this and the next chapters, however, goes beyond the examination of the effects of social context on music production to assert an identifiable relationship between forms of society and forms of music *itself*. Thus for Ballantine, the very essence of the sociology of music consists in the elaboration of this relationship, as it undertakes 'an investigation of the ways in which social formations crystallize in musical structures, indeed even in their inmost cells' (1984: xvi). As Frith puts it, the sociology of music 'has usually rested on more or less crude reflection theories: the music is taken to reflect, to be "homologous" to, the society or social group that makes it' (Frith, 1983: 269).

As Frith's remark implies, however, there are problematic aspects of the claim that there are close connections between sound structures and social structures. Durkheim's notion of the *conscience collective*, for example, was developed in the context of an analysis of simple, undifferentiated societies, and, as I have suggested, is not easy to reconcile with modern complex ones where a plurality of contrasting cultures may coexist. Indeed, serious doubts have been expressed about the usefulness of regarding *any* culture as a system, a relatively integrated totality; there is, too, the associated danger of reifying such concepts as 'culture' and 'society', treating them as if they were real entities. And the attempt to explain any social activities – such as the production of music – in terms of the general characteristics of society entails a further set of difficulties concerning the nature of human action. If music 'reflects' societal patterns, does this mean that composers and performers are little more than puppets whose strings are being pulled by 'the culture'? What then happens to our cherished notions of creativity and free will? In short the problem lies in the implication that human action is in some way determined by social forces, leading to a conception of people as 'over-socialised' (Wrong, 1961).

It would be unfortunate if, having established the inadequacy of individualistic explanations of musical phenomena, we were to attempt to replace them with equally defective sociologistic ones, and the authors whose analyses we shall consider in this and the following chapter are certainly aware of the theoretical dangers they face. Yet, and this is what has motivated their work, despite the evident difficulties involved in the attempt to specify the relationships between music and society, and despite the diverse perspectives that they develop, they do share a commitment to the belief that linkages and articulations can be found, and that cultures do 'hang together' in more-or-less coherent ways. As I have said, such ideas, in some form or other, are widely held; it remains to be seen whether they can be made theoretically precise without falling prey to the kinds of dangers outlined above. At least one promising point of departure, however, should already be apparent. For Durkheim, as we have seen, the essential feature of the human mind was not the allegedly 'universal' capacities and qualities ascribed to it by rationalist philosophers but the way in which people's thinking was, through the process of socialisation, already imbued with the forms and concepts of their culture. Even the fundamental categories of thought – notions of time, space and so on – were held to be culturally derived (Durkheim, 1915: 440). If this line of argument is accepted, it follows that music, like all other human creations, is the product of minds *already* shaped by particular cultures, and in this sense music could be said to reflect the society in which it was created. Similar points were made time and again by one of the towering figures in the sociology of music, Theodor Adorno (1903–69), particularly in his criticism of 'positivist' analysis and its tendency to take things at face value, to mistake the appearance of things for the reality. For Adorno, the production and reception of most music in modern 'administered' societies was tainted by the fact that people's minds were 'deformed' by the very experience of living in them, alienated from a genuine human consciousness. As an approach to understanding the links between music and society, then, we can do no better than to begin with Adorno's work.

Critical theory

'Herr Professor Doktor Theodor Wiesengrund Adorno was a chubby, bald little man', writes J. G. Merquior. 'Former pupils of his tell that, during his Frankfurt lectures, whenever he felt that he had reached a critical stage in the argument, he stood on tiptoe and entreated the general attention by saying in a raised voice: "*Meine Damen und Herren: das ist sehr dialektisch*" ' (Merquior, 1986: 111). Indeed, Merquior continues, dialectical thinking was the core of the philosophy which came to be identified with the 'Frankfurt school' of critical theorists, among whom Adorno was 'the most sophisticated thinker' (1986: 130).

The origins of the Frankfurt school lay in the Institute of Social Research, founded in 1923 and formally attached to the University of Frankfurt, though privately funded and thus enjoying 'considerable autonomy' (Held, 1980: 29). It was in the period after 1930, however, when Max Horkheimer became Director, that the Institute's members and their associates laid the foundations for what was to become 'critical theory' – a fundamental critique of industrial capitalism and the societies which it had created. It is not difficult to discern the motives of these radical intellectuals, who had spent their formative years in Germany during the years after the First World War. It is often said that the War was a watershed, after which all the cherished beliefs and assumptions of the Victorian era and the age of imperialism were increasingly questioned; doubt and disillusion, however, were not confined to the defenders of the status quo. The confidence and optimism which had inspired the organisation of the labour movement and the formation of socialist groups throughout Europe in the pre-War years were severely shaken after 1914, when, on both sides, men of the proletariat sacrificed their lives in vast numbers in defence of the states which, Marx had asserted, served only to secure the power and interests of their bourgeois masters. The bolshevik revolution of 1917 might have kindled fresh hopes, but these were to be short-lived as the 'dictatorship of the proletariat' turned into a simple, monolithic dictatorship and the stage was set for Stalin's tyranny. The collapse of capitalism, envisaged by Marx and confidently predicted by radical orators, might have seemed imminent after the Wall Street Crash of October 1929, and the unprecedented mass unemployment which followed. But the capitalist class was not overthrown; on the contrary the system gradually reasserted itself while millions of working people suffered. Perhaps most frightening of all for the predominantly Jewish critical theorists, and literally on their doorsteps, was the rise of Hitler and the Nazi party in Germany. The country was fast becoming a fascist dictatorship, and in 1933 the members of the Institute were forced to flee, first to Geneva, then in 1935 to New York, where the Institute was attached to Columbia University and where it was to remain until 1953.

How could the civilisation which had produced Goethe, Beethoven – and Marx – have come to this? It must have seemed to the members of the 'Frankfurt School' that the events of recent history were a conclusive refutation of the deeply-engrained western belief in the idea of progress. Spectacular industrialisation and economic growth in Germany had failed to produce a free and happy people; on the contrary, what they saw before them was increasing misery and repression. In the realm of ideas, German science and philosophy, which once had led the world, had yielded only a vicious and philistine dictatorship. These were not the outcomes predicted by the orthodox ideologies – but in reality both 'communist' Russia and 'capitalist' Germany had become repressive, totalitarian regimes.

We can identify two themes, then, which give a distinctive character to the work of the critical theorists in general, and Adorno in particular – a rejection of the Enlightenment view that science, guided by human reason, will lead to progress in social life, and a similar disillusionment with the Marxists' belief that the proletariat could be a liberating force, emancipating humanity from the alienation of industrial capitalism. In fact, as has often been noted, in these respects the Frankfurt school was closer to Weber than to

Marx. It was Weber who sought to explain why class-based social conflict, while possible, was unlikely to produce a revolutionary transformation, who saw no purpose or ultimate destination in human history, and who feared the 'iron cage' constructed out of the 'inexorable rationalisation of human activity' (Mitzman, 1985: 3). Specifically, Weber wondered gloomily how we might set limits on the 'machinery of bureaucratic administration' in order that we might 'keep a portion of mankind free from this parcelling-out of the soul, from this supreme mastery of the bureaucratic way of life' (quoted in Bendix, 1962: 464).

As Bendix remarks, this is an 'early formulation of George Orwell's 1984' – indeed it is a theme which has resonated through much of twentieth-century literature. And it is from this perspective that the critical theorists viewed the institutions of apparently liberal, democratic societies as essentially totalitarian; they pointed, in other words, to the gulf between 'appearance' and 'reality', and the ways in which the former may have the effect of obscuring or mystifying the latter. In this, of course, the Frankfurt school might be regarded as simply echoing some familiar Marxist ideas, often expressed through the concepts of ideology and false consciousness. In Adorno's hands, however, the theme was relentlessly developed in ways which generated a vast and unique body of work, much of it concerned with the analysis of music.

A fundamental theme was the critique of positivist modes of thought, whether in philosophy or any of the sciences, in which the external appearance of an object, as mediated by the senses, is taken as its essential nature. But such objects have coherence and meaning for us only because we interpret them thus, in accordance with the state of our consciousness:

> The given is mediated in many ways by consciousness. But the structure of the world given to us through consciousness is based, in turn, for Horkheimer and Adorno, on the inner historicality of consciousness itself, which is a result and product of the whole of social practice. (Held, 1980: 164)

We do not simply register 'objects', but *constitute* them, in wasy which can only reflect the particularities of our biographies and our cultures.

But if the error of positivism is to mistake appearance for reality, what is the nature of this reality? Adorno's arguments aimed to transcend both bourgeois idealism and Marxist materialism, instead emphasising the *dialectical* nature of knowledge; in this, as Susan Buck-Morss explains, he was much influenced by the ideas of Walter Benjamin (Buck-Morss, 1972: 138). Benjamin had utilised some of the terms from Marxist discourse, but rejected orthodox materialist interpretations: 'the truth of ideas was not found by reducing them to a common denominator, the economic substructure; instead, contained within the very particularity of superstructure formulations were images of objective, socio-historical truth' (1972: 138–9). For Benjamin, the culture of a society, its institutions and social practices, did not simply 'reflect' its material foundation but was rather, an *expression* of them. All kinds of cultural phenomena, then, even the merest fragments, could be read as 'expressing' the social totality: 'If, as Adorno agreed, superstructure phenomena expressed concrete, material truth, then the philosopher's task became one of *interpreting* that truth.' Only by a dialectical analysis, by seeing the parts in terms of the whole and vice versa, could the truth be 'decoded', for taken-for-granted meanings and subjective intentions were no guide to the 'unintended reality' embodied in cultural phenomena: 'The artwork, not the artist; the philosophy, not the philosopher, was the object of their theoretical inquiry' (1972: 139).

It may be useful at this point to summarise the elements of Adorno's approach to the analysis of culture. All cultural phenomena, he held, bore the imprint of the social totality in which they were created, and thus were expressions of the objective nature of the totality. Their meaning, however, was not self-evident, nor could it be disclosed simply by examining the intentions and beliefs of those who, like composers or authors, were the creators of culture. Musical works, as we shall see, could have an objective social meaning quite at variance with the subjective states of their composers. Further – and this is where Adorno sought to assert his radical credentials, despite the decisive departure from orthodox Marxism – the 'decoding' of such meanings through the active process of interpretation could have the effect of liberating people from the 'realm of ideational abstraction'. 'His aim was demythification', says Buck-Morss, 'freeing men from the bondage of fetishised thought which took on the appearance of second nature' (1972: 140). This was not only the professed purpose of his own work but the criterion which he applied in making aesthetic judgements, asking whether works of art 'affirmed' or 'negated' the ideology of the 'totally organised bourgeois society' which he so despised. Adorno's project and his method can thus be summed up by the title of one of his last books, *Negative Dialectics* (1973).

Art and politics

From the start, Adorno's work distanced him from the Marxist critics and theorists who saw in the new, emerging forms of 'modern' art only the self-indulgent excesses of the decaying bourgeoisie. Far from regarding such forms as 'decadent and counter-revolutionary' (Rose, 1978: 114), Adorno held that it was precisely in radical art that the true nature of capitalist societies, with all their contradictions, could be expressed. Whereas most of the dispute over modernism, however, was concerned with the interpretation of literature – as in the polemics of Lukács and Brecht, for example – Adorno 'thought of himself as an artist' who since early childhood had been committed to music (Buck-Morss, 1977: xiii). Indeed, in addition to his voluminous writings, Adorno composed and taught music for most of his life (Rose, 1978: 110). The crucial formative experience, however, seems to have been the period he spent in Vienna during 1925–6, during which he studied composition with Alban Berg, himself a pupil of Arnold Schoenberg. At this time Adorno 'had serious aspirations to become a composer', but, as Buck-Morss delicately puts it, 'he had little success in getting his music performed' (1977: 16) and before long returned to Frankfurt and philosophy.

Whatever the immediate circumstances of Adorno's stay in Vienna, its timing was propitious and its effects enduring. The city which at the turn of the century had been a 'matrix of cultural creation' (Janik and Toulmin, 1973: 35) was still a centre of artistic endeavour: Adorno attended the première of Berg's influential opera *Wozzeck* and, in his interpretation of the work, developed one of the central themes of his 'materialist aesthetics', the idea that the truth of a musical work did not depend on the composer's conscious beliefs or intentions. Berg was not a Marxist, yet Adorno detected 'a *structural* convergence between this music's inner logic and a Marxist critical understanding of the reality of contemporary society' (Buck-Morss, 1977: 23). The influence of both Benjamin and Marx, says Buck-Morss, is apparent in Adorno's work in the post-Vienna period, yet perhaps the single greatest influence on Adorno was still living in the city, working on the twelve-tone technique of composition which was to earn him even greater notoriety – Arnold Schoenberg.

Schoenberg was always an innovative composer, and his first performances often provoked a hostile reaction – 'a sort of minor riot which was accepted as a ritual element in Viennese concert life' (Rosen, 1976: 12) – yet his career was moderately successful until the 'atonal' music of the period after 1908 created a 'scandal' and 'moral outrage' (1976: 16) among the musical public. Yet, Rosen argues, the works were not intended simply to shock: 'the stylistic revolutions of those years were merely the exploitation of already existent possibilities within the artistic languages, the drawing of unavoidable conclusions' (1976: 16). Moreover, Schoenberg had elaborated a coherent philosophy of music which laid great emphasis on the necessity for new compositions to be rooted in, and derived from, the works of the great masters of the past (Janik and Toulmin, 1973: 107). For him, as for Hanslick before him, the essence of composition lay in 'the authenticity of the musical idea and its articulation according to musical logic' (1973: 111), rather than the evocation of extra-musical associations or conformity to comfortable conventions. Thus Schoenberg found fault with the Romantic composers of the second half of the nineteenth century, who had deliberately written pieces that would be acceptable to the public, and with the audiences, who didn't know anything about music but knew what they liked; the combination had perverted the true course of musical progress. So Schoenberg took his task to be that of 'breaking through the limits of a bygone aesthetic' (quoted in Janik and Toulmin, 1973: 107). 'Viewed from this perspective,' Janik and Toulmin comment, 'all of Schoenberg's compositions represent attacks on the pseudo-sophistication of bourgeois aestheticism. His work as a composer becomes, simultaneously, a critique of society' (1973: 111). The immense attractions to the young Adorno of Schoenberg's music and ideas should be evident; certainly the consequences were profound. According to Susan Buck-Morss 'Schoenberg's revolution in music provided the inspiration for Adorno's own efforts in philosophy ... For just as Schoenberg had overthrown tonality, Adorno's Husserl study attempted to overthrow idealism, the decaying form of bourgeois philosophy' (1977: 15).

By choosing to write a thesis which was a critique of Husserl's philosophy, Adorno revealed something of his general strategy: in order

to demolish the claims of what he took to be bourgeois philosophy
– to negate it – it was necessary to confront it in its most advanced
and sophisticated form. We can see too the parallels that Adorno
drew between radical composers like Schoenberg and his circle, and
the work of the critical theorists. Schoenberg's achievement, for
Adorno, was the negation of the prevailing form of bourgeois music
– tonality – through an essentially dialectical method that transformed it from within, by respecting its inherent logic yet working
on it so as to draw, in Rosen's words, 'inescapable conclusions'. Similarly, critical theory, in analysing the cultural products of capitalist
society, could accomplish a radical demystification by exposing the
inherent contradictions of the dominant ideology, and thus 'robbing
the present of its ideological justification' (Buck-Morss, 1977: 36).
Yet it is immediately apparent that such criticism would be the work
of, and would appeal to, an intellectual elite rather than the labour-
ing masses in whose name it was often justified. Thus there were
grounds for a split between Adorno and contemporaries such as Benjamin, who identified aesthetic validity with political correctness,
and Brecht, who chose to compare Schoenberg's deeply unpopular
music 'with the neighing of a horse about to be butchered and
processed for bockwurst' (Buck-Morss, 1977: 34).

   Throughout his long and prolific career, Adorno would never yield
to the proposition that aesthetic value is a function of political ideology; on the contrary, for him artworks, however obscure they
seemed, contained a kernel of truth which could be revealed only by
dialectical analysis. This position, too, helps us to understand why
Adorno's writings, like Schoenberg's music, seem to present so many
difficulties, particularly to the non-German reader. (One collection
of his essays in English carries a preface titled 'Translating the
untranslatable') (Adorno, 1967: 9). Adorno could write clear, conventional prose when he chose to, but mostly he did not, believing
that simple, straightforward messages formulated for the needs of a
wide readership would end up only by affirming the validity of the
established discourse which it was his purpose to negate. 'Defiance
of society', he wrote, 'includes defiance of its language' (1967: 225).
Just as Schoenberg's music demands of the listener 'not mere con-
templation but *praxis*', so the difficulties in Adorno's writings were
'less the product of caprice or inarticulateness than a direct challenge
to the reader to respond with commensurate seriousness' (Jay, 1973:
176).

Indeed, Buck-Morss has argued that Adorno's essays, like Schoenberg's music, should be understood as compositions which reflect in
their form and structure the social structures in which they were conceived: 'the sentences develop like musical themes: they break apart
and turn in on themselves in a continuing spiral of variations. ... But
there is no affirmation, no "closing cadence". The contradictions are
unravelled; they are not resolved'. (1977: 101). In other words,
Adorno's writings were intended to reflect a reality which was itself
fractured and contradictory, and which did not form a 'harmonious
whole' (1977: 100). Moreover, as we shall see, some of Adorno's
most scornful remarks were directed at music which, to this ears, did
'affirm' the existing society by resolving according to conventional
harmonic progressions, or by engendering the sense of a community
of free individuals; for him such music was little more than ideology
in a situation where people were increasingly unfree, enslaved by the
irrevocable 'dialectic of enlightenment.'

So reading Adorno can be difficult – deliberately so, it seems – and
the outlines of his vast body of work can be summarised only at the
risk of distortion and oversimplification. On the other hand, there is
a consistency and continuity in his writing: the principles and presuppositions which are evident in his interpretations of music in the
early 1930s recur throughout his work, and were not subsequently
modified in any fundamental ways. In fact, the 1932 essay 'On the
social situation of music' can still serve as a basic guide to Adorno's
main themes and perspectives (Adorno, 1978). Here we find his fundamental distinction between music which is produced simply as a
commodity for sale in the market, and as such is 'passive and undi-
alectic', and music which 'expresses alienation' (1978: 132). The distinction is not the same as the familiar split between 'light' and
'serious' music, because a great deal of the latter, in Adorno's view,
is itself tainted by its orientation to the demands of the market.
Needless to say, in conditions of industrial capitalism the vast majority of music is of this commodity nature, to Adorno's unremitting
chagrin, and he has some powerful things to say about the ways in
which, as a product of the 'culture industry', it serves only to repress,
stultify, and control people while at the same time giving them the
illusion of freedom and choice. We shall consider Adorno's view of
music and the 'culture industry' below. Firstly, though, it will be
useful to outline his perspective on the 'serious' music which despite
– or rather because of – its unpopularity was a major preoccupation

throughout his life, for it is in this context that we can glimpse something of Adorno's belief that artworks can represent society.

The relentless process of commodification under capitalism,
Adorno argues, has reduced genuine artistic work to a tiny fraction
of cultural production; as such it appears from the perspective of
positivist sociology as virtually insignificant: 'of no consequence to
any approach seeking to register social facts'. Such an approach can
only see in 'advanced modern art ... the outrage of an antisocial attitude', because it fails to examine the 'objective content' of the works
(Horkheimer and Adorno, 1973: 104). In other words, once again
mere appearances are mistaken for the essence of the phenomenon:
this is not only scientifically unsound, but serves to legitimise existing realities and obscure their true nature. In fact, from the point of
view of critical theory, it is precisely the new works of art which
express, in their own terms, the reality of the 'barbaric environment'
of modern rationalised societies (1973: 105). In the present context,
we may note three aspects of this general perspective – firstly the
retention of the category of 'art' as a distinct sphere within the field
of cultural production; secondly the notion that works have an
'objective content' which is independent of the ways in which they
may be socially appropriated; and thirdly the claim that authentic
art, however distant it may seem from the consciousness of the
masses, nevertheless can serve to defend the vision of another, better,
reality. As Jay puts it, 'genuine art acted as the last preserve of
human yearnings for that "other" society beyond the present one'
(Jay, 1973: 179). Moreover, it is the very shock of the new, in pro-
voking 'the rage of the normal ... which betrays something of the
falseness of this normalcy' (Horkheimer and Adorno, 1973: 105). We
shall return to these points in due course.

Typically, Adorno's perspective contradicts two schools of aesthetic thought which were, and remain, influential – the idea that art
expresses the subjectivity of the individual artist, and the belief that
art can reflect eternal truths. In Adorno's scheme of things, says Jay:
'The work is neither a reflection of the soul nor the embodiment of
a Platonic Idea. It is not pure Being but rather a "force-field"
between subject and object' (Jay, 1973: 177). The subject is the artist,
in this case the individual composer who brings his or her creativity
and imagination to the work; these resources, however, are neither
unlimited nor unrestrained, since all individuals are imbued with the
culture of their society, and, moreover, since the autonomous subject

of bourgeois ideology has been all but liquidated in the 'totally organised' society. The object is the 'musical material' which confronts the composer; again this is not freely chosen nor randomly provided:

> This material is traditionally defined – in terms of physics, or possibly in terms of the psychology of sound – as the sum of all sounds at the disposal of the composer. The actual compositional material, however, is as different from this sum as is language from its total supply of sounds. It is not simply a matter of the increase and decrease of this supply in the course of history. All its specific characteristics are indications of the historical process. (Adorno, 1973a: 32)

Adorno is arguing that composers must inevitably orient themselves to a pre-existing system of musical expression, whether they wish to accept or reject it, and that this system, this 'compositional material', inherently represents the historical processes and social forces through which it has been developed and reformulated, rather than the universal characteristics of the human mind. Thus fundamental social structures and processes find their expression in musical structures and processes; the 'musical material' is 'sedimented Geist' in Hegel's sense of the 'objectifications of past subjectivity' (Jay, 1984b: 134, 184). The great work of art will represent, in its own fashion, the social totality, with all its conflicts and contradictions, rather than simply reflect the interests or values of a particular social class. As we have seen, it was the work of Arnold Schoenberg which provided Adorno with his model of how radical art could function in the 'totally organised' society, despite the hostile reception which it had received, and its subsequent marginalisation. I shall suggest later that Adorno's interpretation of Schoenberg displays his understanding of the ways in which great music can be the bearer of social truth; the point is central to his analysis of the relationship between music and society. At present, though, I wish only to emphasise certain general aspects of Adorno's aesthetic theory which must be borne in mind when considering this analysis. It should be clear that for Adorno it was not possible to make a distinction between aesthetic and sociological issues. As Gillian Rose has put it, in Adorno's view the 'sociology of culture is inseparable ... from criticism (aesthetics) because the social origin, content and function of a work of art can only be fully understood by examining the internal formation of a work, that is, the way meaning is structured' (Rose, 1978: 109).

For Adorno, as we have seen, the meaning of music cannot be disclosed by examining the intentions or beliefs of composers, far less their social class origins. Moreover, the ways in which music functions may bear little relation to what he takes to be its original, social, meaning. Thus, for example, Beethoven's works, genuinely revolutionary in their time, have come in a later period to function as elements of bourgeois ideology, expressing the *ideal* of the free individual and harmonious community in a society which is in reality totalitarian. And Chopin's 'aristocratic' music has, in the twentieth century, achieved mass popularity; in such ways 'a music's social function may diverge from the social meaning it embodies' (Adorno, 1976a: 61–2).

For Adorno, all cultural products embodied some kind of 'social meaning', whether they belonged to the realms of 'autonomous art' or 'mass culture', a meaning which could be deciphered by dialectical analysis. As we have seen, his fundamental position was that aesthetic value itself was a function of social content: the crucial question was whether a work tended to 'affirm' or to 'negate' existing society. As a relentless dialectician, he held that nothing was either completely positive or completely negative in its social meaning; all cultural objects would reveal, on interpretation, elements of 'both ideology and truth' (Buck-Morss, 1977: 149). In general, though, his criterion of great art was that it expressed the realities of the social totality with all its inherent contradictions: thus Schoenberg's music, like critical theory, was predominantly an effective negation. By contrast, popular culture was overwhelmingly affirmative, accepting society, and, through an ideological misrepresentation of it, reconciling people to it. It follows from this that it could have little aesthetic merit.

So the starting point of Adorno's cultural analysis is a sort of dialectical reversal of the commonplace proposition that the social whole is made up of its parts; for Adorno, the parts also embody the whole. Early in his intellectual life Adorno had been impressed by the idea that 'the seemingly insignificant details of modern life' may reveal significant social truths: one of his mentors, Siegfried Kracauer, had been much influenced by the 'microsociological analyses' of Georg Simmel (Jay, 1984b: 245). Thus, as Rose has suggested, Adorno's concern with the formal properties of cultural objects, and particularly musical works, is in many respects consistent with Durkheim's analytical method: 'Sociological investigation of musical forms in this sense has affinities with Durkheim's approach to the elementary forms of religious life, with the way in which Durkheim argues that religious forms present (reinforce) and represent (interpret) society' (Rose, 1978: 112). Moreover, while relatively little of Adorno's work was concerned with 'popular' forms of music, and he was evidently not particularly interested in them (Hullot-Kentor, 1991: 109), it is wrong to conclude that he did not take popular culture seriously. On the contrary, the various forms of mass culture have an incalculable effect on the consciousness of people in modern society, and so 'it was precisely here', as Buck-Morss puts it, 'that he riveted his philosophical gaze, under which appearance was dialectically "redeemed", transformed from ideology into social truth'. (Buck-Morss, 1977: 109).

The culture industry

The fourth chapter of Adorno and Horkheimer's *Dialectic of Enlightenment*, written in America during the Second World War, is entitled 'The culture industry – enlightenment as mass deception' and is a sustained – some would say definitive – critique of the culture of industrial capitalism. Much of its undeniable effect stems from frequent rhetorical flourishes – 'the culture industry perpetually cheats its consumers of what it perpetually promises' (Adorno and Horkheimer, 1979: 139) – and its relentless critical bombast: 'the people of today have already forgotten that there ever was a notion of what human life was. For centuries society has been preparing for Victor Mature and Mickey Rooney. By destroying they come to fulfil' (1979: 156). Drawing on the material provided by the radio, films and popular music of the 1930s and 1940s, Adorno and Horkheimer make no effort to conceal their sense of betrayal that the culture of enlightenment, of Kant, Hegel and Beethoven, has inexorably generated that of dance band crooners, The Lone Ranger and Donald Duck, a culture which is itself a product of industrial mass-production and which, driven on by the ceaseless requirement of profit, deforms the consciousness of every individual. Indeed, it effectively destroys the free individual, reducing people to membership of a conforming, consuming mass and eroding their capacity for genuine thought or feeling. The discussion of the 'culture industry' also illustrates well Adorno's method of interpreting small details in terms of grand themes:

Life in the late capitalism era is a constant initiation rite. Everyone must show that he wholly identifies himself with the power which is belabouring him. This occurs in the principle of jazz syncopation, which simultaneously derides stumbling and makes it a rule. The eunuch-like voice of the crooner on the radio, the heiress's smooth suitor, who falls into the swimming pool in his dinner jacket, are models for those who must become whatever the system wants. Everyone can be like this omnipotent society; everyone can be happy, if only he will capitulate fully and sacrifice his claim to happiness. (1979: 153)

For Adorno there was a 'unity', an unbroken continuity, running through historical events, no matter how disjointed they may appear: 'the unity of the control of nature, progressing to rule over men, and finally to that over men's inner nature' (Adorno, 1973b: 320).

Unlike Walter Benjamin, then, Adorno did not believe that 'the age of mechanical reproduction' offered new hope of liberation; on the contrary, the production of mass culture on an industrial scale was held to be no more than a new and powerful means of social control (Rose, 1978: 118). While constantly invoking the myth of a community of free individuals, and engendering feelings of belonging, the culture industry was in reality imprisoning people in the unthinking conformity of the totally 'administered' world, systematically depriving them of the authentic experience of the pre-modern era, and blocking off the opportunities to conceive of things in alternative ways. Its power was all the more insidious in that, unlike earlier forms of domination, it did not work principally through coercive or economic sanctions, or the appeal to supernatural authority, but – in often imperceptible ways – by limiting and 'deforming' consciousness. As far as music was concerned, this could be seen in the 'regression of listening' typical of people in modern industrial societies who, largely through being saturated by the pop music pumped out by the culture industry, no longer had the ability to listen intelligently and perceptively to musical works (1991a). Mass popular music, he wrote, 'helps to maim the consciousness of those exposed to it' so that it 'undermines ... autonomy and independence of judgement – qualities which a society of free men would require' (Adorno, 1976a: 38). In particular, what is lost is the capacity to discern the structural integrity of a piece as a whole, and to appreciate the ways in which the various elements of the work are, in a successful composition, coherently related to each other. This comes about because it is precisely this structure, this cumulative interrelationship of parts, which is lacking in popular music. Adorno calls this 'standardisation': 'the overall theme is clearly stated at the beginning of the piece, but ... the details do not develop the theme, they merely repeat it, and have no special status within the whole work' (Rose, 1978: 133).

Thus the technical grounds for Adorno's rejection of popular music are not its relative simplicity in comparison with 'serious' music; on the contrary, he pointed out that the latter is often much more limited in respect of both rhythm and melody, and, as far as harmonic development is concerned, 'the supply of chords of the so-called classics is invariably more limited than that of any current Tin Pan Alley composer' (Adorno, 1990: 305). The fundamental flaw, as he saw it, was that popular music involved the imposition of a standard formula, endlessly repeated, just as in any other sphere of the industrial production of commodities. For Adorno, 'good serious music' was that in which

> the detail virtually contains the whole and leads to the exposition of the whole, while, at the same time, it is produced out of the conception of the whole. In popular music the relationship is fortuitous. The detail has no bearing on the whole, which appears as an extraneous framework. (1990: 304)

In other words, in a good composition the parts and the whole stand in a dialectical relationship, which each giving meaning and form to the other. In popular music, the individual integrity of the structured whole is replaced by simple repetition of single elements according to a rigid, standardised, pattern: the thirty-two bar song with its AABA form and regular, insistent rhythm are only the most obvious aspects of the formula. Indeed, Adorno detects this pattern of repetition in all aspects of mass culture, in, for example, the rise and fall of singers and film stars: new names must keep appearing to sustain the illusion of novelty. Appearances proclaim innovation, choice and freedom; the reality is standardisation, conformity and the crushing of the individual by the collectivity.

In such a society, trivial departures from established patterns become treated as though they were real differences – just as little novelties in new pop songs give, briefly, the impression of innovation, so tiny variations in individuals' appearances, in hairstyle for example, are regarded as if they were matters of importance. In fact, from time to time Adorno employs the argument – which some have found slightly perverse – that observed departures from expected forms are simply exceptions which prove the general rule. Overall, however, he is unequivocal about the effects of mass culture in general and popular music in particular:

> Music today is largely a social cement. And the meaning listeners attribute to a material, the inherent logic of which is inaccessible to them, is above all a means by which they achieve some psychical adjustment to the mechanisms of present-day life. (1990: 311–12)

Through the pressure of mass culture, often concealed but effective for this very reason, we are pressed into an invisible mould; for the individual this produces a regression to a childlike state of dependency and innocence of the surrounding realities, and for society as a whole it is a reversion to a primitive era when the individual was totally determined by the group.

Adorno's view of popular culture has been widely influential, not least because his critical onslaught derived from a radical, rather than a conservative, perspective. There were echoes of his work in the debate about 'mass society' which followed the publication of David Riesman's book *The Lonely Crowd* in 1950, and in the 1960s it was the Frankfurt School's view of the 'dialectic of enlightenment' which provided the foundation for Herbert Marcuse's critique of modern civilisation in *One-Dimensional Man* (1964). Yet Adorno himself cared little about popular music. Given the theoretical presuppositions he brought to it, this is not surprising; moreover, from the point of view of a 'serious' composer and committed musicologist, as Hullot-Kentor has put it, 'the music itself is not interesting' (Hullot-Kentor, 1991: 109).

Inevitably though, however marginal they are to his work as a whole, Adorno's ideas about popular music have themselves attracted strenuous criticism. His view of the 'culture industry', with all its totalitarian implications, was formulated during the period from the late 1920s to the early 1940s, a time when, as we have seen, totalitarian states were emerging in both 'capitalist' and 'communist' countries, and when the modern mass media – particularly films, radio and recordings – were enjoying an unprecedented rate of development. It is these tendencies which, above all else, are reflected in Adorno's view of popular music as a means of ideological coercion (Paddison, 1982: 209). More recently it has been argued that although Adorno (like Weber and Marx before him) was correct to identify the pressures towards rationalisation and 'standardisation' which are inherent in the development of capitalism, the consequences have not been entirely as they expected. While it is true that 'the various cultural industries' have become increasingly centralised, Volpacchio has argued, this has been accompanied by a significant 'differentiation of the market machinery. ... A few large corporations now oversee a growing diversity of recording artists' (1991: 120), a view consistent with that of Lopes (1992). Others have concluded that the image of modern capitalist society as 'a directed, planned, and tightly controlled corporate machinery extending from the state to the dance hall ... was an exaggeration and a fantasy' (Berman and D'Amico, 1991: 74).

It has also been suggested that, largely owing to his own ignorance and lack of interest, Adorno failed to notice that some forms of 'popular' music have displayed exactly that critical potential which he took to be the hallmark of great art. Paddison has argued that 'radical' popular music, which has, in Adorno's terms, attempted to resist its fate as a commodity, has itself inevitably confronted 'the alienation faced by all avant-garde music' (1982: 218). A similar fate has befallen many modern jazz musicians who since the 1940s have themselves rejected the values and conventions of the music business, and whose work has been interpreted as radical in the sense that it leads them to challenge the legitimacy of prevailing musical, economic and political structures (Kofsky, 1970; Litweiler, 1985). Moreover, as Paddison and others have pointed out, the dominant influence on the development of popular music in the second half of the twentieth century has been the African-American tradition; it is simply wrong to assume, as Adorno did, that the music of the 'culture industry' simply reworks and re-presents outmoded elements drawn from European 'serious' music. Indeed, some have argued that cultural resistance is inherent in 'black' musical forms, and ascribed to them a role not at all unlike that which Adorno reserves for the serious avant-garde: 'it is just that refusal to conform to any preconceived (i.e. European) patterns or rules that is one of the chief virtues of Black or African-American music' (Wilmer, 1977: 9). Moreover, and even more telling from Adorno's point of view, it has been argued that political and cultural alternatives may be inherent in the structure of such music. Schoenherr rejects Adorno's claim that the individual autonomy and social harmony celebrated in popular music are necessarily an illusion or a 'parody ... of a future collective process': jazz composers such as Charles Mingus, he argues, seek above all to reconcile the individual and the collectivity (Schoenherr, 1991: 94). Inevitably, this involves challenging established conventions and traditions.

Finally, it is worth mentioning Adorno's views on 'jazz', since, according to Buck-Morss, 'his analysis of jazz provided a model for all Adorno's later critiques of mass culture' (1977: 109). Yet it is clear that by 'jazz' he did not mean the improvised music which emerged from the African-American tradition but rather the 'essentially commercialised mass music' of the 1920s and 1930s. Adorno's essay on jazz was written in England in 1936 (and subsequently published under the pseudonym of 'Hektor Rottweiler'); it is doubtful if, at this stage, he had paid much attention to the work of the early soloists who brought the art of improvisation back into western musical culture. For Adorno, then, jazz was the 'sweet' music of the big dance bands and broadcasting orchestras: precisely the music from which the 'hot' jazz players and their early fans sought to distance themselves. Indeed, it is ironic that Adorno's critique of commercialised popular music has regularly been matched, and surpassed, by the vitriolic condemnation of it which has emanated from jazz purists. Despite occasional hints that he was aware of the difference between 'real' jazz and commercial pop music, Adorno never reformulated the basic views which, in this sphere as in others, were largely shaped by theoretical conclusions reached by the early 1930s. Besides, as we have seen, his major concerns lay elsewhere, in the field of 'serious' composed music, and it is here that we may discover Adorno's general view of the relationship between music and society.

Music and representation of society

Frederic Jameson has nicely caught the spirit and the ambition of Adorno's relentlessly dialectical analysis of culture:

> for a fleeting instant we catch a glimpse of a unified world, of a universe in which discontinuous realities are nonetheless somehow implicated with each other and intertwined, no matter how remote they may at first have seemed; in which the reign of chance briefly refocuses into a network of cross-relationships wherever the eye can reach, contingency temporarily transmuted into necessity. (Jameson, 1971: 8)

To perceive this 'unified world', we must abandon the dominant

theoretical mode of the modern world – positivist philosophy – and
cease looking at the social world as if it were made up only of a mass
of isolated, independent objects, each of which, as in the manner of
science, may be classified, measured and so on. By contrast, a dialectical analysis will not separate the object from its cultural context
but will seek to grasp the relationship between them, keeping both
in view; the result, as Jameson puts it, is 'a constellation of unfore-
seen uniformities, ... a socio-economic style which can be *named*'
(1971: 8). It is in just this way that Adorno sought to illuminate the
links between music and society: following, as we have seen, Benjamin's idea that even fragments of culture may be seen as 'expressing' the social totality, he dismissed claims that musical
developments are independent, or only accidentally related to the
societies in which they take place. For Adorno music not only reflects
the social totality but reformulates social conflicts and contradictions
'within its own structure'. (1978: 130).

Of course, not all music could do this. As I have suggested above,
it was precisely the lack of structural development in the market-ori-
ented commodities produced by the 'culture industry' which, for
Adorno, rendered them worthless as music. Thus popular music was
inherently affirmative, lacking that power to negate the existing state
of affairs which is Adorno's criterion of aesthetic value in the totally
organised society. In this sense, great art and critical theory have a
common purpose and justification. Whereas the latter aims, dialectically speaking, to negate the ideological basis of existing society, the
former not only reflects social tendencies 'but simultaneously and
actively opposes these tendencies by its negation of standardised
meaning within its own structure' (Paddison, 1982: 207). Both, as a
consequence, may be incomprehensible to all but a minority; again,
as we have seen, Adorno accepted this conclusion, arguing that, in
order to resist 'neutralisation', true art might have to alienate society
by being 'difficult': sacrificing 'surface intelligibility ... in order to
retain the integrity of what Adorno calls the essence or 'latent structure' (Subotnik, 1976: 264).

It is thus in the *form* of artistic works – their 'latent structure' –
that Adorno seeks to reveal their critical potential, rather than in
their apparent content. Indeed the idea that musical structures are
somehow the embodiment of social structures is one of Adorno's
most fundamental sociological claims. How does this process of
'expression' or 'representation' come about? It may be useful to iden-

tify various aspects of the process, before focusing specifically on the activity of composition, or, as Adorno regarded it, 'musical production'. Firstly, as we have already seen, composers do not confront their musical material in a totally fresh, unrestrained manner. Already they have been socialised within a particular cultural context, and – whether they see themselves as conformists or radicals – may find it hard not to display its influence, in the realms of either general ideology or specific musical conventions. Secondly, Adorno insists on the point that the musical materials themselves are not idiosyncratically chosen from all available sounds but present themselves already pre-structured, so to speak, in an established system of which western tonality is the outstanding example (and certainly the only one that interested Adorno). As we have seen, he regarded the actual compositional material available to the composer as being as different from all possible sounds 'as is language from its total supply of sounds' (1973a: 32).

In arguing thus, Adorno emphasises the important sociological theme that both the composer and the material are 'socially constructed' before a single sound has been produced. He also wishes to dismiss claims that great music reflects 'natural' laws, eternal truths or the pure subjectivity of its composer: the form of a musical work is ultimately derived 'not from the artist's own imagination but, unconsciously, from the formal categories and models of the world outside of the art work' (Subotnik, 1976: 247). Thus far, few sociologists would dissent from this general formulation, and many would applaud Adorno's impatience with those who have advanced theories which presuppose cultural or psychological 'universals'. He, however, wishes to go further, in a step which is decisive for his general position and much more theoretically contentious: this is the belief that social structures and processes, conflicts and contradictions are somehow represented in musical forms and structures. Thus, as Subotnik has put it, 'the essential tendencies of a given historical moment become translated into the formal aspects of great art'; this occurs through 'a complex process of mediation, which Adorno does not pretend to understand or elucidate adequately' (1976: 247).

If this claim is accepted, thirdly, it follows – for Adorno – that, by working on and reformulating the materials, the composer is creating a sort of coded representation of society, which will have greater aesthetic value the more it manages to embody the inherent structure of the totality, with all its conflicts and contradictions. The implications of his view are nowhere clearer than in his treatment of the 'new music' of Schoenberg, whose greatness lay in his ability to produce a dialectical negation of conventional forms:

> here and now music is able to do nothing but portray within its own structure the social antinomies which are also responsible for its own isolation. Music will be better, the more deeply it is able to express — in the antinomies of its own formal language — the exigency of the social condition and to call for change through the coded language of suffering. It is not for music to stare in helpless horror at society. It fulfills its social function more precisely when it presents social problems through its own material and according to its own formal laws — problems which music contains within itself in the innermost cells of its technique. The task of music as art thus enters into a parallel relationship to the task of social theory. (Adorno, 1978: 130)

Unlike the social theorist, however, the composer of genuinely critical music need not be consciously concerned with social issues; indeed neither Schoenberg nor Berg was particularly sympathetic to Adorno's theoretical interpretations. Rather, says Adorno, composers fulfil their artistic purposes the more they concentrate purely on the musical material which presents itself to them, since this material is itself an embodiment of social structures and processes. Here again, Adorno emphasises that the inherent meaning of a work has nothing to do with the subjective intentions of the artist, and everything to do with its status as a representation of social reality. Accordingly, he strongly approved of Schoenberg's description of himself as a craftsman rather than an artist.

But what does the actual production of this 'craftsman' consist of? Essentially, he holds, it is a dialectical process in which the subject — the composer — confronts the objectivity of the musical material, 'itself a crystallisation of the creative impulse, an element socially predetermined through the consciousness of man' (Adorno, 1973a: 33). The process of musical production is thus a particular form of the general situation in which acting individuals, with their own unique subjectivities, confront established social structures and institutions, which appear to them as objective facts. Composers cannot ignore such structures any more than anyone else can, yet as creative artists they must refuse simply to accept what is given, and try to transform them – ideally by the production of a new synthesis in which subjective and objective elements are reconciled. From this perspective, it is clear why Adorno had such a high regard for Schoenberg, who claimed to have transformed tonality from within, and why he responded with such antipathy to Stravinsky, who believed that 'In the pure state, music is pure speculation' (1942: 49).

Not since the time of J. S. Bach, says Adorno, has the composer enjoyed a sense of freedom from the demands of established tradition: the inexorable dialectic of enlightenment gradually erodes the autonomy of the individual in this sphere, as in all others. Whereas Bach, armed with the power of reason, enjoyed 'the possibility of freely choosing from all the objectively available procedures of the epoch', the very process of rationalisation not only turned music into a commodity but generated structures and conventions which progressively denied this freedom to his successors (Adorno, 1967: 140–1). Moreover, by the late nineteenth century the accumulation of stylistic innovations was threatening to undermine the whole system: intervallic relationships which were once prohibited as dissonant gradually came into use, weakening the 'pull' of the tonic centre and giving its chord an old-fashioned, formal, sound. Structurally, the use of dissonance as a means of creating tension involved movement to related – and then to remote – keys; the unanticipated, and often unwanted, consequence was 'the long, gradual breakdown of tonality'. 'The concept of modulation', writes Charles Rosen, 'was eventually to prove the powerful force that corrupted tonality' (1976: 36, 37). By the time Schoenberg arrived on the scene, there were many who felt that there was nothing more to be said in the established language of music; it was this artistic paralysis which the modernists confronted in their various ways. 'More than any other composer', says Rosen, 'Schoenberg faced what he felt was the misery of contemporary music' (1976: 45).

So in his analysis of Schoenberg's work we get as clear a picture as any of Adorno's view of compositional activity. The following passages are in the 1932 essay 'On the social situation of music':

> Schoenberg's really central achievement ... is that he ... never behaved 'expressionistically', superimposing subjective intentions upon heterogeneous material in an authoritarian and inconsiderate manner. Every gesture with which he intervenes in the material configuration is at the same time an answer to questions directed to him by the material in the

form of its own immanent problems. (Adorno, 1978: 135)

These problems, of course, are nothing less than a representation of social problems:

> That Schoenberg's solutions to technical problems are socially relevant in spite of their isolation is proven by his replacement within all his works – in spite and because of his own expressive origins – of any private fortuitousness which might have been viewed quite correctly as a type of anarchic musical production with an objective principle of order which is never imposed upon the material from the exterior, but rather extracted from the material itself and brought into relationship with it by means of an historical process of rational transparence. This is the meaning of the revolution which technically took the form of 'twelve-tone composition'. (1978: 135)

There are some, as we shall see, who might hold that the meaning of this passage is not itself entirely transparent; Adorno's conclusion, however, is both apocalyptic and suitably dialectical: 'In the very moment in which the total musical material is subjected to the power of expression, expression itself is extinguished – as though it were animated only by the resistance of the material, itself "alienated" and alien to the subject' (1978: 135). Although Adorno eventually came to be critical of the uses to which Schoenberg's twelve-tone methods were put, he never lost his high regard for the composer who had negated bourgeois music, not in an arbitrary way but by transforming it from within; in doing so Schoenberg expressed 'not the power of the sovereign subject ... but rather the *Angst* accompanying its breakdown' (Jay, 1984a: 150). Whatever their opinion of it, there are few who would dispute that Schoenberg's music may be heard as an expression of Angst; for Adorno these sounds gave voice to the spirit of the times, in which the individual, who has been liberated in the Age of Reason, was inexorably crushed under the weight of the rationalisation which was its consequence. The music itself, in its very structure, achieves that unity of subjective and objective elements which, for Adorno, is the criterion of greatness in composition; moreover, like all great art, it has an inherent and fundamental social meaning, expressing both the anguish of modern society and aspirations for another, more human, reality.

Adorno nowhere provides a systematic outline of his view of the development of western music – indeed the very idea would have been anathema to him. In his writings on composers and their works, however, we can discern a coherent general perspective, reflecting those basic theoretical commitments which he developed early and retained throughout his career.

Music, for Adorno, meant above all the composed works produced in western Europe during the period 'from Monteverdi to Schoenberg' (1967: 137), and in his interpretation of these works his criterion of aesthetic value is the extent to which they bear inherent social meanings. Thus two particular composers stand out from all the others – Beethoven, who in his music and his life exemplified the ideal of the liberated, independent individual of bourgeois ideology, and who also came to anticipate the destruction of this heroic figure, and Schoenberg, who confronted the crisis of tonality which had been inevitable ever since Beethoven's masterworks. For Adorno, then, the rise and decline of western tonality is, ultimately, a musical representation of 'the great achievement of human history ... the crystallization of reason and self-consciousness into the concept of the free individual' (Subotnik, 1976: 244) and the gradual, inexorable crushing of this individual in the rationalised, totalitarian society of modern industrial capitalism.

A great deal of Adorno's work is concerned with the free individual's tragic trajectory. Thus he hears in the works of J. S. Bach some of the first flowerings of newly-liberated Reason, and is concerned to rescue Bach from appropriation by those who interpret them as an echo of a bygone age – 'of the time-honoured bounds of tradition, of the spirit of medieval polyphony, of the theologically vaulted cosmos' (1967: 135). Even worse, they have been taken as an expression of 'the order of Being as such'. Clearly, this will not do for Adorno, and he sets out to re-establish Bach as, for his day, a fundamentally modern composer who, as the very title of The Well-Tempered Clavier suggests, did much to advance the rationalisation of music. In this and other works Adorno hears not the resonance of the old order but 'differentiation, individuation, freedom' (1967: 137), not static recapitulation but significant dynamic elements. Adorno agrees with Schoenberg that Bach's 'technique of the developing variation ... became the basic compositional principle in Viennese Classicism' (1967: 139) but characteristically goes beyond this to emphasise the social meanings which may be deciphered in Bach's works. What 'the technique of the developing variation' involves, he argues, is the 'decomposition' of the thematic material into its individual elements and its productive reconstitution; in this it parallels

> the change in the work-process that took place during the same epoch
> through the emergence of manufacturing, which consisted essentially in
> breaking down the old craft operation into its smaller component acts.
> If this resulted in the rationalisation of material production, then Bach
> was the first to crystallize the idea of the rationally constituted work,
> of the aesthetic domination of nature. (1967: 139)

Of course, there are 'archaic' and 'ancient' elements in Bach, but
Adorno insists, firstly, that these are not the dominant ones in his
works, and, secondly, that their very presence must be heard as evidence of Bach's emancipation from the old order:

> As early as Bach the rationalisation of compositional technique, the pre-
> dominance of subjective reason, so to speak, brings with it the possi-
> bility of freely choosing from all the objectively available procedures of
> the epoch. Bach does not feel himself blindly bound to any of them but
> instead always chooses that which best suits the compositional inten-
> tion. Such liberty vis-à-vis the ancient ... can hardly be construed as the
> culmination of the tradition, which instead must prohibit just that free
> selection of available possibilities. (1967: 140)

Once the power of rationality has begun to corrode the traditions, it
acquires its own momentum; at the same time, says Adorno, compositional work continues to represent – indirectly, dialectically –
more general social processes. Thus Haydn's work reflects 'the exu-
berance of the nascent bourgeois era' and Mozart 'so clearly echoes
the passage from enlightened late absolutism to the bourgeoisie'
(Adorno, 1976a: 69).

It is in Beethoven, however, that Adorno detects not only the cul-
mination of bourgeois individualism – in a society of liberated
equals, where individual and collective interests are in harmony – but
also the first clear indications that such a harmonious totality cannot
be sustained, indeed that it will be destroyed by the same values of
scientific rationalism which made it conceivable in the first place
(Subotnik, 1976: 245). The great achievement of social development
– the reconciliation of individual and collective interests in a harmonious whole – 'came close to realisation at one unique moment in
history, represented in music by Beethoven's second-period style'
(1976: 245). The essential formal feature of this style, according to
Adorno, was the 'sonata allegro' in which the musical subject is
developed, transformed and yet in a thoroughly dialectical way

returned to itself through recapitulation and ultimately reconciliation. What this signifies is the 'attainment of the musico-historical
moment when individual freedom finally overtakes externally given
order as the most manifest governing principle of objectively existing structures' (1976: 249). Moreover, it is Adorno's claim that this
musical representation of the ideology of the new bourgeoisie was
itself in tune, so to speak, with the tastes of the members of the
emerging class: his works, at first considered radical and difficult,
had become accepted and highly popular. This was not because
Beethoven set out, in the manner of the modern culture industry,
simply to please the public but because 'for a time his individual
artistic interests and the artistic interests of society genuinely coin-
cided' (1976: 249).

However, as the dialectic of enlightenment dictates, this representation of the reconciliation of subjective and objective, individual
and society, was ultimately an illusion. Indeed, says Adorno,
Beethoven's second-period style, like any cultural object subjected to
dialectical analysis, displays the seeds of its own destruction and the
elements which will eventually negate it. He identifies 'negative
moments' and 'resistances' which will finally force the recognition
that complete freedom may be 'incompatible with form' and indicate
'the incipient transformation of freedom into force' (1976: 251). Thus
the music of Beethoven in his last years – 'radically different from
his previous works', says Wilfrid Mellers (1988: 647) – was heard by
Adorno as a 'critique' of the middle-period style: it recognises the
impossibility of the harmonious synthesis represented in the earlier
music 'and is, for this reason, the most realistic of Beethoven's styles'
(Subotnik, 1976: 250). Enlightenment rationality, and music from
Bach onwards, had decisively rejected God as the source of order in
the world; now the free individual who had replaced Him was also
seen to be impotent. 'With both eliminated,' as Subotnik puts it, 'the
individual would find itself [sic] subject to an external reality (the
source of form), which was characterised by contingency, or in other
words was essentially irrational' (1976: 252). Thus freedom, as ever,
turns into its opposite, enslavement – in the third period, the development of the subject is recognised as nothing more than the imposition of 'arbitrary, externally derived convention' (1976: 259). And
what was once reformulation and recapitulation in the music gives
way to simple repetition (1976: 260).

It is in Adorno's analysis of late Beethoven, too, that we can see why, unlike contemporaries such as Benjamin and Brecht, he remained a steadfast defender of 'autonomous art'. In the second period, Beethoven's works, as we have seen, were held to affirm the possibility of a liberated harmonious society while simultaneously showing that it had not yet been realised. It was thus, like all great art, a reflection of the totality, embodying both its positive and negative elements, in other words both affirmative and critical. With the collapse of the idea of the free individual, however, Adorno held that affirmative music could only serve to defend 'repressive social arrangements; authentic, critical music which would retain the ideal of human freedom would have to negate these by asserting 'the impossibility of aesthetic wholeness and harmony':

> By exposing some irreconcilable dichotomy within itself, Beethoven's late music could call attention to the concurrent external disintegration of human integrity, to the enslaving dehumanising compartmentalisation (for example, into individual and social identities) forced upon man by society. (1976: 254)

Adorno's conclusion was that music could best serve the cause of liberation by becoming more autonomous, turning inwards on itself and neglecting the conventions and institutions of the – increasingly – administered society. In doing so, the works of the greatest composers would represent, for the reasons discussed above, the social totality and all its contradictions. Yet, and here we come back to the disputes with Brecht and Benjamin, while it was essential that such art-music should provide a critical negation of existing society, there could be no doubt that their very isolation and autonomy left artists virtually impotent. Adorno, as we have seen, was under no illusions about the general acceptability of Schoenberg's work.

There have been many criticisms of Adorno's interpretation of Beethoven, some of which are taken up below. For the present, though, it is worth noting the way in which his treatment of Beethoven's late period exemplifies his approach to the question of the links between the character of music and the society which produces it. The idea that there is a significant stylistic break between 'middle' and 'late' Beethoven has been widely accepted (until recently), but most commentators tend to view this in terms of Beethoven's personal or artistic development – Mellers, for example, contrasts the 'years of revolt against destiny' in the second period with the 'new-found humility' and profoundly religious experience of the final one (Mellers, 1988: 657). Many, too, have noted the likely effects of Beethoven's deafness towards the end of his life. For Adorno, such personal details are secondary: what is foreshadowed in the second period and made explicit in the last is a fundamental social change, mediated through Beethoven's own consciousness and represented in music as the outcome of his heroic struggle with the musical materials which confronted him (1976: 122). It is in this sort of way, according to Adorno, that authentic music echoes the fundamental patterns and processes of the society in which it is produced: out of the relentless struggle between composers and the musical material that confronts them come works which inherently 're-present' the wider society, but in their own terms. Just as with prisms, the process is one of refraction rather than reflection.

Adorno's interpretation of nineteenth century music develops many of the themes familiar from his discussion of Beethoven. Just as the free society is doomed, so tonality is heading towards inevitable breakdown, an event both heralded and hastened by the works of such progressive composers as Wagner and Mahler. In Mahler Adorno hears – as others have heard – an all-pervading pessimism which clearly anticipates his own outlook; for him this is

> a prescient music which, in terms of melodic procedures coalesces from a swell of folk tunes, marches and banalities which are fractured, distorted, dismembered, and then tellingly reconstituted in the course of intractable structures which unpredictably move between the expression of despondency and nostalgia, the shriek and the wistful, between transparent trifle and utter chaos. (Blumenfeld, 1984: 524)

Accordingly, Mahler's works are, for Adorno, the embodiment of social truth; Mahler accepts the forms and structures which sustain existing reality, says Adorno, but through his compositional methods he 'burns it out from within' (1991b: 83), revealing that 'the fate of the world no longer depends upon the individual' (1991b: 83). For Wagner's life and works, on the other hand, Adorno expresses nothing but contempt, insisting that there was an 'essential continuity between Wagner's anti-semitic, racist beliefs, his sado-masochistic, authoritarian personality, and his music' (Jay, 1984a: 147). Generally suspicious of opera, as opposed to pure instrumental music, Adorno heard Wagner's music as ideology, creating the illusion of genuine community while simultaneously blinding people to the realities of their atomised, impotent existence. In this respect, he held, Wagner's works were 'an anticipation of fascism' (Buck-Morss, 1977: 145). Far from Wagner's translating Beethoven's achievements into the opera house, as some have argued, Adorno heard in him nothing of the genuine subjectivity expressed by Beethoven, nor the sort of thematic development in which he excelled. Instead, Wagner's operas portrayed 'late bourgeois man's capitulation to reified forces outside his control' (Jay, 1984: 147) and, in the technique of the *Leitmotif*, only a static and non-developing method which, like so much else in modern culture, can only be repeated indefinitely (Blumenfeld, 1984: 526).

Most nineteenth-century music, for Adorno, was similarly ideological, inasmuch as a great deal of it aimed to recapture the 'unity' of Beethoven's middle-period works; indeed these works themselves took on an ideological character as their essential social meaning was forgotten and they became mere emblems of the late nineteenth-century bourgeoisie. There was another respect, too, in which Beethoven's achievements were subverted, as 'the principle of musical autonomy which emerged with Beethoven becomes a fetish of art as religion, in which the creator (the genius) takes on the ontological aura that has become musically problematic' (A. Williams, 1989: 198). Adorno deplored the way in which Wagner obscured the particular social and psychological origins of his music, representing it as though it had sprung from a 'natural' source – the deep, unconscious spirit of the people. This sort of 'deception', as Jay puts it, is 'characteristic of much authoritarian thought' (1973: 194); for Adorno it was above all another way in which Wagner anticipated the fascist dictator.

Yet, consistently with his belief that artistic works embodied the contradictions of the social totality, Adorno did detect certain negative, critical elements in Wagner's work. In particular, his chromaticism 'abandons the tonic-centricity of tonal harmony' and thus prepares the way for the final breakdown of tonality. (A. Williams, 1989: 198). However, as we have seen, it was in the work of Schoenberg that the authority of the tonal centre was finally undermined. Schoenberg spoke of the 'emancipation of the dissonance'; for Adorno the equal status accorded to each of the twelve tones in Schoenberg's rows was a representation of the 'equal yet nonidentical, individual citizens in the hoped-for classless society' (Buck-Morss, 1977: 130).

Some of the essential aspects of Adorno's interpretation of Schoenberg have already been indicated. It was Schoenberg who confronted the final breakdown of tonality, immanent and inevitable ever since Beethoven, and presenting a stark parallel to the equally inexorable degeneration of bourgeois society. By the end of the nineteenth century, both music and society displayed an *ideology* of community and the harmonious reconciliation of disparate interests; the reality, in contrast, was disintegration and contradiction.

Schoenberg's new music, however, was not to be understood simply as a reaction against the decadence of the music of the late nineteenth-century bourgeoisie. It was essential, Adorno argued, to hear it as a dialectical transformation of that music, in which the new sounds emerged as an extrapolation of the logic underlying the old. Schoenberg's genius, then, consisted in bringing about a critical negation of the established musical system, just as critical theory's project was the negation of orthodox philosophy, and with it the ideology of the administered society. So Schoenberg was to be regarded as a master craftsman – rather than the inspired 'artist' of Romantic mythology – who transformed the musical materials according to their own logic, yet did so in ways which embodied the fundamental realities of his own time and place: 'The objective truth revealed by Schoenberg's musical innovations, which accounts for its identification with the anguished suffering of expressionism, was the collapse of the basis for traditional artistic totalisation, the active bourgeois subject' (Jay, 1984: 253).

The works themselves, then, emerge out of the dialectical tension between the 'objective' resistance of the materials and the 'subjective' will of the composer. (Just as, in any social situation, the freedom of the individual is constrained by the force of established practices and institutions – yet, occasionally, great innovators emerge to change things.) It is in this context that we can understand something of Adorno's vehement antipathy towards Stravinsky, a hostility which otherwise may seem arbitrary. For Stravinsky, as we have seen, the composition of music was above all an exercise of the free intellect; clearly such a premise was anathema to Adorno, resting as it does on some notion of a pre-cultural 'intellect' which is not constituted by its social environment. Indeed, Adorno drew a parallel between this idea and the concept of a realm of 'authentic being' in the work of the phenomenological philosophers, whose work he regarded, of course, as the vanguard of bourgeois ideology. In both cases, he wrote, 'the product arising from the subject is vested with the dignity of the natural ... it is a matter of the chimerical rebellion of culture against its own essence as culture' (Adorno, 1973a: 140).

So while it has sometimes seemed – particularly to those whose main concern is with the actual sound of the music – that Adorno's praise of Schoenberg and condemnation of Stravinsky is capricious, to say the least, it is clear that Adorno's critical position can be seen to be derived directly from his general theoretical presuppositions. Moreover, it is hardly surprising that his interpretation of Stravinsky's works stems also from the same underlying commitments: what could more powerfully affirm the annihilation of the free individual than *The Rite of Spring*? For Adorno this was 'the virtuoso composition of regression ... an attempt to gain control of regression by offering an image thereof' (1973a: 148); moreover, despite the widespread feeling that Stravinsky's work is 'radical from the standpoint of surface sound', it always 'implies the conditions for a re-employment of tonality' (1973a: 151).

As usual, then, Adorno's position rests on his fundamental theoretical presuppositions, and he condemned Stravinsky's later 'neo-classical' work in which, as Jameson puts it, he was 'speaking through the fossilised subjectivity of dead composers' (1971: 33). Yet Adorno's admiration for Schoenberg's achievements did not remain unequivocal. In particular, the development of the twelve-tone row and the total organisation of the musical material are themselves 'symptomatic of an objective tendency in the socio-economic structure of the modern world itself' (1971: 35) – that is, the emergence of monopoly capitalism and its relentless pressure for the rationalisation of social life. The wholly administered, totalitarian state of society is echoed in artistic practice:

> the absolute conscious control which modern artists seek to establish over the last remnants of free-floating contingency reflects this increasing autonomy of institutions, this increasing 'conquest' of both nature and society that they feel at work in the historical moment around them. (1971: 36–7)

Before long, serialism in music, originally intended as a means of integrating its horizontal and vertical dimensions, had become simply a 'mathematical system of rules that predetermined all intervals' (Hullot-Kentor, 1988: 88). Irrespective of what the music actually sounds like, it is clear that such a system involves not a dialectical exchange between composer and material but the domination of the former by the latter: the element of subjective expression is excluded.

It is in criticism of what Adorno called this 'deluded system' (1988: 99) that he once again weighs in against the belief that musical material can have any intrinsic or inherent meaning, that it can 'speak for itself'. 'To be sure the material does speak,' he writes, 'but only in those constellations in which the art-work positions it; it was this capacity to organise the material and not the mere discovery of individual sounds that constituted Schoenberg's greatness' (1988: 104–5). But many of those who have followed Schoenberg – such as Boulez and Stockhausen – have, like the helpless individuals in the totally rationalised society, themselves become slaves to the system. Just as the dialectic of enlightenment transforms science from a vehicle of human liberation into an all-encompassing means of oppression, so the idea that music can be organised according to 'scientific' principles does not represent progress but rather its opposite:

> Vain is the hope that through mathematical manipulations some pure musical thing-in-itself might come into being. One thinks that one is following the laws of nature, whereas the organisations of the material, however cosmically they gesture, are themselves already the product of human arrangements as are tempered tuning and the equality of the octave. Deluded, man sets up something artefactual as a primal phenomenon, and prays to it; an authentic instance of fetishism. This mentality has something infantile about it, for all its purity of intention. It is the passion of the empty, perhaps the gravest symptom of aging. Alienated and preestablished rules are blindly followed – as a good schoolboy might follows them – excluding any tension with subjectivity, without which there is as little art as truth. (1988: 109–10)

Thus Adorno's conclusion about the fate of western music is a characteristically grim one. To the extent that the 'new music' is based on the principle of serialism, Adorno must conclude that works produced in the tradition of European 'serious' music have become as alienated and inhuman as those in the 'popular' field which he so despises. A bleak prospect, but one which is in every way consistent with Adorno's chilling critique of modern society and its culture.

The legacy

It would be difficult to argue that the works of Adorno and the Frankfurt school have become a dominant intellectual force in the years since his death. The tide of cultural criticism which carried

Herbert Marcuse to a position of some celebrity in the late 1960s has certainly ebbed, yet, even so, critical theory is far from being a spent force. The works of Jürgen Habermas, widely seen as the outstanding intellectual heir of the Frankfurt school, have become increasingly influential, and there are clear signs of a revival of interest in Adorno himself. Fredric Jameson, for example, has argued that late capitalism has brought about precisely that ultimate rationalisation of social life that Adorno both prophesied and dreaded, and thus that his work is 'consistent with and appropriate for the current postmodern age' (1990: 229). Susan McClary, too, has emphasised the continuing relevance of Adorno's musical analyses (1991: 28). Moreover, and of particular significance in the present context, increasing interest in the analysis of cultural objects as social products has entailed a reconsideration of Adorno by both musicologists and sociologists. As we have seen, a central theme running through his work was his insistence that music can be understood only as expressing the fundamental structures and processes of the society in which it is created, rather than universal truths or the inner soul of the composer.

In this respect, Adorno is undoubtedly a 'sociological' thinker. Not for him the Romantic – he would say ideological – notion of musical experience as a higher, spiritual realm which transcends the everyday world. So, inevitably, his works have come under fire from musicians and aestheticians who resist the conclusion that musical forms reflect, or are even determined by, social ones. Defenders of Adorno tend to respond that this was not at all what he had in mind, emphasising his consistently dialectical view of valid musical production as the reconciliation of objective and subjective elements. Yet, for all his theoretical virtuosity, it is far from clear that Adorno did in fact provide a coherent account of the relationship he claimed between musical and social structures; indeed, in his unremitting efforts to relate the whole to the parts he leaves unresolved the familiar problems encountered in any attempt to explain individual action in terms of macro-sociological structures.

What is at stake her is what Adorno himself called 'the method of deciphering the specific social characteristics of music' (1976: 62). As I suggested at the start of this chapter, the idea that there is some sort of relationship between the characteristics of societies and the musical forms which get produced in them is widely accepted, and not only by sociologists. The difficulty is to specify the details of this relationship: in John Shepherd's words, it is the problem of showing 'how the social gets into music' (1991: 77). In the remainder of this chapter I will raise some of the issues presented by Adorno's ideas, and in the next consider some more recent discussions of the links between social structures and musical ones.

It should be said straight away that there is much of value in Adorno's perspective from a purely sociological point of view. As we have seen, he effectively demolishes the belief that western tonal music is grounded in the inescapable laws of the natural world, and disposes too of the notion that it expresses either Being in general or the particular consciousness of its composer. Composers, performers and listeners are all – to return to the language of academic sociology – socialised in certain cultural contexts: thus they think, hear and feel in specific, mutually recognisable ways: it is precisely this that allows them to 'understand' or 'make sense of' music in the first place. Similarly, music is not created afresh by each composer: on the contrary, composers must take account of the pattern of established conventions governing the legitimate ways in which sounds may be combined; Adorno makes the point with sparkling clarity when he describes the resources with which the composer must work, which are very much less than the sum of all sounds, just as languages involve a selection from the possible range of sounds. In these and many other examples the implication is clear – that everyone who makes music or listens to it, and indeed the music itself, has been formed within a specific cultural and historical context, the effects of which are inescapable. Thus far, I trust, no sociologist could disagree, and, as we shall see, some interesting work has been done on these topics. But Adorno insists that we go further, recognising that the fundamental forms and forces of social life are re-presented *in* the music, or at least in that music which as achieved the condition of 'autonomous art'.

As we have seen, Adorno had little time for the notion that valid music would simply reflect the interests or values of a particular social class; he took issue, too, with the idea that the social class origins of composers, or their political beliefs, could disclose the social meaning of their music. Rather, it seems that for Adorno the crucial dialectical 'moment' in which music is imbued with the qualities of the social totality occurs in the process of musical production, that is, composition. I have already referred to some of the significant passages in which Adorno describes this process: in the first part of his 1932 essay 'On the social situation of music', for example, where he writes of the confrontation between the 'psychic drive' of the composer – in this case with Schoenberg in mind – towards 'uninhibited expression', and the 'objective' musical material – that is, the tradition he has inherited from Wagner and Brahms (1978: 134). For Adorno, Schoenberg's greatness lies in his refusal to resolve this confrontation 'expressionistically', that is, in an arbitrary or authoritarian manner. On the contrary: 'Every gesture with which he intervenes in the material configuration is at the same time an answer to questions directed to him by the material in the form of its own immanent problems' (1978: 135). So for Adorno social conflicts and contradictions are represented in musical forms, since within the musical material 'the contradictions of this society are defined as technical problems' (1978: 135).

There is an equally revealing glimpse of Adorno's notion of the dialectics of musical production in his much later analysis of the point at which, in Beethoven's final, troubled, period, the inexorable process of the breakdown of the tonal system was set in motion.

> The musical experience of the late Beethoven must have become mistrustful of the unity of subjectivity and objectivity, the roundness of symphonic success, the totality emerging from the movement of all the parts; in short, of everything that gave authenticity up to now in the works of his middle period. ... He must have felt the untruth in the highest demand of classical music, that untruth which asserts that the essence of the contradictory motion of all the parts which disappears in that essence is itself positive, the affirmative. At this moment he transcended the bourgeois spirit whose highest musical manifestation was his own work. Something in his own genius, the deepest part of it, refused to reconcile in a single image what is not reconciled. (Adorno, 1976b: 122–3)

Beethoven's stylistic development, then, is to be understood ultimately as a result of the historical necessity which brings about fundamental changes in society, rather than as a consequence of the contingencies of his own biography or intellectual development. Beethoven's 'musical experience', says Adorno, 'must have become mistrustful', he 'must have felt the untruth' ... and so on. This would seem to mean either that the fundamental structure of social reality somehow imposed itself on Beethoven's consciousness with a kind of sociologistic determinism, or that he, as a great artist, had a unique insight into the essential social forms of his world. It is certain that

Adorno would have dismissed the first alternative as undialectical; the second, however, may be equally problematic, as Subotnik has suggested. The process of mediation which Adorno presupposes as the link between 'artistic structure' and 'objective reality', she writes, is 'indirect, complex, unconscious, undocumented, and rather mysterious' (Subotnik, 1976: 271). Others too have noted the vagueness of Adorno's formulation of this fairly crucial process. J. G. Merquior, for example, is similarly unimpressed with the way in which Adorno treats the 'mediations' which he posits between the artistic object and its cultural context, or rather, fails to treat them: 'Adorno habitually alternated microscopies of musical detail with sweeping, caricatural indictments of the social whole, with virtually nothing in between ... his correlation of results with historical trends often has an arbitrary, almost eerie quality about it' (1986: 134).

What we see here, of course, is a general, and familiar, problem faced by all efforts to specify the connections between cultural particulars and the social conditions of their production. Clearly, any adequate sociology of artistic production must bring such social conditions into the foreground, considering market conditions, available resources, working techniques, conventions and traditions, and so on, as well as the all-important networks of influence among the artists themselves. However, as Raymond Williams has argued in considering Marx's brief treatment of these matters, bringing such factors to the centre of the analytic stage does not constitute a demonstration that the 'artwork' therefore embodies or represents the elements of its wider context. Indeed, Marx's own discussion is deemed to be unsatisfactory:

> it is in that gap, in that area of inter-sections between a material process, general social conditions, and the unmentioned assumptions about the purposes and content of art within those conditions, that the decisive questions about the art itself are to be found. By including the specific social and historical conditions Marx has usefully broadened the scope of the enquiry, but he has not then made it. (R. Williams, 1983: 43)

As we have seen, Adorno's attempts to explicate the dialectical links between the detail and the totality are, theoretically speaking, fairly crucial to his whole project. But does he fare any better than Marx? Perhaps the closest we can get is in his description of the process of composition as 'a type of deciphering (or also of self-remembering); the "text" is looked at long enough until it illuminates itself and that sudden flash of illumination, the spark in which the "meaning" lies, is the productive moment' (quoted in Jay, 1984a: 138). Although in this context Adorno specifically emphasised that he did not wish 'to deny the subjective side of the dialectic' (1984a: 138), we are left with an account which seems to suggest that the demands of the 'text', or the musical 'materials', somehow impose themselves on the consciousness of the composer. It is worth recalling in this context Adorno's insistence that composers' own consciousness, their perception of what their music is about, are not to be trusted; his account seems to imply that, for example, through working on the materials which confronted him, Beethoven was led into a situation in which he could do nothing other than produce a representation of a fundamental – though invisible – pattern of social change, thus expressing a 'truth' of which he may have known nothing. If this is the case, then, for all his theoretical virtuosity and dialectical intentions, Adorno may well have ended up by effacing the free individual subject that, throughout his works, he is so anxious to cherish. Indeed, from a more general perspective, there is an altogether too neat and tidy look about the close parallel he detects between the rise and fall of the bourgeoisie and the remarkably similar career of tonal music, an interpretation which has even been considered 'a sometimes crude sociological account of reflection between music and social structure' (Berman and D'Amico, 1991: 71). This is a telling criticism of one who, as we have seen, persistently rejected the attempts of others to simply 'reduce' music to external social factors.

It is, moreover, hard to deny that Adorno's interpretations, despite his philosophical virtuosity and the density of his writing, occasionally approach the commonplace. Right at the start of the modern era, he hears in Bach the emergence of the rational order in which craft production was replaced by manufacturing – but the simple parallels between the ordering of the music and the rhythms of the workplace can be drawn with ease by any moderately interested listener. What is perhaps of more significance is that other music which displays some of the characteristics of Bach's is simply excluded from Adorno's consideration. The traditional music of Ireland, for example, has developed with highly regular structures and forms, strict conventions governing metre, symmetrical melodies and phrases and so on, yet there are few who would argue that the ethos of the dank bogs and misty mountains is that of rationalised modernity. I would not wish to push this example too far, but it will serve to illustrate two points of importance from a sociological perspective. Firstly, Adorno's view – whatever it was – of the relationship between musical structures and social structures was in fact restricted to a small area of music production (western composed tonal music from the late seventeenth to the early twentieth century) when viewed from a global historical perspective. It is scarcely, therefore, an adequate basis for the sociological analysis of links between 'music' and 'society'. Secondly, we must consider the possibility that the kind of correspondence between musical forms and social ones which Adorno presupposes may not exist; in other words that similar musical practices and conventions may be found in different sorts of societies, and vice versa. This is a proposition which calls into question the very nature of the 'sociology of music' as it has often been conceived, and it is a theme to which we will return.

Just as Adorno celebrates Bach for ushering in, in musical terms, the modern bourgeois era, so Schoenberg, as we have seen, is held to have given voice to its disintegration. Once again, there are those who find this sort of interpretation naive, despite the elaborate theoretical scheme from which it is derived. The use of dissonance, or other cultural shock tactics directed against established conventions, may or may not be effective, but it is hard not to feel that there is a rather unsophisticated, even adolescent, aspect to it. Moreover, the limitations of Adorno's musical horizons are evident here too: Paddison (1982) has argued that certain sorts of music which have emerged from the 'popular' domain may have radical, oppositional, intent, and Richard Middleton similarly notes that elements within blues, jazz and rock have been widely regarded as 'a radical subversion of the culture represented by Tin Pan Alley song ...' (1990: 43). Indeed, many recent analyses of popular music have explicitly rejected the 'mass society' analysis which finds expression in the Frankfurt school's view of the 'culture industry', and emphasised instead the ways in which the meaning and significance of the music may be contested, reformulated and appropriated by listeners for their own ends (e.g. Pratt, 1990: 5–6; Bradley, 1992: 97). From this perspective, the discourse of popular music ceases to be simply an ideological imposition on the exploited masses, and becomes a 'site of struggle' over meanings.

Adorno's interpretation of Schoenberg in terms of the decay of bourgeois individualism is also a reminder – if one were needed – of the prominence of this theme in his analyses. The process by which the heroic free individual is inexorably reduced to a slave of ratio-nalised production is presaged, as we have seen, in the music of Beethoven's late period and consummated in that of Schoenberg. Music which does not somehow express this fundamental theme is for Adorno false, or ideological, in that it affirms – literally – a har-monious society which does not in fact exist, or seems prematurely to resolve social contradictions which persist, in the case of the indi-vidual and the rationalised society, as unreconciled elements. Thus Wagner and Stravinsky are condemned, but so also are jazz and dance band music: these, and more besides, are seen as achieving 'musical dictatorship over the masses' by means of 'pseudo-individ-ualisation. The more strictly the listener is curbed, the less he is per-mitted to notice it' (Adorno, 1967: 125–6). Thus Adorno denounces a vast range of music which to most people's ears sounds very dif-ferent, in terms of the *same* critical principle: Stravinsky and the dance band crooner, Wagner and the jazz soloist, are all ultimately expressing in musical form the same social process, the obliteration of the free individual. It seems far-fetched to claim that the real social meaning of such diverse sounds, produced by different people in dif-ferent times and places, for a variety of purposes, could be, in the last analysis, the same. Could it not be that it is only in terms of Adorno's own theoretical presuppositions that such a diverse array of cultural phenomena could be similarly categorised, and casti-gated?

It is therefore in terms of his theoretical presuppositions that we can, I believe, distinguish between Adorno's work and a genuine sociology of music. As we have seen, Adorno's initial and lifelong commitment was to the composition of music, and his intellectual training was in philosophy, rather than in sociological work; late in his life he remarked that 'I approached the specific field of the soci-ology of music more as a musician than as a sociologist' (quoted in Tar, 1985: 171). In this respect, it may be said, he is by no means alone; for present purposes, though, the point which should be emphasised is that the general view of music, its production and con-sumption, which does inform his approach is derived from a partic-ular, and characteristically Germanic, mode of philosophical speculation. It is true, as Jay has shown, that Adorno's work marks a break with the idea of society as a more-or-less integrated totality which, following Hegel, finds expression in much Marxist thought (Jay, 1984b: 259), and it is also true that Adorno flatly rejected the very idea that any one philosophical system could comprehend the whole of social reality. On the other hand, important elements from the Hegelian–Marxian tradition did remain fundamental to Adorno's thought, as Buck-Morss has emphasised:

> it cannot be denied that acceptance of notions like historical necessity, Geist, and musical subject probably requires an acceptance of the Hegelian dialectic, a principle which to Adorno and many other Europeans commands Beethovenian heights in the history of philosophy but which has as yet gained little recognition in Anglo-American criticism. (1977: 273)

It is this intellectual field which provides the context for the emergence of Adorno's 'strong, and often undoubtedly biased, value judgements' (1977: 272). 'The aesthetic reflex of this ground position of inter-larded pessimism and determinism', writes Blumenfeld, 'is the categorical imperative that high art spontaneously mirrors the evils of a society seen as hopelessly alienated and degraded' (1984: 533).

Adorno's 'ground position', then, casts him inescapably as a social philosopher or social critic rather than as a sociological analyst. Not that this would have worried him unduly: the sociological work which he encountered during his stay in America, and which he took to be typical, was in his view irredeemably positivistic, not only generating spurious 'facts', but doing so on behalf of the dominant agencies of social control. (The job which Paul Lazarsfeld had got him on the Princeton Radio Research Project came to an end after Adorno realised that he 'was being asked to subordinate his intellectual activity to the interests of the mass-media industry') (Buck-Morss, 1977: 166). The empirical findings of such research, he and Horkheimer later wrote, deal with 'mere epiphenomena' rather than the 'essential laws' of society; indeed 'that which is essential is frequently presented in a distorted fashion, if it is not obscured entirely' (Horkheimer and Adorno, 1973: 121). Yet there is more to sociological work than the procedures that C. Wright Mills, with some justice, called 'abstracted empiricism' (1959: 50–75); indeed, Mills's central point was that such empiricism represented a withdrawal 'from the tasks of the social sciences' (1959: 50) as they sought to grasp the connections between the personal experiences of real individuals and the socially structured contexts in which they live.

What thought of the claim that no style of social research can achieve the condition of 'value-freedom' which authentic science demands? We may recall in this context Adorno's view of the inseparability of aesthetic and sociological concerns, and indeed his contention that there are fundamental and inescapable parallels between artistic work and social analysis; for, as Gillian Rose has put it, 'the task of the composer or writer is explicitly or implicitly analogous to that of the sociologist. He chooses a form in which to work , and all form expresses society in a more or less critical way' (Rose, 1978: 109). In many ways this is a more profound and consequential problem than Adorno's equation of sociology with abstracted empiricism, and the whole question of the separability (or otherwise) of 'facts' and 'values' in social research has generated a voluminous literature. Clearly, the issue cannot be debated here; yet it seems appropriate simply to draw out the implications of Adorno's own position, which, if conceded, implies that all depictions or descriptions of the social world are relative, depending on the standpoint of the observer and reflecting his or her values and assumptions. It follows, of course, that Adorno's own position is thus relativised.

Once again, there is an important sense in which Adorno, presumably, would have accepted this. As a dialectical thinker, he did not seek the essential nature of things but aimed to capture the process of becoming, of change and of transformation; he distrusted the appearances of things, seeing tensions and contradictions beneath their apparent unity; he warned against conventional ideas and beliefs – ideology – which served only to conceal the real flux of events. As I have suggested, several commentators have argued that his tortuous writings are evidence not of stylistic limitations but, on the contrary, a sophisticated attempt to capture in his prose something of the splintering, ambiguous and evanescent reality which confronted him. Yet for all that there remain ambiguities and contradictions within his work which are not so easily disposed of. He does, as we have just seen, speak of the 'essential laws' of society, and makes what appear to be categorical claims about the nature and social function of art, which 'always was, and is, a force of protest of the humane against the pressure of domineering institutions, religious and otherwise, no less than it reflects their objective substance' (quoted in Jay, 1973: 179). In this last short quotation there are in fact three assertions which are both problematic and, in the present context, of some significance: firstly the (implicit) notion that there is a specific realm of cultural production which can be called 'art' and which has distinct and unique qualities; secondly the idea that these qualities largely involve an inherent opposition to 'domineering institutions'; and thirdly that the 'objective substance' of these institutions is reflected in art. A short consideration of each of these may help to clarify both the relationship between Adorno's work and sociological analysis, and the problem of the connections between forms of music and forms of society.

One of the important respects in which Adorno's social philosophy may be seen to diverge from more specifically sociological concerns is in his attachment to the concept of 'art'. It will be recalled that Adorno's prime concern was to insist on the necessity of deciphering the social content of works of art, thus presupposing the validity of the distinction between art and non-art, rather than taking the latter as a sociological problem. In this, as in many other aspects of his work, he betrays an apparently unexamined commitment to the values of the culture in which he was himself nurtured; indeed, it is more than a little ironic that such a relentless scourge of bourgeois culture should display so many of its preconceptions in his work. In view of his commitment to avant-garde 'serious' music and his dismissive attitude to more popular genres, it was inevitable that Adorno would often be accused of elitism, but – as several commentators have pointed out – it would be more accurate to characterise his perspective as, in Middleton's words, 'ethnocentric and culture-centric' (1990: 44). The consequence is that Adorno 'takes a socio-aesthetic stance which binds him to one music and deafens him a priori to all others' (Blumenfeld, 1984: 534). The further art, or literature, or music were from the conventions of fashionable intellectual circles in early twentieth-century Vienna, the less Adorno liked them, or was prepared to take any interest in them. It should be clear that such a position cannot constitute the foundation of a valid sociology of music; it is equally unclear why the one form of music which Adorno espouses should be the only vehicle for the expression of the – apparently terminal – human condition (1984: 535).

Despite his insistence on the cultural, as opposed to the natural, origins of human conventions, then, Adorno repeatedly defined art in terms which leave little room for an appreciation of its socially constructed nature. As we have seen, he held that the fundamental

criterion of 'authentic art' was that it, like critical theory in philosophy, was inherently a negation of the dominant institutions in the
'totally organised' society. This is an interesting idea, and one which
is central to Adorno's more general theoretical perspective; from a
sociological point of view, however, we immediately recognise that
it is only one of a (very large) number of ideas which have been
advanced concerning the nature or essence of 'art'. It is for this
reason that I argued in Chapter 1 for an understanding of 'art' not
as a specific quality which we will one day be able to agree is present
or absent in an object or a performance, etc., but as a *claim* that such
things should be accorded special status. Sociologically, our interest
is not in judging the factual validity of such claims – even if such a
thing were possible, for no universally accepted criterion has
emerged in the last two hundred years or so – but in examining what
we might call the 'careers' of such claims. Whose claims are successfully established? Whose fail? What resources are necessary for
success? And so on; in the present context the point is that Adorno's
aesthetic theory and its implications for music may be seen as an
example of the process by which understandings of 'art' are socially
constructed. As such it has its opponents, such as Eisler, who wrote
of Adorno's 'abstract nonsense' (Buck-Morss, 1977: 42), and supporters, such as Ballantine when he writes of the 'great advances'
made in Adorno's analyses of music (1984: 22). Like all the others
who develop aesthetic theories or interpretations of music, Adorno
was a protagonist in a never-ending war over meanings; as sociologists our role is not to take sides but to analyse the constant struggle.
In short we must treat claims about the nature of art or the meaning of music as topics for analysis, rather than the resources with
which to carry it out (Zimmerman and Pollner, 1971).

It may also be added that there is an element of tautology about
Adorno's perspective on art, which, appropriately enough, mirrors
Schoenberg's dictum that 'If it is art it is not for all, and if it is for
all, it is not art'. For Adorno the criterion was the oppositional character of the artwork: 'affirmative' works couldn't be art, art couldn't
be 'affirmative'. But who is to decide, and by what procedures? As
we have seen, Adorno was vague about these matters, although his
own value-judgements flow smoothly enough from his prior theoretical position, and it is clear that only a handful of like-minded
intellectuals could respond sympathetically to his claim (Buck-
Morss, 1977: 41). It is also apparent that, in this respect too,

Adorno's understanding of art music reveals the extent to which his own perceptions were those of haute-bourgeois culture: as Middleton puts it, 'The very concept of autonomous music ... is a construct of the culture' (1990: 41).

Adorno had little interest in the music of cultures other than his own (Jay, 1973: 187), and as we have seen he shows little inclination to concede that any of the 'popular' genres may themselves represent opposition to the dominant institutions. But Adorno's perspective is sociologically problematic even in relation to the 'serious' music which he does invest with such great significance: 'just that art may best serve human emancipation which detaches itself from the controlled and levelling interrelations of a consumption, the democratic nature of which now only serves as ideology' (Horkheimer and Adorno, 1973: 107). The role of real, autonomous art was to 'denounce the dominant forms of intercourse as tools of destruction' (1973: 106); this was its 'objective content' (1973: 104). The difficulty here is not so much in deciding whether some or other form of music either is or is not a 'negation', but in the assumption that *any* music can have an inherent meaning of this kind, an 'objective content'. Despite Adorno's insistence on the 'historical' – as opposed to the 'natural' – genesis of western music, and his recognition that the interpretation of works may change radically as time passes, there remains the notion that works somehow embody, as 'sedimented Geist', the cultural forms and contradictions of the society in which they were created, and that it is the task of the critical theorist to decipher these meanings (Adorno, 1976; 223; Buck-Morss, 1972: 139). It should be clear that such a view of analysis as a sort of decoding of an 'objective content' is hard to reconcile with the sociological insight that meaning is not to be located within the cultural object, but is rather socially constituted.

There remains, finally, the question of how music represents social institutions. I have already suggested that Adorno's treatment of the process through which social elements permeate musical composition is not altogether satisfactory from a sociological point of view: despite his emphasis on mediations, and the complexity of his conceptual armoury, the picture which emerges is of a fairly straightforward reflection in music of the rise and fall of bourgeois individualism. Despite Adorno's refusal to accept the concept of social totality as it developed in the Hegelian–Marxist tradition, he still holds that music 'reflects the class relationship in toto' (1976: 69) and thus represents the fundamental antagonisms and contradictions in a society. But, as Middleton has argued (1990: 40), it is not clear just how the autonomous development of compositional techniques will necessarily encapsulate the underlying dynamics of a whole society. In general, says Jay, Adorno 'made little real attempt to investigate the concrete social forces and forms between [the] individual and the totality. Micrological stress on the smallest detail went hand in hand with macrological emphasis on the largest whole' (1984b: 271–2). We are still left with the problem of specifying how 'the social' gets into music.

   I have argued that Adorno fails to establish just how the process of composition, or musical production, leads to the representation of 'social problems' in its 'innermost cells' (1978: 130), and that the idea that this is its 'objective content' may well be inconsistent with his commitment to a dialectical, as opposed to an essentialist, epistemology. As such, it is one of many apparently anomalous elements in his work, though this might not have dismayed him unduly, given his refusal to accept that any one system of ideas could adequately comprehend reality. As Jay has put it, Adorno's negative dialectics 'must itself be understood as an untotalised 'forcefield' of apparently contradictory statements, which both reflects and resists the reality it tries critically to analyse'. Yet this 'forcefield' was organised throughout Adorno's prolific career around certain fundamental commitments which, I have suggested, largely determined the character of his interpretations of music: thus Schoenberg's work 'leaves all other music of the age far behind' (1978: 134), and in modern times 'popular music is bad, bound to be bad, without exception' (1976: 225). Interesting as they are, however, Adorno's particular philosophical presuppositions and his explicit value-judgements scarcely provide a secure basis for the sociology of music. Just as there is more to sociology than that which Mills (1959) called 'abstracted empiricism', so too the 'grand theory' which underlies Adorno's work is rarely useful in the task of understanding the actions and interactions of real people in real situations – the heroic individual of the bourgeois era and the alienated wage-slave of modern mass society are theoretical caricatures set up to illuminate an all-encompassing, and thoroughly bleak, view of the decline and decay of humanity.

   Sociologically, the task is not – as Adorno saw it – the 'deciphering of music' so as to show how it is determined by the social circumstances of its production (1976a: 223), but rather to understand the processes by which sounds are creatively organised, and invested with meanings by listeners, musicians, composers, critics, promoters and so on. It is thus not so much a matter of taking meanings out, so to speak, as of seeing how they get put in.

So what remains of Adorno's claim that essential social forms are represented in musical ones? I have suggested that his beliefs about the connections between the two, and about the inherently social meanings of music, rest ultimately on the acceptance of certain philosophical, or more accurately metaphysical, assumptions, and that these can hardly be said to constitute an adequate basis for a systematic sociology. Yet the feeling persists that there is *some* sort of relationship between social structures and musical ones, and that the sociology of music ought to be centrally concerned with elucidating it. It is thus useful to consider some more recent works which focus, from rather different angles, on the links between musical and social forms.

4

Social structures and musical structures

Raphael as much as any other artist was determined by the technical advances in art made before him, by the organisation of society and the division of labour in all the countries with which his locality had intercourse. Whether an individual like Raphael succeeds in developing his talent depends wholly on demand, which in turn depends on the division of labour and the conditions of human culture resulting from it.

Marx and Engels (1974: 108)

This, as far as it goes, is an identifiable 'sociological position' ... emphasis is given to general factors of social environment and demand ... But there is then an evident gap, between the briefly mentioned technical dimension ... and a general environment. And in fact it is in that gap, in that area of actual intersections between a material process, general social conditions, and the unmentioned assumptions about the purposes and content of art within these conditions, that the decisive questions about the art itself are to be found. By including the specific social and historical conditions Marx has usefully broadened the scope of the enquiry, but he has not then made it.

Raymond Williams (1983: 43)

Ballantine: music as microcosm

Perhaps it is not surprising that Adorno's vast and complex body of work has not inspired a distinct school of followers, though it remains influential, and is echoed in the writings of several authors who have attempted to elucidate the links between music and society. Christopher Ballantine, for example, takes the task of the sociology of music to be 'an investigation of the ways in which social formations crystallize in musical structures' (1984: xvi), and holds that the main factor which has impeded an understanding of the social nature of music is the 'neutralised consciousness' – the phrase, inevitably, is Adorno's – which eliminates 'social meaning and value' from the analysis of music and which is 'actively propagated by the dominant class interests of advanced capitalist society'. (1984: xvi–xvii). Accordingly, Ballantine adopts as his project the creation of an alternative, Marxist, aesthetics with another phrase of Adorno's as its slogan: 'social critique accomplished through that of art'. (1984: xviii).

For Ballantine, as for Adorno, 'the musical microcosm replicates the social macrocosm'. (1984: 5). The replacement of Bach's essentially static style by Beethoven's dynamic sonatas, for example, reflects 'the collapse of late feudalism and its replacement by the bourgeois democratic order' (1984: 5), indeed the sonata form itself is to be understood as the 'musical analogue' of the Hegelian dialectic – 'the highest musical articulation of the idea of forward movement through conflict' (1984: 32). However, while Hegel's dialectic stood in need of correction – by Marx, who inverted it so that ultimate reality is conceived as the material world of people and objects, rather than the realm of ideas – Beethoven saw things correctly from the start: 'the struggles of his music begin and end with the concrete struggles of real life' (1984: 44). Once it had achieved a position of dominance, however, the bourgeois class gradually abandoned the democratic principles which it had one championed. Dialectical modes of thought which emphasised conflict and contradiction were dropped in favour of those which saw matters in terms of 'smooth and uneventful evolution' (1984: 47), not least in music, where the 'musicological positivism of the academic watchdogs' denies the 'true and concrete nature' of the social content of Beethoven's work (1984: 48).

The imprint of Adorno's thought is hard to mistake in such passages. Yet while his own work develops some of Adorno's main themes, Ballantine is not committed to the particular set of theoretical preconceptions which gave Adorno's work its specific character. He expresses doubts, for example, just as Brecht did, about the social value of the 'serious' avant-garde: even though such music may represent a negation of prevailing rationality, and express the alienated condition of modern life, it has become the property of a group of specialists who exercise a sort of 'technocratic tyranny' (1984: 95) which precludes effective communication with the rest of society. It is true, as we have seen, that Adorno did express similar concerns in his discussion of the 'ageing of the new music' (1988); what he did not do, however, is pursue the idea that some forms of popular music could give voice to an oppositional ideology. For Ballantine this is a realistic possibility: the best rock music, he suggests, does just this, and its social value is all the greater in that, unlike the avant-garde, it can generate a mass audience. Moreover, again in contrast to the composers of new music who have abandoned their human creativity to the dictates of the computer, the rock musicians are the first 'to have humanised twentieth century technology' (1984; 96). Just as Paddison (1982) and Middleton (1990) have argued, Ballantine suggests that not all popular music is ideological, in Adorno's sense, and that we must recognise the contrasting values which are articulated in its various strands and styles. Sure enough, the 'total sell-out of disco music' can be held to confirm all of Adorno's worst fears, yet its contemporary in the 1970s was the punk movement which offered 'brittle and authentic criticism of the repressive social order' (Ballantine, 1984: 5).

Ballantine's perspective on rock music, then, usefully extends Adorno's critical method beyond the boundaries of 'serious' music, and incidentally demonstrates one of the important ways in which Adorno's theoretical preconceptions acted to stifle his sociological imagination. At the same time, though, it once again reveals some of the method's problematic features. Firstly, it remains unclear precisely *how* the 'social macrocosm' is reconstituted in the 'musical microcosm'. As with Adorno, the links between the levels are unspecified, and – perhaps as a consequence – there are occasional hints of a distinctly undialectical determinism as a means of bridging the gap: 'the shrinking of the horizons of change that characterise the 1970's determine the altered structures of the typical popular music of the 1970's' (1984: 5). It is as if mysterious – or perhaps I should say Durkheimian – social forces somehow predisposed people to act in such ways as to bring about certain appropriate forms of music, and the impression is strengthened by Ballantine's contention that: 'it is today quite remarkably difficult for ordinary men and women to *see* the whole, to grasp the social reality behind the ideological veil' (1984: 7). Given Ballantine's explicitly Marxist epistemology, it is reasonable to detect here a model of society as a more-or-less integrated totality, which operates in ways of which most people are ignorant, and in which the economic base ultimately determines the cultural superstructure. The implication, too, is that only Marxist theory can give access to the reality behind the veil. Clearly, some familiar problems arise. Are people's thoughts and deeds determined by invisible social forces? If so, what is the nature of such forces, and indeed of the presumed social whole of which they are parts? Could it not be that, far from describing these nebulous entities, it is the theory which *creates* them? The first set of difficulties, then, concerns the tendencies in this sort of account towards a form of sociological determinism which effaces the consciousness and free will of human actors, and the reification of such concepts as society and social structure, by taking them to be real things rather than ideas.

The second set of difficulties will also be familiar, since it arises from claims that Beethoven's music is 'activist and revolutionary' (1984: 45) or that punk rock expresses 'authentic criticism of the repressive social order' (1984: 5). Once again, the point is not to debate whether Ballantine is correct in his characterisation of such music as radical, but to question whether *any* kind of music can be said to have an inherent meaning. As we have seen (in Chapter 2, and in considering Adorno) such claims are fundamentally incompatible with a recognition of the socially constructed nature of meaning: meaning does not reside within these or any other cultural objects but is assigned to them (indeed, they are constituted) by the collaborative practices of real people in real situations. We will return, before long, to these problems.

Lomax and cantometrics

Given the inevitable difficulties confronted by any theorist who seeks to establish connections between cultural particulars and social wholes, it is not surprising that efforts to link forms of music and forms of society display some of the fundamental commitments and contrasts which characterise more general sociological theory. As we have seen, Adorno's – and Ballantine's – perspectives incorporate some major elements of the Marxian tradition; by contrast, Alan Lomax's attempt to correlate folk song style and social structure echoes, in both its theory and its methodology, some of Durkheim's central ideas.

Lomax's point of departure is the assumption that folk song style in any culture is a symbolic representation of the core elements of the culture; this implies, moreover, that music is not a secondary or inconsequential aspect of culture but is a powerful, and universal, means by which shared values and a sense of belonging are evoked in human beings (Lomax, 1968: 6–7). The 'chief function of song', he writes, 'is to express the shared feelings and mold the joint activities of some human community' (1968: 1). In much of his life's work, Lomax was concerned to record and thus preserve indigenous music traditions, in a world where many were threatened by what he called the 'cultural grey-out' which follows the spread of western technology and communications (1968: 4). Apparently it was on field-trips, first to Spain and then to Italy, that he noticed how vocal performance styles seemed to vary systematically with other aspects of culture, and in particular with the strength of norms governing women's pre-marital sexual conduct. In the southern areas where pre-marital sex was strictly forbidden, and punishments severe, 'a piercing, high-pitched, squeezed, narrow vocal delivery was culti- vated which made choral performance all but impossible'. On the other hand, in more northern areas 'where sexual sanctions were mild', there was 'a strong preference for well-blended choirs singing in open and low-pitched voices' (1968: viii). Together with the anthropologist Conrad Arensberg, Lomax went on to develop two more general hypotheses: '(1) Solo song characterised highly cen- tralised societies, and leaderless performances were most common in societies with simple political structure; (2) Unified choirs occurred in highly cohesive societies and diffuse choruses in individualised cul- tures' (1968: ix).

During the 1960s, Lomax directed an ambitious research pro- gramme which aimed not just to investigate such correspondences but to test systematically the hypothesis that song performance style varies with the basic structural patterns of a society. For this he developed the method he called 'cantometrics', in which thirty-seven different characteristics of songs were rated to produce a profile which represented their salient features, and a total of 3,525 songs drawn from 233 cultures were analysed. The results were very much in line with Lomax's expectations, showing firstly that the geo- graphical distribution of song styles reflects what is known of the history of human migrations and patterns of cultural development, and secondly that 'some traits of song performance show a power- ful relationship to features of social structure that regulate interac- tion in all cultures' (1968: 3–4). In particular, as Durkheim might have expected, the appearance of collective singing styles is inversely related to the degree of social differentiation in a culture. Moreover, as the complexity of a society increases, so does the 'information load' of its song texts, the precision of enunciation, the size of musical intervals used, the degree of embellishment, the number of phonetic elements, and the number of instrumental types found (1968: 128). In general: 'The principal discovery in cantometrics is that a culture's favoured song style reflects and reinforces the kind of behaviour essential to its main subsistence efforts and to its central and controlling social institutions' (1968: 133).

Lomax's conclusion is implicitly Durkheimian: song style 'reflects' the essential cultural forms, and also 'reinforces' patterns of functionally adaptive behaviour. The echoes of Durkheim become explicit in Arensberg's characterisation of the cantometrics project. Cultures are taken to be integrated wholes, which evolve through stages, and which may be studied by the methods of natural science (1968: 303–8). There is even, as in Durkheim, a concern to demonstrate the inadequacy of individualistic explanations: 'Art is not invented in lonely self-realisation, as we are prone to think from modern experience. Song likewise was and is mostly public.' (1968: 305). Thus for Arensberg, and Lomax, art in general and song in particular were to be understood not as the expression of individuals' emotions but as the collective symbolisation of dominant cultural patterns. Folk songs, argued Arensberg, 'seemed to evoke not the actual behaviours of everyday life, but the models in terms of which everyday social activities are structured' (1968: 305). As such they are essentially symbolic – collective representations, as Durkheim put it – and their origins are in the elementary forms of religious ritual (1968: 306); their effect is to evoke and affirm the authority of society in the minds of individuals.

The assumptions which underlie Lomax's cantometrics, then, are clear enough; inevitably, however, the theoretical and methodological problems of Durkheimian structural sociology are also displayed with great clarity. The apparently rigorous analysis of the songs, which yielded an immense array of statistics and tabulations, ultimately rests on some questionable methodological procedures, as Steven Feld has suggested. In attempting to apply Lomax's methods to the analysis of the songs of the Kaluli people of Papua New Guinea, Feld was led to conclude that there was 'so much intracultural variability and subtlety that it is virtually impossible to code a normalized profile for them' (Feld, 1984: 385). This is not, it should be stressed, simply a matter of the difficulty of selecting a sample of ten songs which is supposed to represent the general pattern of all of them: beyond the thorny problem of 'sampling' there is the even more troublesome assumption that any such songs can be abstracted from the cultural context in which they occur, in order to be 'analysed' independently of it. Such 'decontextualisation', as Feld suggests, amounts not to an analysis of cultural patterns which may be observed in the real world but to a fragmentation of them on the basis of the 'analyst's' preconceptions. The Kaluli, for example, are one of the many peoples who, as we have seen, do not have a concept of 'music' in the western sense; rather 'the structure and meaning of Kaluli sounds ... are inseparable from the fabric of Kaluli social life and thought' (1984: 383). These will be understood, says Feld, better through detailed and intensive ethnography than through 'decontextualised trait lists' (1984: 385). Moreover, and equally important, it follows that the analysts' interpretations of the cantometric song 'data' need not accord with the perceptions of those whose cultures are being characterised: indeed, the considerable measure of agreement among those who 'rated' the cantometric data may reveal less about the properties of the songs than about the cultural preconceptions of the raters themselves. The voice quality of 'oriental bardic singers', for example, is 'generally tense, high, thin, feminine and placatory' (Lomax, 1970: 64), whereas the 'nasal resonance and throaty burr' of the American Indian singer 'is expressive of a full-blown and unrepressed masculinity' (1970: 66). Such conclusions, it may be suggested, tell us more about the conventional representation of gender in modern American society than about the songs and their place in the cultures from which they have been arbitrarily plucked. (We will return to the question of gender representation in music below.)

The 'scientific' methods employed in cantometric analysis, then, may be somewhat problematic. In the present context, however, the theoretical assumption that cultures can be understood as more-or-less coherent, integrated entities must be regarded as equally troublesome. The way that the Kaluli organise and use sound, says Feld, cannot be predicted on the basis of their 'mode of production and techno-economic complexity', nor can the argument be reversed to explain social structures on the basis of musical forms, since 'similar surface musical forms are found in societies of widely varying social complexity'. What requires emphasis here, however, is that such musical forms 'have greatly divergent meanings and identities in these separate historical and geographical settings'. In short, 'it is difficult and confusing only to argue from objectified social structures to musical structures; the result is a nest of reifications' (Feld, 1984: 405).

If we accept that it is not possible to use a small sample of songs to represent the musical style of a whole culture, it follows that the characterisation of whole societies on the basis of a few of its cultural patterns is equally invalid. Few social anthropologists today accept the theory or methods underlying G. P. Murdock's classification, in the 1960s, of world cultures on the basis of 'social structural' data, yet it was with Murdock's *Ethnographic Atlas* that the cantometrics data was correlated (Lomax, 1968: 118–19). Similarly, few sociologists still accept Durkheim's notion of society as a reality 'sui generis', or as an integrated totality existing independently of the actions and interactions of real people: following Max Weber, G. H. Mead and others, the idea of the priority of society has been opposed by a view of social order as an outcome of the interactions of individuals as they pursue their interests. As Rochberg-Halton has argued, much of modern social thought may be understood in terms of a fundamental opposition between perspectives which view societies as structures or systems, on the one hand, and those which emphasise actions and situations, on the other; a good deal of recent theorising has aimed to transcend the perceived limitations of this pervasive dichotomy (Rochberg-Halton, 1982).

It would be unkind, though not entirely unfair, to describe Lomax's cantometric analyses as just the sort of (American) social 'science' which so enraged Adorno – as naive positivism which mistook superficial appearances for the real essence of phenomena, and which concealed its vacuity behind a smokescreen of jargon and statistics. However, as I have suggested, some recent theorising has sought to establish more sophisticated models of social order, and we should consider whether these discussions of the links between music and society have overcome the difficulties encountered so far.

John Shepherd: the musical articulation of social reality

The central thread running through all of John Shepherd's work is the idea that 'any significance assigned to music must be ultimately and *necessarily* located in the commonly agreed meanings of the group or society in which the particular music is created' (1977 *et al.*: 7). Inevitably, such a claim has led him to develop forceful, sociologically informed critiques of the view that music's meaning and value are inherent, and of the notion that it can be understood in terms of the psychology of individuals. Indeed, it is an important part of Shepherd's case that such misapprehensions of the real, social, nature of music (views, it should be said, which echo the empiricist and rationalist positions discussed in Chapter 2) are a direct consequence of the predominant 'world-sense' of capitalist industrial societies, a mode of experiencing the world which, as we shall see, privileges visual and rational modes of communication at the expense of aural and emotional ones. It follows that music itself has become a marginal rather than a central activity in such societies; moreover, only those aspects of musical communication which are amenable to visual representation and rational manipulation – the 'melody, harmony, and rhythm' which can be depicted in western notation and which usually serve as a formal definition of 'music' – are taken seriously in those institutions which preserve and reproduce the dominant 'classical music' tradition of modern western societies. For Shepherd, this is an absurd and a troubling state of affairs, for music is primarily and essentially a *sonic* means of communication which affects us in ways that are simply not reducible to visual or verbal representations. What western notation cannot deal with – the specific timbre of individual voices or instruments, for example, or the minute and often irregular variations of both pitch and rhythm which are characteristic of most non-western musical styles – are precisely those elements which give musical communication its intensity and immediacy, and, for Shepherd, its importance (1991: 90). Above all, he argues, what music communicates is a sense of 'human relatedness' (1991: 3) which is implicitly denied by the rationalised tonality of the western classical tradition: 'Alienation of self by a central and remote controlling power finds musical expression through the alienation of the individual notes of the harmonic-rhythmic framework by the key-note' (1991: 134). Thus Shepherd's project is not only to demonstrate the inherently social nature of music but in so doing to rescue it from the theoretical straitjacket forced on it by academic musicologists, and thereby to undermine the hierarchy of musical styles which is sustained by the 'authorities' in musical and educational institutions. In turn, this should lead to a renewed understanding of the unique power of music as a medium of communication (1991: 214) and in particular to an overdue recognition of the cultural importance of popular music styles, especially those that have developed in the twentieth century out of the African-American tradition, since 'the people of fundamentally oral cultures within industrial capitalism relate to their world with an 'emotional rationality' not totally unrelated to that of pre-literate cultures' (1991: 139). In marked contrast to Adorno, then, Shepherd sees popular music not simply as trivia which serve only to domesticate the masses but as having a real potential to overcome the alienation of industrial capitalist societies by regenerating a more immediate, more spontaneous mode of 'human relatedness'.

The general framework within which Shepherd elaborates his view of the relationship between music and society in general, and of the links between social change and musical change in the modern West, was provided – unusually, but significantly – by the work of fellow-Canadian Marshall McLuhan, whose ideas attracted considerable attention in the late 1960s. Best known for his slogan 'the medium is the message' (1967: 15), McLuhan was concerned above all to suggest that human consciousness – and social organisation – are affected more by the *way* in which communication occurs, in other words by the nature of the media involved, than by the content of communications. Pre-literate peoples, for example, live in a world of sound which is 'essentially a unified field of instant relationships' (1967: 293) since all their communications are of an oral–aural nature. By contrast the closeness and immediacy of such communities was shattered by the invention of phonetic literacy, which as a visual medium both 'diminishes the role of the other senses' and entails the 'lineal structuring of rational life' (1967: 94). 'The breaking up of every kind of experience into uniform units in order to produce faster action and change of form (applied knowledge) has been the secret of Western power over man and nature alike' (1967: 95).

Like McLuhan, John Shepherd contrasts the 'world-sense' of pre-literate peoples with that of those whose relationships were mediated first by phonetic literacy, then by the technology of printing. For the former, experience is aural–oral, immediate and primarily collective; for us in the modern world, on the other hand, it is predominantly visual, distant and increasingly individualised. Above all, literacy facilitates and encourages 'a divorce between meaning and symbol'

(Shepherd, 1991: 27) and leads to the form/content, objective/subjective dichotomies which are so central to modern western thought, and which serve to distance people from each other and from their environment. Everything that cannot be visually represented is turned into 'non-knowledge', and the subjective immediacy of the pre-literate world is transformed into the search for rational control over it. It is in these cultural conditions, Shepherd argues, that music becomes devalued and marginalised as a means of communication; in so far as it is theorised at all, it is inevitably, as I have suggested, understood as the product of individual minds, or as having inherent meaning and value.

These orthodox perspectives on music, Shepherd argues, simply fail to comprehend that music is socially constructed: 'because people create music, they reproduce in the basic qualities of their music the basic qualities of their own thought processes' (1991: 12). Such thought processes, as we have seen, are fundamentally shaped by the nature of the media of communication; moreover, different cultural contexts generate and are 'articulated by' different forms of music. Shepherd is arguing, then, just as Adorno did, firstly that the production and reception of music can be understood only once it is realised that individual composers, musicians and listeners are always and inevitably operating within the parameters and constraints of an established cultural context, and secondly that the characteristics of musical styles are related in complex but identifiable ways to the basic characteristics of the societies in which they are created. Like Adorno, too, Shepherd seeks to demonstrate this relationship in an analysis of the development of the tonal music of the West (although, as I have suggested, his conclusion are rather different):

> There are those media which communicate implicitly and those which communicate explicitly. There are those world-senses (such as the 'pre-literate') which tend towards the implicit and those (such as that of industrial societies) which tend towards the explicit. Music is capable of implicitly coding an explicit world-sense, a process evidenced throughout the entire tradition of functional tonality. (1991: 84–5)

The history of the dominant tradition of western music, Shepherd argues, is the history of the emergence and development of functional tonality, and this, as a musical system, must be understood as part of the general pattern of social change since the early medieval period. The 'world-sense' of society in the early Middle Ages was 'articulated musically through structurally implicit monody' (1991: 96). However, as feudalism gradually gave way to capitalism, the 'implicit monody of plainchant began to disintegrate' (1991: 96), and eventually 'the emerging explicitness of late medieval and early renaissance polyphony gradually syncretized into the homogeneous and explicit structure of functional tonality' (1991: 97). For the sake of illustration, we may contrast medieval plainchant and functional tonality, as Shepherd characterises them, in order to identify the ways in which, he suggests, the organising principles of each are 'dialectical correlates' (1991: 102) of the fundamental forms of social organisation. It is in this sense that, Shepherd argues, there is a 'structural homology' between forms of music and forms of society (1991: 89).

It is basic to Shepherd's discussion that medieval music (such as plainchant) is regarded as organised in terms of pentatonic (five-note) scales, and that each note in the scales is heard as being equally important and independent. (In contrast to functional tonality, that is, there is no fundamental note, no 'tonal centre' or keynote to which a melody will eventually return, and consequently no hierar-chy of notes determined by their relationship to the keynote.) A chant can start or finish on any of the five notes. Shepherd's argu-ment, then, is that 'the pentatonic structure underlying much medieval music in itself serves to articulate the *ideal* feudal structure' (1991: 109). The elements of feudal society, like the notes of a pen-tatonic scale, are separate but equal; it is 'decentralised and localised' rather than centralised and organised into a coherent hierarchy (as in functional tonality). Medieval music, too, conveys a sense of immediacy and belonging which is consistent with the 'world-sense' of pre-modern peoples, and contrasts with the sense of distance and separation which, as many have noted, is characteristic of industrial cultures: 'From the standpoint of industrial societies, the music of medieval people seems to negate the individualism which is a dialectic correlate of these societies' dominant world sense' (1991: 110).

With social transformation, the form of music also changed. The system of functional tonality, Shepherd argues, did not emerge spon-taneously out of the old pentatonic conventions as a development of it; both patterns of musical organisation were elaborated in ways which bore the imprint of the dominant cultural patterns:

The phonetically literate concepts which instigated and facilitated the creation of functional tonality were themselves instrumental in changing the very structure of society and consciousness. Evolving functional tonality represented a creative articulation and encoding of that change. (1991: 116)

As we have seen, functional tonality, which has become the predominant musical 'common sense' of people in modern western societies, contrasts with pentatonicism in important respects. The notes of the scales are no longer autonomous but must form a hierarchy dominated by the 'tonic', or keynote. Melodic lines and harmonic movement must eventually return to affirm the tonic, thus creating a sense both of progress towards a conclusion (musicians talk of 'harmonic progressions') and of tension and release when 'remote' or otherwise alien elements are introduced and then 'resolved' or in some way reintegrated into the system. The sense of 'magnetic pull towards the key-note', writes Shepherd, 'provides the quintessential articulation of the concept of progress' (1991: 124). Much western music, too, is organised in terms of regular rhythms which are based on simple arithmetical patterns; its harmony, as we shall see when we consider Max Weber's essay on western music, is a culturally unique system which attempts to 'rationalise' the natural properties of sound. In this respect, the contrast between modern western music and that of pre-industrial, pre-literate peoples is of fundamental significance: instead of being dominated by natural forces, or having a sense of being part of them, the industrial 'world-sense' predisposes us to achieve control over them.

In its hierarchical and centralised nature, then, in its expression of time as linear (rather than cyclical) and above all in its representation of the notion of progress, functional tonality is seen by Shepherd as 'encoding' the 'industrial world-sense' (1991: 122): 'Both pentatonicism and functional tonality are grounded in the relationships of the harmonic series,' he writes, 'but both structures are extended and directed in different ways as dialectic correlates of the social structures of the time' (1991: 126). There can be little doubt about the pervasiveness of functional tonality as the fundamental musical system of the modern West. For Shepherd, its influence is 'hegemonic', as 'the established ... music of powerful interests' and in addition 'through the harmonic-rhythmic framework it "supplies" to most genres of popular music' (1991: 128). It is taken for granted

as 'natural' by most members of western societies and, as I have suggested in Chapter 1, deviations from its rules are immediately perceived as 'wrong', even by non-musicians.

Yet it is important, Shepherd suggests, to recognise that tonality
does not express the central or core values of western societies in the
same way that Durkheim regarded established cultural patterns as
reflecting the fundamental principles of social organisation (see pp.
76–81 above). If functional tonality is an expression of the 'world-
sense' of industrial societies, and specifically of *capitalist* industrial
societies, then it follows that the values it expresses are those of
'powerful interests' – in short, the dominant class – just as it implicitly denies the values of those who are dominated and powerless.
That is, the ascendancy of functional tonality has come about not
because it is an expression of the Durkheimian *conscience collective*,
but because the dominant class has the power to impose its values
and standards on those who are politically and economically subordinate. 'The ideas of the ruling class', as Marx and Engels put it,' are
in every epoch the ruling ideas, i.e. the class which is the ruling *material* force of society, is at the same time its ruling *intellectual* force.
... The ruling ideas are nothing more than the ideal expression of the
dominant material relationships, the dominant material relationships
grasped as ideas' (1974: 64). From this perspective, which sees industrial societies as fundamentally divided on the basis of social class,
the dominant musical ideas express the values of the ruling capitalist class, and are likely to be embraced by others who accept such
values or aspire to membership of the dominant class; others again
– indeed the majority – will not experience the same 'intuitive' resonance between the predominant musical forms and their own
lifestyle and social position. (A somewhat similar theme has been
developed by Pierre Bourdieu: 'nothing more clearly affirms one's
"class", nothing more infallibly classifies, than tastes in music' (1984:
18).)

It is consistent with Shepherd's argument that echoes of pre-industrial times are still to be heard in the music of certain groups who
are far removed from modern urban centres of power – in the resid-
ual 'folk' traditions of western countries, for example, which often
display pentatonic scales and are relatively untouched by the imper-
atives of tonality – and, perhaps most significantly, in early recordings of rural blues singers in the United States. Indeed, it is of
immense importance for Shepherd that the twentieth century has

seen the development of African-American styles, which have come
to constitute the single most powerful influence on popular music.
As we have seen, Shepherd rejects the view of most academic musicology that only tonal music of the western classical tradition is
worthy of serious consideration, emphasising that there are good
sociological grounds for the contention that this is not the music
which most people in industrial societies either listen to or create.
Similarly, he dismisses the claims of Adorno and the critical theorists
that popular music is simply mass-produced to ensure the continuing docility of the commodity-consuming millions. On the contrary,
the overwhelming influence on popular music now is not, as Adorno
supposed, the 'light' classical music of the nineteenth century but the
African-American tradition in all its stylistic variety.

Of course it is true that much 'pop' music is simply – often cynically – produced like any other commodity, with the aim of realising profits. Shepherd's argument, however, is that this is only a part
of a much more complex picture, and that the vital process in
twentieth-century popular music has been the various ways in which
the African-American tradition has emerged out of the confrontation, in the Americas, between European tonality and the African
elements which remain part of the cultural heritage of black people.
As we have seen, functional tonality is the dominant organising
framework, one which is 'structurally homologous to the overall
symbolic environment'. Shepherd's claim, however, is that people's
response to this framework varies according to their structural loca-
tion in society: 'as different groups and cultures relate differently to
this environment, according to such variables as class, generation
and ethnicity, so their musics articulate that relationship through the
way they utilise and articulate the harmonic-rhythmic framework'
(1991: 133). With its hierarchy of notes and its pursuit of 'pure'
sounds, western tonality expresses the 'alienation of self by a central
and remote controlling power.' In the African-American tradition,
however, matters are different: 'The dirty timbres and inflected notes
articulated *within* the harmonic-rhythmic frameworks of much Afro-
American music ... speaks of a less alienated, more intimate relationship to both self and others' (1991: 134). Whereas functional
tonality symbolises the subordination of individuals to a unified,
controlling system, the *use* of this framework by musicians in the
African-American traditions renders it 'little more than a given conceptual scheme within which to make personal, immediate state-

ments' (1991: 136).

The various stylistic strands of black music in the twentieth century, then, are derived from the experience of people located at different points in the social structure: in general, the more remote (and therefore the more subordinated) people have been in relation to the dominant power-centres, the less they have been obliged to reach an accommodation with the demands of functional tonality. Thus in the rural blues its influence is relatively weak, in the later urban 'rhythm and blues' styles it provides a more explicit framework, while in the black 'avant-garde' jazz of the 1960s there was a deliberate attempt to set aside its constraints and conventions. It is in such ways, Shepherd suggests, that black music has sought to 'formulate disaffection towards the social structure' (1991: 143); moreover, the growing appeal of popular music styles influenced by the African-American tradition since the Second World War can be understood in terms of the increasing number of *white* people experiencing 'material, intellectual, and ... emotional dispossession' (1991: 144) and for whom, therefore, the elements of black music styles had greater resonance. It is from this perspective that Shepherd seeks to understand the commercial success of a series of white artists who have drawn on black music sources. 'The singing of Presley and Buddy Holly', he writes, 'reveals a marked innuendo of virile, individualistic, masculine sexuality eminently successful in flouting the propriety of middle-class sensibilities' (1991: 146), while 'progressive' rock represented a search for 'alternative social and cognitive modes' by predominantly middle-class youth (1991: 147), and 'punk' challenged the established orthodoxies by imbuing their symbols with contrary meanings.

Shepherd's conclusions are clear. Firstly, popular music styles are in an important sense the music of 'the people' in industrial capitalist societies, and that musicologists and sociologists should be aware of the far-reaching implications of this seemingly obvious point. Secondly, despite the highly commercialised nature of popular music production, and its potential as 'an agent of social control', it does retain the ability to generate an oppositional consciousness which may challenge and subvert the implicit premises of the 'industrial world-sense':

> The potential for avant-garde jazz and progressive rock to collapse the
> literate and oral worlds, to collapse intellect and emotion, thought and

action, into one another, and so evolve a new social-musical reality
would not exist but for the ability of past black cultures to turn a white
mask to white society and preserve an inviolate sense of that which was
essentially spiritual and cultural'. (1991: 149)

As I have suggested, certain important sociological themes are developed in Shepherd's work. In emphasising the socially constructed
nature of music, he demonstrates the weakness of those orthodoxies
which take the production and reception of music to be understandable in terms of individual psychology, or which take value and
meaning in music to be inherent in the works themselves. There is,
too, his valuable insistence on the point that the analysis of music as
a cultural product must be concerned with all the music of a society,
and that 'popular' music styles may have a significance not usually
recognised by academic musicologists. Inevitably, of course, Shepherd's large-scale effort to illuminate the relationship between forms
of music and forms of society invites challenges, especially from
those musicologists who may feel under attack. From a more
specifically sociological perspective, however, there are two general
areas in which Shepherd's work seems to raise critical questions.

The first of these is the issue of the nature of musical communication, or in other words how music can be said to 'convey' meanings. We have noted Shepherd's commitment to the idea that musical
meaning is neither inherent nor a consequence of the universal structures of the human mind. Rather, it is to be understood as 'socially
constructed', through processes in which musical sounds – just like
the sounds of words – become symbols, invested with meanings
through the collective actions of people in different cultural contexts.
Yet we have also noted Shepherd's emphasis on the specific qualities
of sonic, as opposed to visual, modes of communication, and his
contention that European functional tonality, on the one hand, and
African-American styles, on the other, express fundamentally different modes of human experience: both 'progressive' and 'punk' rock,
for example, share 'an emphasis on the experiential richness of the
here and now, on the inherent potential of people to exist fully in
the world, which is *essentially* denied by the social-musical reality of
functional-tonal music' (1991: 150, emphasis added). Moreover,
Shepherd is unequivocal about what it is that music communicates.
'Music, as sound, *cannot help* but stress the integrative and relational
in human life' although the ways in which it is marketed and used

'all too often neutralize what may be taken as the *inherent social meaning* of a piece of popular music' (1991: 217, 150, emphasis added).

The point to be emphasised in the present context is that there may well be some incompatibility between the notion of the 'inherent' meaning of music and a commitment to the idea of the 'social construction of reality'. As I have suggested in Chapter 2, the fundamental implication of this latter perspective is that sounds – and any other phenomena which may become cultural symbols – are essentially meaning-less, in the sense that their meanings are not inherent but arise only in and through the processes by which people attach significance to them. The 'social construction' perspective has developed in various ways, drawing on elements of several intellectual currents, notably the 'interpretive' sociology of Max Weber as reformulated by Alfred Schütz (Berger and Luckmann, 1971), Wittgenstein's philosophy (Coulter, 1979), and American symbolic interactionism (Blumer, 1969). In discussing the contribution of the philosopher G. H. Mead to the interactionist tradition, Herbert Blumer made what is, in the present context, the essential point: 'for Mead objects are human constructs and not self-existing entities with intrinsic natures. Their nature is dependent on the orientation and action of people toward them' (1969: 68). In order to discourage a misunderstanding which has become tediously familiar, it should be said immediately that this view does *not* imply that human beings are therefore free to define or interpret objects in any way which they choose; on the contrary, in their different ways Schütz, Wittgenstein and Mead all emphasised that the generation and sustenance of 'meanings', or any kind of communication, presuppose that individuals are members of particular cultural communities, and that in what they think, say and do they must orient themselves to the established conventions and practices of such communities. One implication of Wittgenstein's later work, for example, is that 'language is a public, collective thing, something that is passed from the community to the individual and not built up from individuals into a common thing' (Anderson, Hughes and Sharrock, 1986: 193).

We shall return to the matter of the ways in which human actions and meanings presuppose membership of cultural communities in the following chapter. At this point, however, it should be clear that Shepherd's commitment to a 'social construction' perspective may not be entirely consistent with his view of the nature of musical communication. Can music have an 'inherent social meaning', irrespective of the many ways in which it may be heard, appropriated, redefined or ignored in specific social contexts of interpretation? Is it the case that music 'cannot help' but express human relatedness? Such a claim would seem to depend on the assumption that sonic modes of communication do indeed work in non-discursive ways, conveying their message without our conscious awareness of them. At best, such a view seems inconsistent with the whole tradition on interpretive sociology, with its emphasis on the *activity* of human beings as they collaboratively create and sustain meaningful social contexts; at worst, we could be led into just the sort of simple behaviourism which Shepherd has done so much to counter, in which a musical 'stimulus' produces a behavioural or emotional 'response'. (Indeed, this suggestion has been made by Bradley, also writing about the effects of popular music: 'music can articulate aspects of world-sense *without benefit of* a [*sic*] conscious analytical work ('words') by the listener's mind' (1992: 27). While it is certainly true that our knowledge of the ways in which music can affect people is inadequate, the postulation of inherent meanings may point not to a clearer understanding but to an unacceptable determinism. In contrast, the acceptance of a 'social construction' perspective implies a view of musical meaning as 'arbitrary', in the sense in which Bourdieu uses the term: as contingent rather than inherent, as established, sustained and challenged by real people in real situations, yet *experienced* by them as 'natural' rather than cultural (1977: 95).

In some of his most recent work, however, Shepherd has reaffirmed his commitment to the idea of 'musical-social articulations which are *purely* intrinsic to musical processes'. It is possible, he writes, 'for people to both create and know about aspects of their world which may not be available to them initially through any other medium than 'music' (1991: 214). Thus Shepherd argues against the idea that musical meaning is 'arbitrary' in Bourdieu's sense: such a view, he suggests, seems to imply that 'the inherent sonic qualities of music are of little or no consequence to the articulation of meaning' (1991: 221). Yet the fact remains, and here we return to points raised in the discussion of musical meaning in Chapter 2, that sounds produced in he context of a musical culture which is alien to us do not – at least at the level of consciousness – communicate meanings to us in the ways which they do to someone who has been socialised into that culture. Indeed, while we may find the sounds interesting, or seek to impose some sort of significance on them (usually on the basis of our prior assumptions), they may nevertheless seem sense-less. Moreover, even within our own culture it is evident that the 'meaning' of music may change – some of the 'progressive rock' sounds which Shepherd saw as having a certain emancipatory poten-tial, for example, are now used as part of the mass-marketing of cars and clothes through television advertising. Further, it may be sug-gested that there is an important distinction between regarding the meaning of cultural symbols as arbitrary, in Bourdieu's sense, and treating them as random. Although all kinds of sounds, in human cultures, have come to have all kinds of meaning, it is clear that some will seem more appropriate than others in particular situations: there are, after all, certain functional requirements of music which is to be used as part of work routines, or for dancing, or to accompany rit-uals and so on. The rhythms of nature, and particularly the human body, may also exert an influence on the shaping of sound patterns. Far from the association between sounds and meanings being random, then, it is perhaps more useful to think in terms of the 'elec-tive affinities' through which compatible cultural elements become associated. Once cultural configurations are established, as Bourdieu insistently reminds us, they come to seem 'natural'; the fact that people in all cultures associate certain sounds with certain social meanings is inevitable if there is to be any kind of collaborative prac-tice called music. This does not, however, make any particular asso-ciations necessary or natural.

The implications of these points cannot be pursued here. What I have tried to do, however, is to suggest that there may be some ten-sion between John Shepherd's argument for the specific qualities of music as a medium of *sonic* communication, and the implications of the idea of the 'social construction of reality'. From the latter per-spective, there is a deep suspicion of any suggestion that behavioural or emotional effects may be produced in individuals at pre-or uncon-scious levels. As Blumer put it, the social actor 'has to construct and guide his action instead of merely releasing it in response to factors playing on him or operating through him' (1969: 15).

The second set of questions raised by Shepherd's work concerns his conceptualisation of social structures. As we have seen, penta-tonicism and functional tonality are treated as 'dialectical correlates of the social structures of the time' (Shepherd 1991: 126) since there is an underlying 'structural homology' (1991: 88–9) between the form taken by musical organisation and the form of social organisation. It is evident, too, that for Shepherd the use of the term 'structure' is neither simply heuristic nor metaphorical: 'there is an order, a logic which underpins the activities of a society, and which can be teased out by analysis of different social institutions whose relationship, on the surface, may seen tenuous' (1991: 87). The implications of this would seem to be, firstly, that societies may be regarded as more-or-less integrated totalities, and, secondly, that their fundamental 'order' or underlying structure may be unambiguously described by the diligent analyst.

Shepherd's characterisation of feudal society may serve to illustrate these points. It is basic to his argument that the feudal social order was 'highly decentralised and localised', comprising 'small social units' which were 'mutually dependent' (1991: 108); the parallels with the organisation of medieval pentatonicism have already been outlined. Shepherd is drawing attention here to interesting aspects of feudal society (particularly in comparison to modern industrial ones). What is not so clear, though, is whether his account of feudal social order may be taken as unproblematic, or whether it exhausts all the descriptive possibilities. In discussing pre-modern political organisation, for example, Benedict Anderson writes that the literati of Europe were 'adepts, strategic strata in a cosmological hierarchy of which the apex was divine. The fundamental concepts about 'social groups' were centripetal and hierarchical, rather than boundary oriented and horizontal. ... Kingship organises everything around a high centre. ... states were defined by centres' (Anderson, 1983: 22, 25–6). Clearly, it is difficult to reconcile this with Shepherd's perspective.

In the present context, it is not my intention to join a debate about whether feudal society was 'really' centralised or decentralised. What I do wish to do, however, is to suggest that *any* such characterisation not only is a retrospective construct rather than a literal description but is inevitably partial and selective. As such, it may be useful as a guide to research, as Poggi has argued in relation to contrasting interpretations of feudalism (1986: 226–7). What such a characterisation is *not* is an objective description of 'the' social structure. Indeed, the notion that there is an 'order' or a 'logic' underlying 'the activities of a society' seems at odds with a 'social construction' perspective which emphasises the ways in which social order is actively created and sustained, and with the tradition of interpretive sociology generally. In short, what we are considering is one of the fundamental differences between Durkheim's and Weber's conceptions of social order. For Durkheim, the very forms and categories of human thought are ultimately representations of the underlying principles of social organisation, and society is 'not a nominal being created by reason, but a system of active forces' (1915: 447). Despite Shepherd's affirmation that there is no such 'thing' as society (1991: 87), his postulation of an order which underlies social life seems to take him close to a Durkheimian structuralist position, with its attendant dangers of the reification of 'society' and seeing individuals as determined by the 'system of active forces'. For Weber, on the other hand, society was to be considered not as some sort of real structure but as a concept useful in describing the patterns of social order which emerge out of the actions and interactions of real people as they pursue their interests (Weber, 1978: 13–18). From this interpretive perspective, then, it is not the social order that shapes 'the activities of a society' but rather social action which generates the sense of social order.

The dangers of Shepherd's position emerge when we turn from the conceptualisation of society to his account of social change, and to the idea that 'modes of thought and social organisation in industrial societies are dialectical correlates' (Shepherd, 1991: 60). It is clear that in introducing the notion of 'dialectical correlates' and in emphasising the importance of 'active negotiation' of meanings (1991: 97), Shepherd is concerned to distance himself from any simple theory that art 'reflects' society. Unfortunately, possibly as a result of his using the concept of 'structural homology', his work has been *taken* to imply a fairly straightforward version of 'reflection theory' (Becker, 1992: 528), in which forms of music somehow come to correspond to (or should it be echo?) structures of society. For all the talk of 'dialectical correlates', Shepherd does seem to posit a fairly close correspondence between social and musical organisation in feudal and industrial societies. Some might suggest that his account accentuates those aspects of both music and society which seem consistent, while ignoring others: some musicologists could argue, for example, that medieval plainchant is *not* fundamentally pentatonic in its organisation. On the other hand, pentatonic music would appear to be compatible with a wide range of social structures: 'This type of scale is one that Europe shares with a large part of the world, particularly with Northern Asia, with the American

Indians, and with Negro Africa' (Nettl, 1973: 44). It would be difficult to sustain the view that all the societies of these regions have been structurally equivalent to medieval European ones. It may be, then, that the relationship between forms of musical and social organisation is somewhat looser than Shepherd's account implies; recourse to the concept of 'dialectical correlates', moreover, seems to offer little in the way of clarification – the idea of correlation could be emphasised when a fairly close correspondence is claimed, and the notion of dialectics is sufficiently vague to cover instances when it is not.

Critics of Shepherd's work also suggest that the idea of a 'structural homology' gives it, however unintentionally, an historicist flavour: as large-scale historical forces necessarily transformed feudal society into industrial capitalism, so, necessarily, a change in musical culture was entailed. Absent from this account, writes Becker, 'is any sense of the process by which these connections actually come about and any attention to the details of the worlds whose features are given such explanatory weight' (Becker, 1992: 529). Similarly, DeNora argues that the emphasis on structural transformations tends to 'reify social action'. When, for example, the 'implicit monody of plainchant began to disintegrate' (Shepherd, 1991: 96), this was not some automatic, predetermined process; it did so, rather, 'in specific contexts of practice, of aspiration, constraint, and probably, conflict between real individuals over time' (DeNora, 1992). In other contexts, too, Shepherd, whatever his intentions, appears to imply a reified view of social structures: 'in order that the centralised structures of industrial societies should not come under scrutiny, they should *actively militate* against the formulation of any social theory for the significance of music' (Shepherd, 1991: 60). It is Shepherd's case that 'they' do, and indeed that 'world-senses' are 'complex totalities which maintain, reproduce and articulate themselves in terms of some deep-seated set of logics' (1991: 93). As I suggested above, such claims would seem to be more compatible with a structuralist view of social order than one based on a 'social construction' perspective.

Susan McClary: music as a gendered discourse

In much of his more recent work, John Shepherd has been concerned to develop his analysis in ways which take account the fact that capitalist industrial societies are stratified not only in terms of social class but also on the basis of gender. The rationalised, predominantly visual, culture of modern western societies is one which privileges written over oral communication and simultaneously institution-alises the domination of men over women; although the significance of music in general is therefore diminished, the dominant forms of music (in both 'serious' and 'popular' traditions) reflect male hege-mony in various ways (1991: 171). This theme also finds expression in the recent work of Susan McClary, who has developed a compre-hensive and challenging reinterpretation of the nature and develop-ment of western tonal music.

Like Adorno, McClary sees western tonality as an historically specific musical system which expresses both the dominant patterns and the tensions within societies: 'its career of rise and decline hap-pens to articulate through musical terms the course of the European bourgeoisie' (McClary, 1987: 21). There are echoes of Adorno, too, in McClary's contrast between the 'ruptured, anxiety-ridden narra-tives of the nineteenth century' and 'easy reconciliations and ... illu-sory hopes' of Enlightenment music (1991: 66). Unlike Adorno, however, McClary sees the task of critical musicology to be the analysis of *all* forms of musical expression, and in terms reminiscent of Shepherd she describes that task as the examination of 'the ways in which different musics articulate the priorities and values of var-ious communities' (1991: 26). Inevitably, then, McClary too is drawn into conflict with many orthodox musicologists; what their preoccu-pation with either formal analysis or historical details neglects, she argues, is any concern with what she takes to be music's essential quality, its ability to evoke 'images or responses' in us (1991: 20). Her complaint, then, is not just that orthodox musicology has been blind to the issue of the representation of gender relations but that it lacks *any* 'theory of musical signification' (1991: 20). This is not, she sug-gests, simply an accidental omission. On the contrary, it is precisely the capacity of music to heighten our experience of emotions in gen-eral and sexuality in particular that make it threatening in the con-text of the dominant discourse of Enlightenment rationality:

> in Western culture, music *itself* is always in danger of being regarded as the feminine Other that circumvents reason and arouses desire. Hence the ongoing academic struggle to control music objectively: just as Carmen must be brought in line with patriarchal demands, so the

musicologist must silence music, deny that it has meaning, and impose
theoretical closure on this discourse that often provokes more than it
can contain. (1991: 79)

For McClary, then, as for Shepherd, the importance of music in
this context is that it can and does communicate in emotional and
physical ways, rather than rational ones: 'it can cause listeners to
experience their bodies in new ways' and exert its effects 'seemingly
without mediation' (1991: 25). McClary is therefore drawn to Michel
Foucault's work, in which he 'locates the efficacy of cultural discourses
in their ability to arouse and manipulate' (1991:29), although, she
argues, the determinism implicit in Foucault's formulations must be
supplanted by a view of culture as 'the terrain in which competing
versions of social reality fight it out' (1991: 29). Two further theoretical strands in McClary's work should be mentioned. The first is
her adoption of the binary oppositions which, according to Lévi
Strauss, lie 'at the foundations of Western thought' (1991: 141). From
this perspective, McClary presents a set of categories which, she con-
tends, reflect the fundamental organising principles of the western
world-view. Basic to these is the opposition between the rational and
the emotional, and the identification of the former with male, and
the latter with female, cultural elements: rationality/masculinity is
associated with strength, control, objectivity, domination and the
mind, while emotion/femininity entails weakness, submission, subjectivity, subordination, the body and so on. As we have seen, it follows that music itself is cast into the latter set; the central theme
running through McClary's work, however, is the illumination of the
ways in which this fundamental opposition is represented *within*
musical discourse. A second theoretical influence is, as in John Shep-
erd's work, that of a 'social construction' perspective. 'Meaning is
not inherent in music', writes McClary, 'but neither is it in language:
both are activities that are kept afloat only because communities of
people invest in them, agree collectively that their signs serve as valid
currency' (1991: 21). Thus McClary firmly resists the notion that
music is any kind of 'universal language' – her interpretation of
Bach, for example, rejects the idea that his works express some sort
of transcendental order or truth in favour of a concern with the ways
in which they 'are indelibly marked with the concerns and conventional social constructs of his time and place' (1987: 55). It is true,
McClary argues, that symbolic codes may display considerable sta-

bility over time, but this is due not to their inherent validity, but to the persistence of the attitudes and values which give them their currency. Such persistence, as we have seen, is likely to result from the cultural dominance of a particular social group, and its consequent ability to impose its frame of reference as both valid and legitimate. Tonality has been the dominant musical form in western societies because it encodes the values of the dominant social class; as a feminist musicologist, therefore, McClary is particularly concerned to demonstrate the extent to which these values are patriarchal, and the ways in which their implicit premises are 'inscribed' even in music which is taken to be 'absolute' or value-free (1991:19).

For McClary, the formative period in the development of the modern western musical tradition came in the seventeenth century, when the 'tonality and semiotic codes' which we now take for granted were initially formulated and institutionalised by the early operatic composers as they sought to develop a musical vocabulary in which to represent dramatic characters and their actions on the stage (1991: 35). Such musical devices, therefore, are neither natural nor universal, and the musical depictions of masculinity and femininity 'were shaped by attitudes prevalent in the societies in which the composers lived' (1991: 37). This was not a simple process, and McClary suggests that the rhetorical devices which Monteverdi assigned to his character Orfeo in 1607 were in later works given to female characters; such a shift reflects a more general social instability, in particular a period of challenges to traditional authority, 'an anomalous moment in culture when power relationships associated with gender and rhetoric were oddly reconfigured' (1991: 51). Gradually, however, powerful conventions for the representation of male and female roles began to crystallise, and there could be no better illustration of these than in McClary's discussion of Bizet's *Carmen* (1875). In the opera, Carmen is 'the dissonant Other who is necessary for the motivation and sustaining of the plot' (1991: 57); she is represented musically in ways which emphasise her physical sensuality (the Latin rhythms which accompany her entrance) and her threat to the high-born Don José. Unlike José's musical discourse, which is 'that of the universal "tongue" of Western classical music' (1991: 59), Carmen the gypsy is given an entry which in its chromatic descent seems to undermine the basic tonal framework. Like the woman herself, it is 'slippery, unpredictable, maddening' (1991: 58). In such ways, Bizet represents the danger that Carmen embodies, both to Don José and the 'unfortunate white, male, high-art "victim" ' (1991: 61) and to the established social order. Both the stability of society, and musical convention, therefore, require that Carmen should be overcome – 'for the flood of chromaticism to be stopped, for stability to be re-established' (1991: 62) – and this is duly accomplished by her death. 'Her principal musical motif', writes McClary, 'is made up of the illicit augmented-second interval that had long been the sign for the Jew, the Arab, and all-purpose racial Other; this is the motif that finally is forcibly expunged by the final [major] triad of the opera' (1991: 64).

McClary offers what is in many ways a brilliant and persuasive analysis of *Carmen*. She is aware of the possible criticism, however, that the analysis of music which is tied to a libretto, or which is intendedly 'programmatic', is bound to disclose devices and techniques whose purpose is representational, and she is concerned not only to meet this objection but to establish that so-called 'absolute' music in the western classical tradition is *also* organised in terms of semiotic codes which portray the overcoming of the threatening female Other. Indeed, she argues, one of the fundamental organising principles of western music, sonata form, encodes precisely this process. Just as it has become conventional to represent masculinity in terms of diatonic scales and major chords, and femininity by chromaticism and minor ones, so the sonata procedure sets up an opposition between a 'masculine' theme followed by a 'feminine' second theme often in an unrelated key, and a final part in which the second is symbolically overcome by the first. This last stage represents the imposition of 'closure', with greater or lesser degrees of 'violence'; even when we experience the second theme as more attractive or memorable, the so-called 'disinterested' formal procedures require it to be reduced to submission (1991: 68–9). For McClary, too, the build-up of 'tension' and its subsequent 'release' which give a sense of movement to both small- and large-scale musical structures must be understood as a symbolic enactment of – specifically male – sexuality: 'In most post-Renaissance music and in virtually all of its critical literature, the climax-principle (like the phallus of the classical Greek column) has been transcendentalized to the status of a value-free universal of form' (1991: 130).

It seems that the work of composers reflected the increasing consolidation of patriarchal structures; whereas Haydn and Handel, writes McClary, seldom produced musical narratives that 'demand sadism', Beethoven and Mahler postpone the release of tension more and more, 'such that desire in their narratives frequently culminates. ... in explosive violence' (1991: 127). Accordingly, McClary hears in the conclusion of Beethoven's Ninth Symphony – a work often asso ciated with 'the dignity of the individual, the sufferings and hopes of mankind' (Matthews, 1985: 167), or indeed with the emergence of 'World Spirit' itself (Dahlhaus, 1989:183) – only the necessity to destroy the utopian and other-wordly visions inspired by earlier parts of the work, notably the penultimate Adagio movement. Culturally, she argues, 'to linger in that pleasurable, semiotically and structurally feminine zone would be an act of intolerable transgression'. In the end, Beethoven 'simply forces closure by bludgeoning the cadence and the piece to death' (McClary, 1991: 129).

The formal procedures laid down by Beethoven, of course, soon came to be regarded as definitive of the symphony, and departures from such procedures have often been taken as evidence of inferiority in a composer. For McClary, however, such departures from the orthodox raise the possibility that some composers were deliberately striving to escape from, or to subvert, the patriarchal implications of the form itself. Thus the first movement of Tchaikovsky's Fourth Symphony is to her not a 'lapse' on account of its formal inadequacy – as Dahlhaus has argued – but is rather a carefully crafted effort to resist the implicit narrative of the form itself. As a homosexual in a homophobic society, says McClary, Tchaikovsky is not so much trying and failing to live up to the highest standards, as to 'tell another kind of story with other kinds of characters' (1991: 76). Moreover, it follows from this argument that the works of women composers can no longer be regarded as inferior on the grounds that they too fail to meet formal requirements, but must be heard as efforts to discover or express alternative possibilities. Thus it has been argued by Julia Moore that compositions by women are deliberately and significantly different: 'men composers demonstrate their socially-established ability to compel events, whereas women composers inject a more egalitarian perspective into patriarchal discourse. Women say "narrative is possible without compulsion" '. Women Romantic composers, Moore argues, display a marked tendency to avoid the conventional movement from tonic (masculine) to dominant (feminine) keys in the exposition sections of their sonatas (a movement which equally conventionally requires resolution in favour of the former); Clara Schumann made strategic moves to the submediant, while others favoured continual modulation, thus avoiding any 'binary harmonic opposition' (Moore, 1992).

Susan McClary's investigations of the alternative strategies pursued by women musicians take her beyond the confines of the classical music field, and her distinctive perspective is evident in a discussion of the singer-composer Madonna who, like Carmen, refuses to be 'framed by a structure that will push her back into submission or annihilation' (1991: 152). Madonna's work in general is seen as rendering problematic the conventional gender stereotypes of popular culture, so that she cannot be defined in their terms, and her involvement in dance serves to emphasise the physical aspects of her performance at the expense of the 'abstracted listening' of mainstream western discourse (1991: 153). In both respects, she presents a challenge to patriarchal assumptions, and just as classical women composers have sought to subvert the hidden message of sonata form, so Madonna resists the different but no less powerful conventions of popular styles:

> Madonna's means of negotiating for a voice in rock resemble very much the strategies of her visual constructions; that is, she evokes a whole range of conventional signifiers and then causes them to rub up against each other in ways that are open to a variety of divergent readings, many of them potentially empowering to girls and women. (1991: 154)

Thus in the song 'Live to Tell', the expected resolution from the key of F back to the expected initial D never comes, and Madonna exploits the consequent uncertainty and ambiguity, refusing to 'reproduce the structure of oppression that informs narrative convention'; the song 'is about staying in motion for the sake of survival, resisting closure where it lies in wait' (1991:160).

It is not surprising that McClary's critique has provoked a considerable reaction amongst musicologists. Temperley has referred to 'the doubting mass of scholars and critics', and made several points which may serve to represent their scepticism. To the notion that tonality encodes the rise and fall of the bourgeoisie, he counters that (whatever has happened to the bourgeoisie), tonality seems still firmly entrenched in all branches of western music; moreover the musical procedures through which, according to McClary, bourgeois values are expressed are procedures common to 'almost any extended music, Western or otherwise'. For Temperley, the works of

McClary and other 'contextualists' who argue that music is socially determined fail to take account both of the individual genius of particular composers and the extent to which musical change and innovation must be understood as a consequence of 'intellectual exploration' rather than the effects of social forces (1987: 685–7).

A similar conclusion could be reached on the basis of Rosen's influential discussion of *The Classical Style*, which, he argues, exhibited a general disintegration through the nineteenth century. We should, therefore, be wary of the assumption that nineteenth-century composers in general were committed to sonata procedures: in Mahler, for example, sonata-forms were accorded 'the same mock-respect that he gave to his shopworn scraps of dance-tunes', and a whole succession of composers 'from Chopin to Debussy. ... gradually altered and finally destroyed the musical language' (1976: 460). If it is accepted that innovation and transformation were widespread, it becomes harder to identify the norm from which women composers are presumed to be deviating. Yet another historian of music, indeed, has not only characterised the mid-nineteenth century as a period of extraordinary stylistic diversity, but has emphasised 'the vast distance that separated music from the central technological and sociohistorical developments of the age' (Dahlhaus, 1989: 193). Such arguments may be deployed in order to resist the contention that music expresses or articulates fundamental social processes, and they lead us back to Temperley's dismissal of the whole enterprise: 'To say that music reflects society is little more than a tautology. To say that its every detail is directly shaped by society is unnecessarily doctrinaire' (1987: 686).

We will return to the issue of the correspondence, or otherwise, between forms of music and forms of society; enough has been said to indicate something of the generally cool – though at times heated – response which McClary's ideas have received from orthodox musicology. The central concern at present, however, is whether, from a more specifically sociological point of view, her perspective succeeds in overcoming the difficulties we have identified in other efforts to develop a social theory of music. It should be said straight away that McClary's explorations of the ways in which the conventions for the representation of gender in music were established represent a very considerable contribution to the field. Her insistence, too, that such conventions, however normal or 'natural' they are taken to be, must be seen as culturally arbitrary (in the sense discussed above) is clearly consistent with a sociological view of music. However, there are points at which McClary herself seems equivocal on this point, suggesting that particular musical passages *require* certain responses from listeners – in the discussion of *Orfeo*, for example (1991: 42), or in describing the effects of Carmen's entrance (ibid: 57). A 'good piece of tonal music', she writes, 'can ... dictate one's very breathing' (1991: 125). Moreover, McClary does not hesitate to define the basic meaning of works: *Carmen* is 'fundamentally a paranoid fantasy' (1991: 59) and, as we have seen, Madonna's 'Live to Tell' 'is about staying in motion for the sake of survival' (1991: 160). The physical gestures that accompanied some early rock music were 'quite rightly perceived as subversive of hegemonic bourgeois values' (1991: 25). In these and other passages it seems as if McClary has abandoned a 'social construction' approach, suggesting firstly that musical texts have inherent meanings which impose themselves on passive listeners, and secondly that she has achieved some sort of final or privileged interpretation of what they are really about.

Equally troubling, from this point of view, is McClary's commitment to the view that music 'can tell us things about history that are not accessible through any other medium' (1991:30) and that its power as a medium of communication derives from the fact that 'most listeners have little rational control over the way it influences them' (1991: 151). As in John Shepherd's discussion, there is some tension between this notion of music as a special mode of communication which produces effects in us, in unconscious, non-rational ways, and any view which holds that meaning-construction is an active process. As I have suggested, the belief that music can 'make' us do things or 'demand' certain responses can lead in the end to a version of behaviourism (all the more so because the responses are held to be culturally rooted rather than innate or universal). In the present context, however, it is enough simply to note that such a belief is inconsistent with a 'social construction' perspective. The latter view, in contrast, implies firstly that meanings cannot reside 'in' musical sounds or any other kind of cultural objects; rather they are constructed, sustained, contested, and so on by real people in the course of their interactions (Blumer, 1969: 2). It follows that the task of the sociological analyst does not involve the attempt to disclose the 'real' or ultimate meaning of a cultural object but to understand meanings-in-use: how certain things are defined in certain ways, how some people have the power to impose definitions which others must accept, how established definitions are challenged or changed, with what consequences, and so on. In other words, attention shifts from a concern with the production of an authoritative reading of a text to the process by which readings are produced and sustained – and to the grounds on which 'authority' is claimed. From this perspective, it is impossible to say what a song 'is about'; what is important is to establish *what it is taken to mean*, by whom and with what effect. Thus to say that Madonna's songs are 'about' ambiguity and resisting orthodoxies is to make a *claim* about them, one which may be rejected by others. From a 'social construction' perspective *all* songs are ambiguous, in the sense that they are potentially available to be interpreted – or appropriated – in various ways for various purposes. 'The meaning of a popular song', writes Denzin, does not lie in its musical characteristics or even lyrics, but 'in the interactions brought [*sic*] to it'. In fact, as studies have shown, there may be little correspondence between intended and imputed meaning and thus 'an art object ... cannot be taken as an *a priori* valid indicator of a group's perspective'. In fact, it is 'in the status and political battles between individuals that art takes on meaning' (1969: 1036–7). We will return to these points below.

A second implication of the 'social construction' perspective follows from the indeterminate and contingent nature of the relation between music and the meanings attributed to it: listeners cannot be considered as passive recipients of non-conceptual messages. It is true, as in every other area of social life, that most people accept prevailing definitions for most of the time, and display culturally predictable responses. But this does not make the responses necessary or inevitable – as we have seen, these may change over time, or be subject to redefinition. They are certainly not evoked in a cultural 'outsider'. We must be wary, then, of arguments, made by people who themselves have a deep commitment to music, that it possesses all sorts of extraordinary qualities and powers to affect us: these are, once again, *claims* made about music by people with a particular interest in it. This is not to deny that people can experience profound emotions or bodily sensations when listening to music, but simply to recall that such effects are not universal or inevitable. The music which McClary finds irresistible may be a matter of great indifference to me (and vice versa), and I am not inclined to accept her contention that it is influencing me in ways over which I have 'little rational control'. Many people, quite simply, are not interested in, or much influenced by music *per se*. Moreover, and this is an important if neglected point, 'listening' to music requires an *active* orientation to it; it cannot be assumed that because someone hears music he or she is unconsciously absorbing its 'effects'. (There is a certain irony in the fact that music which has a great effect on an audience may have little or no effect on the musicians who are producing it, not least because they have done it all before, many times.)

A third implication of a 'social construction' perspective is, as I have said, that no particular interpretation of a piece of music is to be regarded as ultimate or privileged. Whereas the music critic or indeed the musicologist may have a personal or professional interest in arguing for the validity of a particular interpretation – in terms of either a work's meaning or its aesthetic value – the prime concern of the sociologist must be with the interactional processes through which a variety of interpretations may be produced, and the consequent conflicts, challenges, negotiations, accommodations, disputes and so on. These, taken together, constitute the social world which both provides a context in which the various groups and individuals pursue their interests and is a source of the meanings and schemes of interpretation which are available to orient their actions. In this sense, the imposition of meanings, and resistance to them, is to be understood as a *political* process in which competing claimants must either control the resources (material or cultural) with which to overcome their opponents, or reach some sort of accommodation with them. And just as it has been said that 'politics is the art of compromise', so it has been argued that social order can be seen as the outcome of processes of negotiation – on large and small scales – between those with competing interests and claims (Strauss 1978: 235).

Once again, therefore, it seems that there may be some inconsistency in McClary's position, as seen from a sociological angle. On the one hand, and rightly in terms of the points made above, she commends a view which conceives of 'culture as the terrain in which competing versions of social reality fight it out' (1991: 29). On the other hand she is firmly committed to one particular version of that reality: she wants, to take an important example, to replace the established critical view of western musical procedures as purely formal with one which sees them as symbolically expressing the patriarchal domination of women. For McClary, it is not a matter

of purely formal procedures but of sex and violence: the musical discourse of rock 'n' roll is 'characterised by its phallic backbeat' (1991:
154), while Beethoven's symphonies are replete with 'assaultive
pelvic pounding ... and sexual violence' (quoted in van den Toorn,
1991: 285). Rather than offering a detached account of the processes
by which cultural configurations are formed and transformed, then,
McClary presents a *version* of 'social reality'; she is not so much an
analyst of the conflict as a dedicated combatant *in* it. As we have
seen, her version, or in this case the way of hearing that she recom-
mends, has been resisted by many musicologists: for van den Toorn,
significantly, it is a 'crusading ideology' which insists on one particular way of hearing the music (1991: 293–4). In response, and in
defence of McClary, Solie rejects van den Toorn's notion that there
could ever be the sort of direct, 'unmediated aesthetic experience'
through which music speaks to individuals, and which the 'crusading ideology' seeks to subvert (1991: 400). From a sociological point
of view, once again, the interest in such exchanges is not so much to
take sides (although van den Toorn's individualism and aesthetic
presuppositions do indeed seem suspect) as to see how they provide
a context and a set of interpretive resources in which and through
which subsequent discussions of musical meaning will be carried out.
The outcome, moreover, is of some importance, which is why the
writing of both McClary and van den Toorn betrays strong personal
involvement. What is at stake, among other things, is how the music
will be understood, what music will be played, in educational institutions and concert halls, which music will be considered artistically
valid, and why. Following McClary, many women (and men) will
hear Beethoven and rock music in new ways. Only time will tell
whether McClary's critique will be strong enough to undermine the
established orthodoxies; the point to be emphasised here is that our
understanding of the reception and interpretation of music will be
furthered to the extent that we see them as emerging in and through
such disputes.

   For Ballantine, sonata form was a representation in music of the
Hegelian dialectic; for Shepherd, tonal music articulates the world-
sense of industrial capitalism; for McClary it is patriarchal values
and their associated violence which are inscribed in both these fundamental conventions of western music. For many musicologists,
particularly those committed to the notion of 'absolute' music, the
forms and conventions carry no such cultural messages; what they

are held to represent, if anything, is pure intellectual creativity on the part of composers. Such diverse readings may serve as a final reminder that meanings are not 'in' cultural objects; rather the objects themselves, and the various ways in which they are defined, are always the outcome of collaborative social action.

Conclusion

The central theme running through this chapter (and the previous one) has been the idea that forms of music – the ways in which different peoples have developed systems of organised sound – correspond in some way to the central values or the organisational forms of their societies. It is an idea, I have suggested, which is fundamentally sociological, in the sense that the explanation of musical systems is held to lie in social processes, rather than the properties of the harmonic series, the psychology of individuals or some sort of pure aesthetic realm. In their different ways, each of the authors discussed has offered persuasive criticisms of these alternative approaches, and strong arguments in favour of a perspective which emphasises the specifically social aspects of the production and reception of music. I have also suggested, however, that none of these accounts of the links between music and society may be regarded as entirely satisfactory from a sociological point of view.

Two general problems seemed to recur in the discussion. The first concerns the authors' treatments of the question of musical meaning. It was argued in Chapter 2 that the evident difficulties of both empiricist and rationalist accounts of musical meaning may be overcome if meaning is understood as socially constructed – arising, that is, in and through the processes of collaborative social interaction which themselves constitute the social world. It is clear that Adorno, too, had little time for empiricist or rationalist views, constantly emphasising the dialectical nature of meaning, the perpetual interchange between subject and object, the constant flux of experience and so on. Yet we have also detected in Adorno's writings some degree of tension between his dialectical ambitions and his commitment to the idea that music can and does represent the 'essential laws' of society, and that this is its 'objective content'. Adorno accepts that a piece of music may be taken to mean all sorts of different things, yet wishes to retain the authority of the expert like himself who, through analysis, can decipher and disclose the real meaning of the piece. It may well be that Adorno himself would have been untroubled by the presence of contradictions and inconsistencies in his work; for present purposes, however, the commitment to the idea of inherent social meanings in music renders his perspective sociologically problematic. Similar tensions, it was argued, may be detected in the contributions of John Shepherd and Susan McClary, both of whom assert their allegiance to the view that reality is socially constructed, yet who both discuss whole styles or individual pieces of music in terms of their inherent meanings. Both, moreover, retain a view of musical communication which emphasises its non-verbal, indeed unconscious, aspects. While it is true that the whole matter of the effects of music is not well understood, I have suggested that any notion of it as having immediate effects, or as demanding certain responses, is hard to reconcile with a 'social construction' perspective: for music to have any effects at all, normally requires the prior socialisation of listeners, and their active orientation to it.

The second set of problems concerns the conceptualisation of societies and social structures. Once again, there appears to be some tension within Adorno's work between his rejection of the idea of society as an objective totality (which could be comprehended by the methods of positivist 'science') and his insistence that, in some way or other, the social whole is embodied in the authentic work of art, which can therefore represent the true condition of society. In the end, it seems fair to conclude that Adorno's thought remained rooted in the presuppositions of Hegel's philosophy, with its emphasis on the dialectical relations between the social whole and its parts; his analysis of music, therefore, must be read as speculative philosophy rather than sociological analysis. There is an unfortunate irony, too, in the fact that despite their commitment to the notion that musical and social forms are dialectically related, both Adorno and Shepherd have been *taken* as implying that musical structures simply reflect social ones: on this reading, reified social structures are seen to determine the behaviour of individuals. To many in the world of music, this seems to deny the freedom and creativity of the great composers, as when Adorno writes that Beethoven 'must have' become unconsciously aware of incipient social changes and thus expressed them in his work. Adorno's position, it may be suggested, appears as equally unsatisfactory from a purely sociological point of view, appearing to minimise the role of human agency in the processes of cultural production. In short, despite their persuasive criticisms of alternative perspectives, neither Adorno nor the other authors considered in this chapter have produced a sociologically satisfactory account of 'how the social gets into music' (Shepherd, 1991: 77).

It is of course possible to respond to this apparent theoretical failure by taking it as proof that music is, after all, an autonomous form of expression and that the supposed relationship between music and society is illusory. Clearly, however, the arguments advanced so far in this book do not prompt such a conclusion; moreover it is implausible, to say the least, that there is *no* relationship between musical and social forms. What I wish to argue by way of conclusion is that the sociological inadequacies of these accounts derive largely from the weaknesses of the general theoretical perspectives which they presuppose. More specifically, their failings – an inadequate treatment of meaning, reification of concepts such as society and social structure, and a potentially deterministic view of behaviour – are among the failings of 'structural' sociology generally. It is important to emphasise, however, that 'structural' models of the social order do not exhaust the possibilities for sociological analysis – indeed it is precisely the weaknesses of these perspectives that have stimulated and sustained a vigorous alternative approach which, following Max Weber, has been termed 'interpretive'. Interpretive sociologies have come in various guises – 'humanistic', 'interactionist' and so on – but what they share is an emphasis on meaning as constructed in collaborative interactions, on social order as an outcome (not a cause) of such interactions and on individuals as actively involved in the production and sustaining of normative patterns. It should be said immediately that such perspectives do not entail individualism (other than in a methodological sense), subjectivism or a neglect of power and social conflict: on the contrary, as Collins has argued, Weber's intellectual legacy is a general perspective on social order which specifically emphasises conflict and the pursuit of power, wealth, prestige as the normal condition of social life (Collins, 1975: 43 and *passim*).

Societies, then, need not be conceptualised as organic wholes, or cultural systems, in the manner of Durkheim or Parsons. From an interpretive point of view, societies are not systems or totalities existing independently of real people but are rather *concepts* which we necessarily use in order to convey a sense of the social order. It follows that 'society' cannot legitimately be used as the explanation of anything, in the sense that 'it' has caused any particular effects, since 'it' does not exist. It is real human beings that exist, pursuing what they believe to be their interests as best they can in particular circumstances, with resources that are highly unequal; indeed, as I have indicated, conflict over valued resources is central to the whole process through which social organisation is created.

The contrast between 'structural' and 'interpretive' perspectives may be illustrated by consideraing their alternative approaches to the explanation of religion and law. As we saw in the introduction to the previous chapter, for Durkheim both these institutions could be understood as reflecting the fundamental organising principles of society, conceived as a cultural system. For Weber on the other hand, religions must be seen, above all, as social movements in which some groups of people may attempt to convert (or coerce) others to accept their beliefs, in which the beliefs themselves are formulated and modified by a specialised priesthood with its own interests, and which may well be beset by endless internal disputes, schisms and so on. Thus the particular pattern of beliefs, rituals and institutions which characterises a given religion at a particular time is not to be seen as a reflection of the society's basic normative infrastructure but rather as the (temporary) outcome of a perpetual process of conflict, competition, negotiation, coercion and so on. Indeed, the 'society' itself is not an integrated entity but a territory in which individuals and groups – large and small – struggle for advantage: the social order is essentially a balance of power, just as an ecological balance will develop in a given natural environment. Similar points may be made in relation to the analysis of the law: in contrast to the view of Durkheim, and Montesquieu, that a society's laws represent the 'core' of its cultural values, a Weberian perspective takes the establishment of laws as an instance of the ways in which groups – especially powerful groups or classes – attempt to institutionalise their situation or protect their advantages from the challenges of others. As in the case of religion, too, there is a specialist group – the legal profession – which has its own particular interests (though it too may be internally divided) and exerts considerable influence in the ways laws are enacted and enforced. These, and other, considerations suggest that the body of laws in a society does not represent its 'core' values but is rather the outcome of a process of contest and accommodation involving lawyers, judges, the police, politicians and a whole range of special-interest groups, from employers and trades

unions to local action groups. Indeed, in view of the variety of interests involved, it is not surprising that the enactment and enforcement
of laws may ultimately reflect neither core social values nor *any* particular interest. As Lemert puts it, when incompatible values are
involved 'laws and rules represent no group's values nor values of
any portion of a society. Instead they are artifacts of compromise
between the values of mutually opposed, but very strongly organised,
associations' (Lemert, 1972: 57).

The contrast between structural and interpretive perspectives in
sociology cannot be elaborated here; it is sufficient to note that
whereas the former takes society to be some sort of pre-existing
structure or system which produces cultural and institutional effects,
the latter emphasises the ways in which patterns of social organisation are generated and sustained through the collaborative interaction of individuals. The mode of analysis typical of the former
perspective may be termed synchronic, in the sense that the characteristics of any element (for example a musical style) are explained
with reference to the characteristics of others existing simultaneously
in the social whole (for example the pattern of class stratification).
In the latter, interpretive, perspective, analysis is diachronic, in the
sense that cultural and institutional patterns are seen as perpetually
developing in response to new contingencies: there is no *necessary*
connection between, say, the form of music and the class structure
(although the former may well be *interpreted* in terms of the latter,
as we have seen). (See Middleton 1990: 167.) It follows that the
notion of a 'structural homology' between patterns of musical and
social organisation has no place in the interpretive paradigm; of
course there are links and correspondences between different areas
of cultural activity, but, rather than presuppose these, as structural
thinkers generally do, the aim of interpretive analysis is to demonstrate them empirically. It is necessary, therefore, to abandon the suspect notion that social forms or group values somehow or other find
their way into music, and instead to investigate the ways in which
particular musical styles are developed through collaborative interaction in particular cultural and institutional contexts. The reception
and interpretation of music, too, is to be examined empirically,
rather than assuming that its truth or inherent meaning can only be
deciphered by the expert analyst. Some of these topics will be taken
up in the next chapter.

The implication of the interpretive perspective, then, is that the search for correspondences between musical structures and social structures can no longer be regarded as the core business of the sociology of music. Rather, the aim is to analyse empirically the social organisation of musical activities, abandoning the general supposition that art 'reflects' society, so as to reveal why cultural objects take the forms that they do, and why they are interpreted by particular people in particular ways. As Howard Becker has put it, the emphasis of an empirical sociology of music is on

> occupational organisation, the development and maintenance of traditions, the training of practitioners, mechanisms of distribution, and audiences and their tastes. The basic imagery in this kind of sociology is of art as something people do together. Sociologists working in this mode aren't much interested in 'decoding' art works, in finding the works' secret meanings as reflections of society. They prefer to see those works as a result of what a lot of people have done jointly. (1989: 282)

Accordingly, Becker's main concerns, which will be considered in the following chapter, are with the collective action of people in specific cultural communities – or 'art worlds' – and with the ways in which artworks must be understood as the result of their collaborations.

By way of conclusion, it is instructive to consider Cerulo's unusual study of classical music compositions produced during the Second World War in six countries, some of which were in 'combat zones', and others not so immediately affected by warfare. Cerulo's findings were that the works of composers in the combat zone did indeed differ from those in other areas: 'melodies written by composers residing in the Combat Zone became lengthy and conjunct (smooth), while compositions emanating from musicians in the Noncombat Zone contain melodies that remain comparatively shorter and more disjunct (jagged, leapy)' (1984: 890). At first sight, it might appear that this study involves just the sort of 'reflection' theory which has been found unsatisfactory, since general social conditions are said to have had a direct effect on the nature of the artworks produced. Moreover, Cerulo's work could also be taken as an instance of the sort of positivist analysis which Adorno condemned, with its 'sampling' of composers and their works, its abstraction of musical elements from their contexts, its categorisation of melodies as smooth, jagged and so on. Yet, in the present context, Cerulo's discussion of her findings is of considerable interest. In fact, she does not explain the changes and differences in compositional styles primarily in

terms of the direct and obvious effects of war – destruction, danger
and so on. Rather, her emphasis is primarily on the social isolation
experienced by war-zone composers and their consequent inability to
sustain normal networks of communication with their colleagues:

> The loss of contact with peers experienced by Combat Zone writers
> destroyed their professional community. This, in turn, caused the
> unravelling of the normative prescriptions that govern techniques of
> composition. Consequently, in the absence of both a supportive system
> and the enforcement by contemporaries of normative adherence, com-
> posers deviated from their current pattern of musical construction.
> (1984: 900)

The implication is clear: even the apparently solitary composer must
be seen as operating within a specific social context, a community of
musicians, or in Becker's terms an 'art world', in which certain conventions and expectations are established which will ordinarily exert
normative control over the process of musical production. Even if
composers wish to reject or destroy these conventions, they none the
less have to take account of them in what they do. Cerulo's point is
that general social disruption may bring about the collapse of the
network of communications through which control normally operates, weakening its effects and allowing – or requiring – the composer to innovate or deviate from conventional practices. If we are
to make sense of the idea that music is socially organised, we need
to abandon the belief that it somehow expresses general social values
or represents social structures, and instead examine the ways in
which it is created, performed and heard by specific people in specific
social contexts. It is this theme which is developed in the following
chapter.

5

Music as social action

A theory of cultural production cannot be properly developed unless we possess an adequate account of the nature of human agents.

Anthony Giddens (1987: 214)

every morning when you woke up and realised that you were in New York City you felt a big thrill just from being there. But ... [what] Elmer Williams and I were really concerned about was where we were going to play music. The most important thing for us was making contact with the other musicians and people in show business. That was the problem we had to figure out first.

Count Basie (1986: 51)

Interaction and social order

The two quotations above may be taken to indicate different aspects of the central theme to be developed in this chapter – the notion of music as social action. In the first, Giddens is concerned to alert us to the evident failure of 'structural' and 'post-structural' theorists to develop an adequate understanding of the social actor generally. Social life does not come about through the operations of invisible structures or macro-sociological forces that play on individuals and produce responses in them. On the contrary, institutional patterns and our 'normal' sense of orderly activity are created, sustained, and changed through the processes of social interaction. Human action, Giddens continues, 'does not unfold as the result of programmed impulses' as much structuralist and post-structuralist theorising has implied. Rather, following Harold Garfinkel, Giddens argues that

human life must be understood in terms of 'practical action' in interactional contexts, in which – quite literally – we make sense: 'meaning is produced and sustained through the use of methodological
devices' (Giddens 1987: 214–15). Interactionist and, more particularly, ethnomethodological analyses have been concerned with the
nature and use of these 'methodological' devices, and we will touch
on some of this work later. For the present, however, the central
point is to suggest that social life must be understood in terms of
actual interactional processes and practices rather than hypothetical
structures.

Rochberg-Halton (1982) has displayed the contrast between structural and interactional orientations in the course of comparing the
theoretical presuppositions of Durkheim and G. H. Mead. For
Durkheim, the elementary form of society provides 'the a priori
foundation of meaning, the underlying structure upon which all later
developments appear as "secondary", mere "accretions" and "luxu-
riant vegetation" ' (1982: 463, quoting Durkheim). For Mead, however, societies could not be understood in terms of an 'underlying
structure' which was independent of real, active people, and which
somehow animated them; Mead's alternative view, as we shall see,
takes patterns of social order to be the outcome of our fundamental
human capacity to think reflexively, that is, to anticipate imaginatively the likely responses of others to our own words and acts. By
taking others into account in the formulation of our own acts, and
in becoming the sort of person that others expect us to be, we are
led to act in regular, normal and predictable ways, at least for most
of the time. Thus, as Rochberg-Halton puts it, 'Mead ... defined
structure itself as a communicative process of role-taking'. From this
perspective, structure 'is not a timeless, passive entity ... but an *ability*' (1982: 465) and the creation of orderly social life is seen as an
interpretive, or communicative, process. It should be emphasised that
this focus on the acting individual and processes of interaction does
not entail a move from the 'macro' to the 'micro' level of analysis.
As Giddens puts it, it is important to insist on the distinction
between human agency and individual subjectivity (187: 214). The
latter is of interest to sociology only in the sense that it is to a great
extent constituted by experience of the former, that is to say, in interactional encounters. Indeed, the whole thrust of Mead's work is to
transcend what he took to be two false dichotomies: by understanding mind as a capacity rather than a substance or quality he chal-

lenged the orthodox Cartesian mind–body dualism, and by insisting on the fundamentally social nature of the self he rejected the opposition of the individual and society. As Baldwin has put it: 'Mead's primary focus was on social processes, showing the unity and interaction of the mental and physical components involved in micro and macro social phenomena' (1986: 36). In this chapter I will consider some of the implications of this focus on social process for our understanding of the organisation of musical activities.

The extract from Count Basie's memoirs is also significant in this context. Here were two keen young players in the 1920s, newly arrived in the big city which they knew to be the centre of the musical world they were desperate to belong to. But how should they go about participating in it? Playing music involves more than just a technical ability; it is necessary to be part of a network of social relationships for any kind of performance to occur. At a commonsense level this is an obvious, even trivial, point. However, its implications often seem to be neglected: in theories, for example, which pass from the concept of society or social group to the nature of the music without any reference to the actions and interactions of the people who produce it, as if music happened spontaneously. We have come across this sort of issue already in discussing, for example, Adorno's difficulty in specifying *precisely* how a composer's work comes to represent the form of a total society. Moreover, and this theme will be developed in the present chapter, the networks of social relationships in and through which music is created and performed are not simply incidental to it but themselves exert some influence on the nature of the music itself. Consider the alternative views of musical composition which emerge from Adorno's work and from Cerulo's discussion. In the former, the composer engages in a dialectical confrontation with the 'musical materials', out of which emerges a work which somehow embodies the state of society; despite Adorno's scorn for the Romantic idea of the true artist as an individual genius, he still seems to regard the composer as a social isolate. Cerulo's emphasis, on the other hand, is on the composer as a member of a musical community, a group with its own standards, expectations and conventions, which individual members will take into account in the course of their own activities. To use a term to which we will return, the other members constitute the 'reference group' to which individuals orient themselves as they formulate actions, make decisions and plans and so on. Through this process, individual composers are able to anticipate the likely reactions of others – musicians, audiences, other composers and so on – to what they write, and to decide whether to conform to established expectations or not. Some – like Schoenberg – may set out deliberately to follow a particular artistic commitment, irrespective of the hostility and outrage it may provoke. Others may aim only to write music which will appeal to as many people as possible. Most, perhaps, are found somewhere between the two extremes, balancing their personal artistic vision with the necessity to attract sufficient listeners. Irrespective of the choices made, however, the essential point is that it is through their ability to locate themselves and their work in relation to the expectations of a reference group that individual composers can make the choices which, cumulatively, give their work its character.

The point is illustrated nicely by some remarks of the composer Paul Hindemith, taking issue with those who have argued that music expresses the inner feelings of its composer:

> Music cannot express the composer's feelings ... Here is what he really does: he knows by experience that certain patterns of tone-setting correspond with certain emotional reactions on the listener's part. Writing the patterns frequently and finding his observations confirmed, in anticipating the listener's reaction he believes himself to be in the same mental situation. (quoted in Storr, 1993: 75)

For G. H. Mead, this reflexive ability to 'take the role of the other' – to anticipate imaginatively the likely reactions of others to our own actions – was fundamental to any understanding of social order in a general sense. In more specific contexts, such as the creation and performance of music, we will tend to orient our conduct to the expectations of 'significant others' – individuals or groups whose responses are important to us, and whose expectations give us a constant sense of what is right and wrong, good and bad, appropriate or inappropriate, and so on. Two points should be made about this perspective in the present context. Firstly, an awareness of these expectations does not mean that our actions are determined by them, simply that, typically, we will take account of them. Secondly, despite this, it is an important part of Mead's scheme that through taking account of others' responses we do come to 'internalise' the conventions and expectations which are dominant in our cultural context: clearly, the process of socialisation in childhood is the period in which we internalise the beliefs, values and habits of thought which are established in our culture, even though the process of learning to participate in new social contexts continues throughout life.

From this perspective, we can begin to develop a sociological understanding of music which takes it to be actively and collaboratively produced in specific social contexts, rather than simply assuming that it represents the values of social groups or reproduces their organisational features. Different musical styles, to take an important example, do not just represent different combinations of musical options in a purely technical sense but are rather created and reproduced by groups of people with different interests, projects, commitments, social locations and so on. As such, they rest on the adoption and maintenance of certain conventions, which may become matters of considerable importance to individuals and which give the style its character. It is in this sense that styles of music may be said to be socially organised: the music does not express the essential qualities of any group or individual (though it may be believed to do so) but is formed and changed in the constant process through which people sustain, modify, transform and abandon conventions. For example, as we have seen, the blues have often been interpreted as an expression of the misery of black oppression, and a cry for freedom (Finkelstein, 1948: 91). Yet in discussing this music Albert Murray is anxious to resist the implication, however well-meaning, that blues music 'does not require artifice but is rather a species of direct emotional expression in the raw'. This view, says Murray 'ignores what a blues performance so obviously is. It is precisely an artful contrivance, designed for entertainment and aesthetic gratification; and its effectiveness depends on the mastery by one means or another of the fundamentals of the craft of music in general and a special sensitivity to the nuances of the idiom in particular' (1978: 87). The idiom may be regarded as 'a very specific technology of stylisation' (1976: 90).

Murray's remarks may serve to alert us to some of the implications of seeing music as collaborative social action. His emphasis is on the musical style as a tradition, as a way of doing things which has a certain authority, which must be learned but which may also be changed as the practitioners, or their audience, change. Major stylistic changes in African-American music have been generated by fortuitous collisions of different traditions (notably European and African) and the periodic development of new technologies, affecting instruments (acoustic and electric), recording (the first 'jazz' record was made in 1917), and reception (notably amplification and domestic hi-fi). Population movements too, particularly the movement of blacks out of the South of the USA, and general economic conditions all play a part in determining which groups of people get together to make music and the circumstances in which they do so: the consequence is the establishment of various styles, each of which must – like jazz – be further subdivided but all of which depend on performers and listeners orienting themselves to certain accepted conventions and a 'specific technology of stylisation'. Through such considerations we can begin to understand the ways in which musical styles are socially constructed, rather than assuming that they are somehow representative of a group's socio-economic position. Of course, music may be *defined* as expressing 'social' messages of one kind or another, but this too, as we have seen, may be understood as a result of the ability or the attempts of some individuals or groups to influence the ways in which the sounds are heard (Wright, 1975). In this way, as Bourdieu puts it, what is in fact social is believed to be natural (1984: 68): the 'technology of stylisation' becomes taken for granted and the music is assumed to express directly meanings which are matters of considerable importance to the adherents of particular styles. As Strauss puts it, in relation to G. H. Mead's perspective: 'Group membership is thus a symbolic, not a physical, matter, and the symbols which arise during the life of the group are, in turn, internalised by the members and affect their individual acts' (1959: xiii).

A sociological understanding of music, then, may be approached through an examination of musical activities as collaborative interactions. It is this perspective which is developed in the work of Howard Becker.

Becker: art as collective action

For Howard Becker, the sociology of artistic work in general, and music in particular, must begin with two distinctive steps. Firstly, the notion of 'art' itself must be rendered problematic: all 'artistic' work involves the collaboration of a whole range of people, only some of whom are conventionally defined as 'artists'. Sociological interest, therefore, must focus on how and when the definition is successfully applied, and on its consequences, rather than assuming that 'art' is some sort of qualitatively distinct realm of activity (see pp. 13–14

above). It follows, secondly, that a sociological concern with the production of artworks will focus primarily on the more-or-less complex division of labour on which they depend. To do this it is
necessary to highlight the whole range of activities which are normally taken for granted as unproblematic, or simply the way things
are. Consider some of the things which are required in order that a
symphony orchestra can give a concert:

> instruments must have been invented, manufactured, and maintained, a
> notation must have been devised and music composed using that nota-
> tion, people must have learned to play the notated notes on the instru-
> ments, times and places for rehearsal must have been provided, ads for
> the concert must have been placed, publicity must have been arranged
> and tickets sold, and an audience capable of listening to and in some
> way understanding and responding to the performance must have been
> recruited. A similar list can be compiled for any of the performing arts.
> (Becker, 1982: 2)

Expressed in this way the routine staging of a concert begins to
appear sociologically interesting, and Becker has only hinted at complex matters such as the financing of the orchestra, the recruitment
of its players and the selection of its repertoire. What the concert
depends on, then, is an extensive and elaborate division of labour
among many people (often remote or taken for granted), of whom
some few may be conventionally designated as 'artists'. This distinction, however, like all the other ways in which tasks are divided up
and assigned to people, is essentially arbitrary, in the sense that it is
sustained only by convention. Yet in practice it is extremely difficult
for any individual or group to change these conventions, since they
constitute the working parameters of all those engaged in a given
arena of cultural production, or what Becker more succinctly calls
an 'art world'. There are a number of important sociological implications of Becker's argument, but in the present context the most
salient of these is the way in which his perspective dissolves the distinction between the artwork and its social context: the latter is no
longer to be seen as the external environment *within* which the
former is produced. On the contrary, by viewing artistic work as
'collective action' it becomes possible to understand how the works
themselves are shaped by the opportunities, conventions and constraints which present themselves in any given 'art world' at a par-

ticular time. It is therefore well worth looking at Becker's discussion more closely.

As we have seen, Becker's starting point is the observation that the production of all artworks depends on the collaboration of a number of people, only some of whom are, by convention, regarded as 'artists'; each work, therefore, presupposes an elaborate division of labour among various individuals and groups. This pattern of social organisation – the specific way in which the work is divided up – is not, however, determined by the nature of the activity. There are, after all, any number of ways in which sounds can be organised as 'music' and 'performed' as such. But in any particular social context, a combination of factors – technological, economic, ideological, aesthetic and so on – will lead to the establishment of a normal, accepted way of getting things done. The standard symphony orchestra and its performance conventions were established in Europe in the early part of the nineteenth century, for example, whereas the orthodox rock band dates from the 1960s. Neither was a necessary or inevitable development, but the outcome of a particular constellation of economic, social and technological influences in which certain individuals' activities flourished, while others did not. However, while the particular form of the division of labour in an art world may be contingent, Becker's contention is that, once established, its inherent conventions and constraints will have important consequences. In general, it must be understood as a social order in which, like any social order, established normative patterns and institutions confront people as the normal, appropriate and proper way of doing things.

There are echoes here of Marx's classic discussion of alienation as the process through which the ideas and cultural patterns which human beings create come to acquire an apparently independent existence, and indeed to dominate their erstwhile creators. A later German theorist, Georg Simmel, saw the process as inevitable, but – unlike Marx – could not envisage a human society in which people could ever escape from the 'tragedy of culture'. Becker's point is more specific: in normal social life, people must orient themselves to accepted norms and institutional patterns, whatever these are and however they have been arrived at. Thus within art worlds, as we have seen, there is considerable variability in the way in which the definition of 'artist' is bestowed, and there is an inevitable growth of groups of specialists who are not themselves considered as 'artists' but on whom the 'artists' are dependent. It is equally inevitable that, from their particular and disparate positions within the overall division of labour, such specialists will not necessarily share the perspectives, goals or interests of the 'artists'. Faulkner's studies of orchestral musicians provide some useful examples of the possible consequences: players may well be 'more concerned with how they sound in performance than with the success of a particular work; with good reason, for their own success depends in part on impressing those who hire them with their competence' (Becker, 1974: 769; Faulkner 1973a, 1973b). In general, there are various ways in which the 'career interests' of the musicians may lie 'at cross-purposes to the composer's'.

The central idea, then, is that the realisation of an artwork involves establishing a working relationship (however fragile) among what are often quite large numbers of specialists, and an orientation to the conventions which have come to be the basis of their activities. It is these conventions, normally taken for granted, which are, as we have seen, the 'commonsense' principles which people have to take account of if they are to act effectively in the social order. Conventions can range from general fundamental principles, such as the use of the diatonic scale, to the smallest details of dress or demeanour, and it should be emphasised, as by Becker, that through them we can understand not only the production but also the reception of music:

> By using such conventional organisation of tones as a scale, the composer can create and manipulate the listener's expectations as to what sounds will follow. He can then delay and frustrate the satisfaction of these expectations, generating tension and release as the expectation is ultimately satisfied. ... Only because artist and audience share knowledge of and experience with the conventions invoked does the art work produce an emotional effect. (Becker, 1974: 771)

Becker's sociological perspective, then, leads to a position similar to that outlined at the conclusion of Chapter 2, where it was argued that to experience music as meaningful depends on membership of a cultural community in which customary practices concerned with the production and performance, and normally accepted modes of representation – in a word, conventions – have been established.

We will return to the idea of cultural communities below, in considering the nature of musical communication; before that, though, it is important to clarify some of the implications of Becker's perspective, if only to subvert certain common misconceptions. Firstly, while the notion of conventions is valuable as a means of highlighting the normal procedures and often tacit organisational premises which underlie any social order, this is not to claim that the actions of individuals are determined by conventions. Rather, what is being asserted is that people must, inevitably, orient their conduct towards accepted practices. For most of the time and for most people this does involve an acceptance of them: the conventions – both social and specifically musical – which surround an orchestral concert in the western tradition are almost universally upheld, even down to the elaborate rituals concerning just when and how the audience should show its appreciation. By definition, conventions are generally observed; if they were not, social order would be impossible. Yet, exceptionally, some individuals may choose to reject them, particularly, as Becker notes, in the contexts of 'art worlds' where a high value is placed on individual self-expression. The composer Harry Partch chose to work with an octave divided into forty-two microtones: for his work to be performed, new instruments had to be invented and built, people trained to play them and so on (Becker, 1974: 772). Similarly, Charles Ives wrote music which, at the time, was outside the normal competence of orchestral players and so was not performed; Ives's response was to abandon the remaining constraints and conventions which governed normal compositional practice, and to compose exactly as he wanted, freed from the obligation of taking into account its preformability (1974: 773). Such cases illustrate the way in which individuals may opt to reject existing conventions (though rarely all of them); they must, however, then pay the price, since rejections usually entail a situation which 'increases the artist's trouble and decreases the circulation of his work' (1994: 773). Indeed, the price of an all-out attack on artistic conventions is so high that few are prepared to pay it: rapid obscurity is the fate of most radical innovators, accompanied (if they are even recognised by those already established) by accusations of incompetence, mendacity, mental instability, publicity-seeking and so on. The point is clear: people can, in theory, choose to abandon the established conventions, but the costs are so great that few do, thus further strengthening the authority of normal procedures. The situation also illustrates the way in which established norms come to acquire a certain aura, a generally accepted feeling that they are right and proper, and that those who challenge them must be mad, or bad, or both.

The theme is explored extensively in the sociology of deviant behaviour: as Becker puts it, an attack 'on convention and an aesthetic is also an attack on a morality' (1974: 773–4).

While theoretically possible, then, wholesale rejection of conventions is rare. What is more frequent, and much more theoretically significant, is the situation in which individuals' orientations to established conventions do not take the form of outright rejection but are concerned with innovations of various kinds. The pursuit of profit, or fame, or careers or artistic vision, and the effects of new technologies are, among others, all sources of instability which may threaten the conventional status quo. Indeed, a process of gradual, incremental change is a normal part of social life. From time to time, however, more fundamental challenges emerge, with effects not unlike those engendered by new political ideologies or scientific theories (1974: 773). As we have seen, the innovative work of Arnold Schoenberg generated 'an enmity, even a hatred, almost unparalleled in the history of music' (Rosen, 1976: 9). The young pioneers of modern jazz attracted bitter condemnation in the American jazz community of the 1940s, not least from white critics and established musicians whose own authority was perceived to be under threat. A few years later, it was the bebop orthodoxy which was itself under attack from the 'free jazz' of Ornette Coleman, whose crednetials and competence were, once again, questioned by those whose commitments were to the now-conventional modern jazz. And in the late 1970s the 'punk' rebellion was understood by many as a deliberate rejection of, and challenge to, some of the otiose conventions which had become established in the popular music business (Middles, 1993, 49–50).

Howard Becker's account of art as 'collective action', then, draws on and regenerates a more general model of the social order – not as an external social structure (for such a view is considered metaphysical) but as the outcome of the actions of individuals and groups as they seek to pursue their interests and accomplish their projects within specific institutional contexts. Social institutions, in this sense, may themselves be understood as complexes of conventions which have become established and accepted as legitimate; none the less, they are sustained only by the constant actions and interactions of real individuals as they conduct themselves, whether voluntarily or under some sort of compulsion, in appropriate ways. In view of the persistent misunderstanding of the interactionist perspective, it is worth emphasising once again that this view does *not* entail the neglect of power and conflict in social life. As Becker puts it, a pattern of conventions is also an 'arrangement of ranked statuses, a stratification system' (1974: 774). Those who accept the dominant conventions, and become expert in their practice, may enjoy careers which bring them financial rewards, esteem and a measure of security; those who do not, as we have seen, may be marginalised or stigmatised. What is at stake is the power of some groups to impose authoritative definitions on others, to accumulate the resources with which to protect their positions and render them legitimate, and to resist challenges to their supremacy. Far from neglecting power, this perspective has a central concern with the ways in which some people are able to impose their definitions of the situation on others; the whole social order, moreover, is taken to be the outcome of perpetual processes of challenge, competition and conflict:

> As conflicts and coalitions develop between minor worlds, so particular and overarching definitions change. Not all are equally important in the determination of that change: the power of different groups affects their ability to mould the emerging forms. Some definitions may be upheld by force, manipulation or structural intimidation. (Rock, 1979: 133)

As Gilmore (1990) has argued, the approach to the analysis of artistic production and consumption which has been developed out of the symbolic interactionist tradition, notably by Becker with the concept of 'art worlds' organised around particular conventions, has much to contribute to an understanding of social order in general terms. Firstly, by focusing on the ways in which institutionalised practices are generated, enacted and transformed, this perspective renders the whole debate over 'micro' and 'macro' levels of analysis irrelevant (1990: 174). Secondly, it has led to a necessary reformulation of the concept of 'social structure', in which this is seen no longer as some sort of framework existing independently of social life but as a metaphor for the ever-changing, yet durable, pattern of relationships among individuals and groups; more graphically, it is a 'snapshot' of the situation at any given moment. The essential point is that this pattern or 'structure' is not the cause of people's activities, but rather their outcome. Thirdly, the 'social worlds' perspective, again as Gilmore shows, is in no way incompatible with a recognition of the centrality of power and coercion in shaping the social order. All individuals and groups are, inevitably, caught up in the perpetual struggle for advantage which is the normal condition of society; it does not follow, therefore, that all have equal access to the resources necessary for success. Indeed, much of the struggle is specifically about the defence of such resources, or the attempt to acquire them. Money, political power, fame, symbolic or professional authority and so on are the sorts of things that people compete for, even though the actual distribution of them is highly unequal. Thus, again as Gilmore suggests, the 'social worlds' perspective is not in any fundamental way incompatible with approaches which have sought to explain artistic production and organisation in terms of social class (1990: 170–1). It would be naive to deny the importance of economic factors in this context; what the 'art world' approach implies, however, is that the social organisation in question is unlikely to be explained entirely in class terms. Above all, and in keeping with its interactionist origins, this approach takes these matters as questions to be answered empirically rather than by *a priori* theorising.

There are many examples of ways in which the unequal distribution of resources, the pursuit of interests by particular groups and indeed the proselytising activities of certain individuals have led to the stratification of musical activities in modern industrial societies; some of these will be considered in the following chapter. Perhaps the most spectacular example is the case of so-called 'classical' music (a useful marketing concept, if ever there was one, which has now come to include all sorts of composed works, including opera). In Britain, this music attracts by far the largest amounts of public subsidy and private sponsorship, in comparison with other musical styles; indeed it could not survive without them. As this suggests, of course, 'classical' music can hardly be considered to be the music of 'the people'. Yet, as we have seen, this is the music which is considered by arts authorities, critics, academics, the media, even politicians, as central to the cultural tradition, as 'serious' and legitimate. (By implication, other forms are not.) Despite some recent reforms around the margins, the whole system of academic music teaching is organised around the values and assumptions of the 'classical' tradition. University departments and prestigious colleges describe what they do as 'music', as if no other sort existed; the same applies to 'quality' newspapers, which often (in so far as they deal with them at all) distinguish between such genres as 'rock', 'country', 'folk', 'jazz', etc. – and 'music'.

From a sociological point of view, and particularly from an 'art worlds' perspective, such a situation is both interesting and problematic. How did this musical tradition (in so far as it is a coherent tradition) come to occupy its culturally predominant position, given that is not, and never was, the preferred music of most people and that its origins – certainly as far as people in Britain and North America are concerned – are both historically and geographically remote. (One outspoken British politician – but only one – has faced the wrath of the cultural establishment by wondering publicly why his taxes should be used to pay for the singing of some 'fat Italians'.) From a sociological angle, this dominant musical tradition cannot be explained as representing the 'core' of the culture or the 'soul' of the people; what it does reflect, however, is the musical taste of certain groups who have occupied dominant positions in society and thus been in a position to establish and legitimise their music through their privileged access to financial, political and symbolic resources.

In the next chapter we will consider some studies of the links between the social stratification of capitalist societies, and the formation of a hierarchy of musical styles within them. For the present, the point to be emphasised is that Becker's 'art worlds' approach to the sociology of music does in fact offer a useful analytic framework within which to examine questions of power and stratification, and as such it is not at all inconsistent with the work of those who have focused on the issue of social class. Indeed, an 'art worlds' perspective is in certain respects more theoretically satisfactory: capable, as I have suggested, of taking account of the effects of economic factors but also able to accommodate non-economic influences on the processes through which cultural patterns and institutional forms are created. It is thus free of the difficulties encountered by 'reflection' theories which see art (and all cultural forms) as representations of underlying structural patterns, such as class divisions. It is true, for example, that there is a relationship between social class and the hierarchy of musical styles, but this does not mean that the latter is determined by the former. The 'art worlds' approach, then, is in many ways consistent with the work of those researchers in the general field of cultural studies who have, following Gramsci, emphasised that the 'cultural field' is above all characterised by 'vigorous and dynamic struggle'. The hegemony of an ideology, that is, is not imposed from above but must be won by the consent of those who are socially subordinate. 'Cultural domination is the product of complex negotiations and alignments of interest' (Turner, 1990: 67). Such a view sees dominant cultural forms as perpetually contested, and there is now a flourishing tradition of studies which have examined ways in which elements of the 'dominant' ideology are challenged, resisted or appropriated for other, more subversive purposes (e.g. Hall and Jefferson, eds, 1976). In their emphasis on contest, contingency and indeterminacy, then, the cultural studies researchers have begun to converge with the interactionist tradition as developed by Becker and his colleagues; the coincidence of ideas is explicit in their recognition that meaning is not inherent in a text or an activity but generated through social practices (Turner, 1992: 112). (For discussions of the affinities between symbolic interactionism and cultural studies, see Becker and McCall, eds, 1990, and Denzin, 1992.)

In the sphere of music, then, the established – hegemonic – tradition of the classical styles neither springs spontaneously from the mass of the people nor is authoritatively imposed by a dominant class. Its institutional pre-eminence depends on state and private sponsorship, which must be won, and its legitimacy constantly reasserted by the media and in the schools. It must be presented as 'great' and 'timeless', and to do this it must be detached from its social origins and perceived as autonomous: 'In this way the collective definition of what counts as music appears not to be a social historical development, but a spontaneous result of music's inherent materials themselves' (Green, 1988: 101).

Such ideological work, though, is only partially successful: as we have seen, despite the experience of schooling most people fail to develop any deep or active attachment to 'classical' music. On the other hand, what is perhaps more important is that even the most disinterested and unmoved have been taught what 'proper' music is. A general acceptance of such definitions is likely to lead to a similar acceptance of the cultural status quo – thus the consent of the majority has been achieved at the same time as their personal experiences have been devalued. Moreover, if a person wishes to be considered as 'educated' or 'cultured', then he or she must learn to like 'the classics': as Bourdieu puts it, 'nothing more clearly affirms one's 'class', nothing more infallibly classifies, than tastes in music' (1984: 18).

As with the social order in general, then, the institutional and cultural patterns which develop within and between 'art worlds' are the outcome of a perpetual struggle among groups and individuals, all seeking to further their interests or defend their advantages against the challenges of others. It is, as I have emphasised, not a game with evenly matched players but a massively unequal contest; none the less, as in other spheres, the pattern of stratification in the music world does change, as some groups' resources – economic, political and cultural – are augmented while others' are diminished. Certain forms of rock music, for example, are now considered worthy of extended attention in the arts pages of 'quality' newspapers – partly, one suspects, because record companies will buy considerable amounts of expensive advertising space but partly too because many of those who grew up with the music in the 1960s and 1970s have now attained positions of editorial influence in the media. Similarly jazz, once considered a 'filthy product of modernity' by Lord Reith of the BBC, is now included among 'serious' music broadcasts and considered worthy of some public subsidy. This only happened, however, as a result of lengthy periods of proselytising and political campaigning by committed individuals and groups, gradually winning concessions from a generally hostile cultural establishment. Such gains, however, are small and insecure, while other styles – 'folk' and other ethnic musics, for example – have made virtually no progress at all.

The stratification of musical styles, then, is generated, sustained and challenged by the activity of interested parties, among whom critics and theorists – like Adorno – attempt to provide ideological justifications for the promotion of their favoured works, composers or performers, and there is little doubt that their opinions can have considerable effects. The ability of some influential critics to influence the fate of Broadway shows is legendary, but the general effect of critics' activities is less spectacular and more diffuse: indicating what is to be taken seriously (and by implication what is not), offering characterisations of works, providing positive or negative assessments and developing aesthetic theories. In all these ways critical writings establish and sustain a meaningful context of interpretation for any particular performance or work. They provide explicit formulation of the conventions which, they believe, ought to govern specific performances, and give listeners a way of hearing, or – to use the terms which we will encounter below in considering Alfred Schütz – a set of 'background expectancies' which we may use to order our experience. Similar points might be made about the effects of being taught about music in formal educational contexts, or perhaps in a 'music appreciation' class. It is important to emphasise that none of this is to suggest that concert-goers, record-buyers or music students will necessarily accept the definitions or verdicts of the critic or the teacher.

Yet the effect of the latters' activities may nevertheless be considerable. As I have suggested, the listener has been provided with a *possible* way of hearing the music, and one, moreover, which claims to be authoritative. Indeed, even in cases of vehement disagreement – a rejection of the teacher's judgement, for example, or a dispute between critics – there is a simultaneous affirmation of the social relationship which links the protagonists. It is agreed, for example, that the music's meaning or value is worth arguing about: indeed, such things matter so much to people that the debates can be intense. It is also the case that to participate in the debate is to share a cultural world – to hold in common assumptions about the nature of music and the concepts with which it can be understood. It is for this reason that Kingsbury has argued that 'musicological discourse is not simply talking and writing 'about music', but is also constitutive of music' (1991: 201). Talk about music conventionally involves the extensive use of 'spatial-architectural imagery' (1991: 196) – terms such as structure, progression, return, bridge – and other metaphorical devices: the composition as an organic whole, the relation between major and minor as gendered, and so on. Yet through extensive usage, and especially as the student in inducted to the conventional ways of the academy, the element of metaphor tends to disappear, and the community of musicology is one in which 'musicians and music theorists ... over time and through continual interaction in terms of these conceptualisations, have come to experience these images not as metaphors but as actual references to the essential phenomena: the 'actual' structure, the 'actual' material of the composition 'itself' (1991: 205). It is these terms, as Schütz would put it, that constitute the 'taken for granted' realities of the social world of the musicologists, and in talking about music, whether affirming or negating conventional interpretations, they are implicitly confirming and enacting their membership of a particular 'art world'. 'What lies at the core of musicological interpretation', writes Kingsbury, 'is not an attachment to any one tropological image – be it organicist, spatial-architectural, or Kaluli waterfalls – but rather an attachment to a fundamental sociological concern, namely the negotiated maintenance of an interpretive community' (1991:211).

It is thus that the social world of the musicologists is created and sustained. It is a community which claims to speak legitimately and authoritatively about music, and in doing so makes its contribution to the stratification of musical styles which is characteristic of industrial societies. By contrast, outside the formal world of the musicologists are the rock critics, who mostly lack institutional recognition and the coherent social network which goes with it: those who chronicle and champion the iconoclastic fervour of successive waves of young rock bands are unlikely to win the respect or gratitude of the musical, or political, establishment. Yet in important respects the work of the rock critics performs similar functions to that of their classical counterparts. Just as the latter, for example, provide symbolic legitimation for the established hierarchy of musical styles, and thus the cultural superiority of dominant social groups, so the rock critics add value to the products of the music industry, and thus promote its economic health. This seems to hold regardless of whether their writings are hostile or not: as the old show-business adage has it, 'there's no such thing as bad publicity'. In the present context, the crucial word is 'publicity' – drawing attention to music and musicians whom they consider to be worthy of attention, and offering a prospective interpretation – a way of hearing – the sounds in question. As in the 'classical' world of the musicologists, too, the rock writers are highly differentiated in their interests and judgements, yet their discourse has the effect of constituting an 'interpretive community'. Moreover, despite the undoubted depth of their aesthetic and personal commitments to their music, rock writers have only rarely challenged the established hierarchy of styles. Beethoven, it seems, has yet to be rolled over.

The work of writers, critics and theorists, then, must be seen as an integral part of the process through which their various 'art worlds' are constantly reconstituted. Other significant actors in these worlds may play parts similar to those described by Becker, in another context, as 'moral entrepreneurs' – those crusading reformers who seek the enactment and enforcement of new rules (1963: 147). They are, in other words, active in pursuit of causes, which they often justify in terms of fundamental ethical, religious or political principles. In the context of music 'worlds', of course, such 'moral entrepreneurs' are much less likely to be concerned with the establishment of laws or formal rules – though they may be, in influencing educational curricula, for example, or in seeking to have certain records 'banned' from the airwaves. More often, though, they

are those who make it their business to promote the status and reputation of a particular artist or musical genre. An outstanding
example of such a 'moral entrepreneur' in the music field is provided
by the career of Cecil Sharp, the autocratic early leader of the English folk music revival, who sought to regenerate the national culture
through revitalising the traditional music of 'the folk'. In doing so,
he not only invented much of the 'tradition' but had considerable
success in getting folk song and dance accepted as part of the school
curriculum, in influencing the thought of dominant intellectual and
political figures, and in shaping the subsequent movement for the
revival of 'folk ' traditions (Boyes, 1993).

The concerns of other 'moral entrepreneurs' may be more specific.
Many leading performers and composers owe their success to the
efforts of other individuals who have effectively proselytised on their
behalf. Around the time that Cecil Sharp was galvanising the folk
music movement, Edward Elgar was becoming accepted as a major
English composer, partly through the efforts of his wife, who
changed him from a humble music teacher who also served in the
family shop to an 'English gentleman'. 'Elgar's career as a serious
composer', writes Meirion Hughes, 'dates from this transformation'
(1989: 43). Even more crucial was the securing of royal patronage
through the activities of Sir Walter Parratt, Master of the Queen's
Music, who regularly ensured that Elgar's music was brought to the
attention of Queen Victoria and her court. 'Although Elgar's emergence may have been in different ways influenced by accidental contingencies, it was also shaped by human agency' (1989: 58). The
career, and posthumous reputation, of another contemporary, Frederick Delius, supplies a further illustration of the ways in which
'human agency' is involved in the selective interpretation and
redefinition of musical works. It was the conductor Sir Thomas
Beecham, on the occasion of Delius's reburial in rural England (he
had lived and died in France), who described Delius's music as
'extraordinarily redolent of the soil of this country and characteristic of the finer elements of the national spirit' (quoted in Stradling,
1989: 70). Yet Delius's origins were in industrial Bradford, rather
than the countryside. He received his musical training in Germany,
and chose to live in France. His 'English' works, argues Stradling,
were a deliberate stylistic departure 'aimed at the English market'
(1989: 90). Despite some success in England (though rather more in
Germany), Delius was widely ignored in Britain during his lifetime.

Once again, it is the work of the 'moral entrepreneurs' who have cleaned up Delius's image and restored his reputation: 'Without his contemporary English supporters, a smallish group of subsequent English advocates, and a fairly select English audience, so far from being a 'great universal' Delius would at best be a minor cult figure, and at worst have been completely forgotten' (1989: 88). The overall shape or pattern of an 'art world', then, must be understood as the outcome of the activities of all these, and other, individuals and groups, rather than as a simple reflection of the inherent qualities of performers or works.

Alongside the moral or cultural entrepreneurs, too, are those whose motives are primarily economic. Indeed, it is often difficult in practice to make a clear distinction between them: those who have a financial interest in a style, or an artist, for example, may genuinely believe in the aesthetic value of the music. After all, most professionals in the particular 'art world' – probably the majority – were drawn to it in the first place by their enthusiasm for music itself. Once involved, however, individuals' artistic inclinations and aesthetic priorities must be reconciled with the demands of earning a living, and some of the consequences of this will be considered below (pp. 205–15). The point of immediate relevance is that economic interests and aesthetic criteria cannot, in the real world, be so easily separated as some critics assume (indeed, the belief that they can is itself the product of a particular artistic ideology). A critic's appraisal of a performance, for example, in so far as it is influential within the art world in question, will inescapably have economic consequences – affecting the decisions of potential listeners about whether to buy concert tickets or recordings, for example, and so affecting, in turn, the potential income of performers, composers, agents, promoters, record companies and so on. (Musicians' frequent mistrust of critics often stems from the belief that these practical considerations, and their serious consequences, are often neglected by the critics; the issue has the potential to generate considerable conflict within the art world.) Other significant figures in the art world are those whose doings are more unequivocally motivated by the prospect of financial reward: as a business, music is a high-risk activity, but the constant prospect of enormous profits for a few people effectively encourages the others.

The theme of music as a commercial activity will be considered more in the following chapter. In this section I have raised some of

the issues arising from Howard Becker's discussion of social organisation as 'collective action', and from his characterisation of 'art
worlds' as arenas in which participants develop commitments and
pursue interests. I have suggested that this perspective can be
deployed so as to show how regularly recurring patterns of action,
institutionalised power differentials and inequalities of wealth and of
prestige can all emerge as a consequence of interactions amongst
individuals. The perspective, then, is not only capable of compre-
hending issues of power and conflict but implies that analysis should
focus on them. What the perspective opposes are theories which take
artworks to be the reflections or embodiments of some underlying
social structure. Instead, cultural products are seen as the outcome
of collaborative action among individuals, who must, however,
orient themselves to the established conventions of a given 'art
world', and respond to the constraints which these inevitably entail.

Conventions and constraints

As we have seen, Becker's analysis of 'art worlds' and artistic
activities as 'collective action' lead him to viewing such activity in
terms of 'conventions'. As in every other area of social life, people
do not participate in such art worlds as innocent individuals; rather,
to get things done 'they rely on earlier agreements now become customary, agreements that have become part of the conventional way
of doing things in that art' (1982: 29). In music, for example, such
conventions range from the most general – such as the taken-for-
granted convention of the diatonic scale – to particular details of the
sorts of sounds which are, again by convention, accepted as appropriate to performances within various 'styles'. Other matters are also
settled by convention – the conduct and dress of performers and their
audience, for example, or the ways in which the latter may show
their appreciation (or lack of it). By such means both performers and
listeners, once socialised into the conventional ways, are able to
orient their conduct with, normally, a minimum of stress and uncertainty: the social world which confronts participants appears to them
as normal, organised and unproblematic. Indeed, Becker argues that
much of the response to artistic work may be understood as arising
from the artist's ability to manipulate the taken-for-granted expectations of the intended audience: often, for example, arousing an
expectation and then creating tension by delaying its eventual satis-

faction. 'Only because artist and audience share knowledge of and experience with the conventions invoked does the artwork produce an emotional effect' (1982: 30). We will return to this point below.

Two further aspects of conventions are discussed by Becker, and it is these which will concern us in the present section. Firstly, the simple but important point that conventions 'make possible the easy and efficient coordination among artists and support personnel' (1982: 30). In the present context, the point to be emphasised is that the necessary orientation to the established conventions itself has implications for the nature of the 'artistic' work which is done: such work cannot simply be separated from the social circumstances of its production. Secondly, and following on from this, it is clear that the acceptance of conventions inevitably involves the acceptance of specific constraints on what can be done, and how it is done.

These points may be exemplified by considering the production of music in two different contexts – the concert world studied by Samuel Gilmore, and the improvising jazz group. Gilmore makes a useful and basic distinction between what he terms 'schools of activity' and 'schools of thought' (1988: 206). The latter are the 'schools' to which artists are assigned by critics, theorists and historians, based on the supposed similarity of their works, but which need not have any existence as actual social groups. The former, with which Gilmore is mainly concerned, are real social groups, in the sense that they are constituted by the actual participants in an art world as they develop and sustain the 'common practices' which make possible an effective division of labour among 'interdependent specialists'. 'Collaborators identify these practices through interaction and exchange, and maintain them in the form of a convention' (1988: 207). Gilmore's extensive programme of interviews with composers and performers, all involved in the production of classical music concerts, suggests that 'artistic identities formed through schools of activity play an essential role in organising concert collaboration' (1988: 208). Whereas the 'schools of thought' identified by critics and theorists were often irrelevant to the actual working practices of the musicians, most composers and performers operated with a particular 'school of activity' which acted as a 'reference group' for the process of artistic decision-making (1988: 209). A 'reference group' consists of those others whose responses an individual considers significant, and who will therefore be taken into account – in interaction or in imagination – when a course of action is being formulated (see Shibutani, 1962: 132). On this basis Gilmore was able to identify three 'relatively distinct' subworlds within the classical concert scene in New York, each representing an alternative school of activity and each exhibiting a distinct set of conventions. It is to one or other of these subworlds that actual or potential participants in this art world have to order their activities.

'Each subworld', writes Gilmore, 'is a wholly encompassed organisation of musical activities with a relatively distinct identity' (1988: 210), and each is concerned with distinctly different sorts of 'musical practices'. The largest, and most visible, of these is the 'Midtown' concert organisation, dominated by performers – some of them very well known – who play pieces mostly from the standard repertory of pre-twentieth-century works, in some of the world's most prestigious concert halls, and who attract by far the largest audiences. Inevitably, there are few opportunities for contemporary composers in this 'world', but their interests are expressed in either the 'Uptown' or academic subworld in which innovative compositions are performed, or the 'Downtown' world of the avant-garde, dedicated to 'radical aesthetic change and … pluralistic forms of cultural activity' (1988: 210). The 'Midtown' concert world is the most formally organised, in terms of the training and recruitment of players, hiring of soloists, promotion of performances and so on: this is possible because the requirements for playing works from the standard repertory, and the likely audience for them, are known in advance. It follows, too, that this concert subworld is primarily concerned with the *interpretation* of works which have already achieved canonic status, rather than the works themselves. In contrast, the aesthetic focus of the other two concert worlds is on composition itself, but they are differentiated by the ideological commitments of the leading figures, and by the degree of formalisation of activities. 'Uptown' composers are primarily academics, whose new works retain standard instruments and notation, and who orient themselves to various established theories of composition. 'Downtown', on the other hand, such matters as instrumentation, performer competence, even the definition of composition itself, are constantly open to challenge and debate; thus the socialisation of participants and the organisation of concerts is irregular and highly informal.

These 'schools of activity', Gilmore suggests, 'act as work reference groups circumscribing conventional orientations in the concert world', and as such 'association with different schools has real pragmatic and aesthetic consequences' (1988: 217). To be recognised as a participant in one or other of these 'worlds' – in other words, to be musically active as a performer or composer – it is necessary to orient oneself to its established conventions; in turn, as a whole tradition of symbolic interactionist studies have shown, conventional ways of doing things, and ways of thinking, are likely to become part of the normal, taken-for-granted perspective of the participating individuals. Thus different outlooks, aesthetic values, musical skills and performance preferences – in a word, identities – are systematically generated as a result of the social organisation of the artistic activities. Thus Gilmore points to the inadequacy of explanations of musical activities, and there are many of them, which focus 'exclusively on the individual', and which neglect the complex web of social relationships in which individual identities are formed and transformed (1988: 218). In the present case, for example, participation in the 'Uptown' and 'Downtown' worlds leads individuals to adopt contrasting musical values – the former committed to interpretation and technical virtuosity, the latter to innovation and radical challenge to established conventions. Indeed, the latter situation is one in which the idea of challenging conventions is itself a fundamental convention underlying the collaboration of musicians and the various projects they are involved in.

In some of his later work Gilmore has developed these ideas, particularly in respect of the standard concert repertory of works which, as we have seen, constitute the musical resources of the 'Midtown' subworld in New York. Indeed, it is widely acknowledged that certain works by a small number of European composers, mostly produced before 1900, have a virtual monopoly on 'classical' concert programming throughout the western world, and, increasingly, beyond it. Although the basis of a standard repertory only began to emerge in the mid-nineteenth century (1992: 7), the process was rapid: whereas it has been estimated that around 1820–5 less than a quarter of the pieces performed by the Leipzig Gewandhaus orchestra were by 'dead composers', during the period 1900–70 fifteen eighteenth-and nineteenth-century composers accounted for 'on average 59% of the orchestral repertory of twenty-seven major American symphony orchestras' (1992: 7–8). Thus the performance of new works is rare, and second and subsequent performances even rarer.

There are two 'standard explanations' for the dominance of this repertory, Gilmore suggests. One is consumer choice – people will buy tickets only for concert programmes that they want to hear, and the orchestras are not in a financial position to ignore them. The other explanation is based on the 'administrative rationality' of orchestral managers, and their constant efforts to keep costs down. Since the major costs of producing concerts are incurred in performers' fees and rehearsal time, managers attempt to minimise these by limiting rehearsal time; they are therefore led to favour 'conservative programming', since the preparation of new works for a concert takes far longer than rehearsing familiar ones. Gilmore accepts that elements of both explanations are important, but argues that they tend to neglect 'the influence of the artists themselves and the artistic community in which they operate' (1992: 3) on the programming process. Drawing on the opposition, mentioned earlier, between the interests of performers (in playing the standard repertoire) and composers (in securing premières of new pieces), Gilmore argues that there is a general coincidence of interests between the managers and the performers, who thus form a dominant coalition. Thus composers (and critics, who often write pleas for innovation and greater variety) are in a relatively weak and marginal position when programming decisions are made, whereas conductors – especially well-known ones – enjoy considerable authority. Though they may encourage a limited amount of innovation, they know that success with audiences usually depends on performing familiar works; moreover, traditional programmes provide opportunities for the display of 'virtuosic technical standards' and a focus 'on the interpretation of composition rather than the evaluation of composition per se' (1992: 17). In general, then, 'it is the alignment of performers' programming with organisational interests in the art world that had the most telling effect on the dominance of repertory' (1992: 15).

In the present context one of the most significant aspects of Gilmore's analysis of concert programming is the way in which he demonstrates how the social order of the art-world – a stable, orderly pattern – must itself be seen as the outcome of a struggle among a variety of groups whose interests may be divergent or indeed conflicting:

> There is a constant struggle in the concert world, as there is in all culture producing worlds, for social control over production resources among groups representing opposing interests. When one set of aesthetic interests gains inordinate control over the allocation of concert

resources and performance opportunities, the artistic character of that art world is altered. (1992: 5)

It is this last point which is of most general relevance: the character of the art world, and thus the art that gets produced, are seen from this perspective not as 'reflecting' the social order generally, nor as the result of the inspiration of isolated individuals, but as the work of people who must participate in, and orient themselves to, specific 'worlds' or, as Gilmore puts it, 'schools of activity'. His analysis shows how, in one situation, a coincidence of interests systematically works to the advantage of some participants, and against the interests of others; the result is that some sorts of music are heard, and often, while others are not. Moreover, the established repertory, by appearing to be a traditional canon of undisputed masterworks, gains in both authority and 'aura' as time goes by (and it is obviously in the interests of its protagonists for it to be legitimated as such). Simultaneously, the difficulties facing the composer of new works multiply, unless he or she manages to obtain an academic post, and beyond the immediate art world of 'classical' music concerts, other forms and styles of music are marginalised and devalued.

Insights derived from symbolic interactionism, then, and developed in Becker's view of art worlds, can be used to illuminate the fundamental processes which shape the production of music and other cultural activities. It is Becker's contention, moreover, that this perspective affords a valuable method of understanding cultural products themselves, or more specifically the processes through which they are created. The cultural products which come to be called 'art' are invariably the results of processes of decision-making by individuals – the moment-to-moment choices which composers, performers, painters, film-makers, photographers, dancers, authors and so on make in the course of their 'creative' work. Such choices, however, as our earlier discussion suggested, are normally made in the context of an already existing art world, and as such will be influenced or constrained by its conventions: western composers, for example, take for granted that that diatonic scale provides the means of organising tones, while musicians in all styles draw on an established canon or repertoire of music. The actions of artists, then, result from their 'acceptance of art world constraints and their internalised dialogue with the art world's other members' (1982: 198). In his use of the notion of an 'internalised dialogue', Becker is drawing

on the theoretical perspective developed by G. H. Mead. It is fundamental to Mead's view of social action that human beings, uniquely,
have the capacity to think reflexively – that is, to see ourselves from
'outside', so to speak, in the same way that we see other objects in
our environment. Through this capacity we are able, in our imagination, to 'step out' of ourselves and view ourselves and our conduct
as other people would see them; it is through this process, according
to Mead, that individuals take into account the values and expectations of others in the course of formulating their own actions. For
Mead, the process is both universal in social life, and of the utmost
significance:

> It is by means of reflexiveness – the turning back of the experience of
> the individual upon himself – that the whole social process is thus
> brought into the experience of the individuals involved in it; it is by
> such means, which enable the individual to take the attitude of the
> other towards himself, that the individual is able consciously to adjust
> himself to that process, and to modify the resultant of that process in
> any given social act in terms of his adjustment to it. Reflexiveness, then,
> is the essential condition, within the social process, for the development
> of mind'. (Mead, 1934: 134)

The process, in short, has come to be known as 'taking the role of
the other' and it is to this that Becker is referring when he talks of
artists having an 'internalised dialogue with the art world's other
members'. Artworks are the product of activities shaped by a constant process of decision-making, of innumerable choices through
which their creators imaginatively take account of the likely
responses of others. This does not imply that artists will simply conform to such expectations – on the contrary, they may consider their
whole purpose to be the challenging or subverting of established conventions. The basic point, however, is that, whether the intention is
to conform or rebel, the artist must know what the conventions are,
must take account of them and must be able, in imagination at least,
to know how others are likely to respond to this or that course of
action. Thus each decision about what to do – the 'editorial moment'
as Becker calls it – occurs in the context of a particular cultural
environment:

> During the editorial moment, then, all the elements of an art world
> come to bear on the mind of the person making the choice, who imag-
> ines the potential responses to what is being done and makes the next

choices accordingly. Multitudes of small decisions get made, in a continuous dialogue with the cooperative network that makes up the art
world in which the work is being made. (Becker, 1982: 201)

Through our ability to 'take the role of the other' and the consequent
'internal dialogue', Becker proposes, we can come to a rather more
satisfactory understanding of the processes of artistic creativity (and
cultural production generally) than that supplied by theories which
take cultural objects to be representations, reflections or expressions
of social 'structure'. As I have suggested, this perspective eliminates
the need to postulate, and then reify, the idea of 'society' or 'social
structure' as some sort of entity existing independently of real
people. Moreover, far from neglecting, or glossing over, the activity
of the individuals who produce and perform the 'works' which define
an area of artistic practice, Becker's approach focuses specifically on
them, seeking to show how the nature and form of such works is the
outcome of 'internal dialogues' in which 'social' and 'individual' elements are synthesised, and how stable patterns of social organisation
emerge from, and are enacted in, the actions and interactions of individuals. Far from neglecting social structure, power and conflict, the
perspective seeks to understand how these are achieved, and what
their consequences are (Gilmore, 1990: 173–4; Rock, 1979: 130–5).

    In conceiving of artistic work in terms of decision-making
sequences, however, it is possible to present an unduly rational picture of the social actor. This, of course, is not at all Becker's intention. While undoubtedly some of the creative work of 'artists'
involves difficult, even tortured, processes of deliberately choosing
among various ways in which to proceed, much of the work –
perhaps most of it – involves the application of routine, taken-for-
granted, normal ways of doing things which, although they might
well be justified and defended with some vigour if challenged, do not
involve conscious deliberation on each occasion of their use. The
point here is that, again as Mead argued, experience of participating
in a particular community will lead individuals to 'internalise' its
values and conventions, that is, to experience them as normal, natural, morally right, and indeed as part of one's own self. Such
assumptions and presuppositions thus pre-empt many potential decisions; this goes some way towards explaining the frequently
observed phenomenon of artists who are both skilled and creative
but find it difficult to describe or explain clearly just what it is that

they do. In every art world, says Becker, 'practitioners use words whose meanings they cannot define exactly which are nevertheless intelligible to all knowledgeable members of their world. Jazz musicians say that something does or does not "swing"; theatre people say that a scene 'works' or does not "work" ' (1982: 199). In both cases, socialisation in the art world has imbued the participants with a strong sense of how things ought to be; a sense which is not easily verbalised but which may be deeply felt – indeed protagonists in the inevitable aesthetic disputes which beset art worlds are notorious for the vehemence, even passion, with which they will defend their sense of artistic propriety.

Becker's view of art worlds organised around conventions, which participants have to take account of, may be illustrated by pursuing his example of the jazz musicians' criterion of 'swing' – ineffable but recognisable – as an important standard by which to judge the quality of a player or a performance. (In the words of Fats Waller, 'If you have to ask, lady, you ain't got it.') Jazz players, of course, do not form a single homogeneous community but are differentiated into numerous 'schools of activity' in which different ideas about the nature of 'swing', or indeed its importance, have become established. For a New Orleans traditional band to 'swing' it must do different things, musically speaking, to those required from a bebop quintet or a big band; in some more recent styles, 'swing' is not regarded as having any particular aesthetic importance. The crucial term here is 'style'. For present purposes, the essence of a style, in this and other forms of music, is not that which may be defined by the musicological analyst, or the historian, but the particular set of conventions and values which the participants in a particular musical 'world' orient themselves to. It is, above all, considerations of 'style' in this sense that guide the decision-making process through which the music is actually produced.

The situation of the improvising jazz musician, in fact, provides a useful example of the process in action. Unlike the orchestral player, or the musician employed to produce 'commercial' music, the jazz soloist's essential task is the creation of original ideas and their instantaneous performance. It is a difficult and demanding craft, both technically and intellectually, but even when players have overcome these obstacles they remain faced with the problem of *what* to play in the moment-to-moment flux of improvisation. Of course, the player's choices are strictly constrained – at least in accepted jazz

styles – by established conventions which govern what is rhythmically and harmonically permissible; playing 'wrong notes', or failing
to 'make the changes', or 'losing the place' are all instantly detectable
by experienced players, and are likely to lead to the offender's competence being questioned. But even rhythmically and harmonically
'correct' playing may not, as Becker points out, sound 'right'. As we
have seen, it may be judged as not 'swinging', or it may be melodi-
cally uninteresting, or recognised as assembled out of well-tried
clichés and devices, and so on. The musician must thus confront the
problem of playing in such a way as to be judged convincing and
interesting by those whom he or she considers a positive 'reference
group', that is, those whose judgement and opinions may be
regarded as worthy and authoritative. And sure enough, the literature on jazz is full of examples of players whose early ambition was
to sound 'like' one of the outstanding innovators; *or* to work out
something deliberately different. The trumpeter Rex Stewart, for
example, later to be a star in Duke Ellington's band, has recalled his
intense admiration for, and desire to imitate, Louis Armstrong (Stewart, 1991: 89). On the other hand, in a famous incident a few years
later, Lester Young was forced out of the Fletcher Henderson
Orchestra because he refused to copy the then-fashionable saxo-
phone style of Coleman Hawkins: 'I had in mind what I wanted to
play,' he explained, 'and I was going to play that way' (Büchmann-
Møller, 1990: 50).

In the present context, the essential point is that the 'style' adopted
or developed by a player is a matter of accepting or rejecting certain
known conventions: even in the heat of the creative moment, in mid-
solo flight, so to speak, the improviser must somehow select from
among all the confusing barrage of possibilities those which will
sound 'right'. It is this selection process, complex and rapid though
it is, that is guided by the 'internal dialogue' of which Becker speaks;
the player evaluates the alternatives from the standpoint of the likely
responses of imaginary others. Of course, the 'reference group', or
the 'significant other' need not be any real individuals, and are more
likely to be a sort of imaginary typification which, through time,
becomes a habitual guide to appropriate action. Thus the experienced player acquires a stock of useful and appropriate phrases
which are known to be effective within a particular stylistic context,
but which may not 'work' at all in others. Both New Orleans bands
and bebop groups, for example, play pieces based on twelve-bar

blues in certain familiar keys, but the sound and phrasing and harmonic choices of the players – in a word, their 'feel' – will be very different. To do otherwise would be to violate the stylistic conventions which make their collaboration possible.

Through his concepts of art worlds organised around conventions, and the internal dialogue which guides the action of participants, Becker has provided a framework for the analysis of music as social action which avoids the difficulties of 'structural' theories. It is also, it should be said, a perspective which appears far more consistent with the experience of real musicians. As with authors, composers sometimes talk of an imaginary (or real) person whom they are writing 'for', and whose anticipated responses they use as a guide at the 'editorial moment', as Becker puts it. Similarly, experienced performers – jazz musicians, concert soloists, rock guitarists, blues singers, orchestral conductors and so on – know what to do in order to elicit a response from their various audiences. What makes all this possible is what G. H. Mead called our capacity, as human beings, to 'take the role of the other'.

The preceding discussion has focused mainly on the ways in which, by being able to conduct an 'internal dialogue', musicians' work is shaped by the anticipated responses of others. Such a focus, of course, presupposes that both musician and hearer share a common cultural context; if they did not, the reactions of others would be impossible to judge. Both musician and hearer, then, may be said to inhabit a particular 'interpretive community' (Kingsbury, 1991: 211) and the focus on musical production must be supplemented with a brief consideration of its reception.

Music as communication

Music has often been likened to some sort of language, even described as a 'universal language', although – as we have seen – most attempts to specify what sort of language it is have been unsuccessful. This has resulted not so much from a misunderstanding of musical communication but from a profound failure to appreciate the nature of language itself (DeNora, 1986). As we saw in Chapter 2, words do not mean anything independently of the contexts of their use, nor can linguistic exchanges be understood as processes of 'encoding' and 'decoding' in which an active 'transmitter' sends clear 'messages' to a passive 'receiver': a sense of meaning is achieved, rather, through the collaborative work of individuals in interaction, and a sociological approach to musical meaning will have to focus on this joint interpretive activity rather than assuming that meanings are either inherent in the 'texts' or self-evident. The departure from traditional theories of language will be even more evident when the specific character of musical communication is confronted – that is, the way in which ideas or emotions seem to be conveyed by meaningful patterns of sounds which cannot adequately be grasped or described by means of ordinary language.

This is the starting-point for Alfred Schütz's notable essay on 'Making music together' (1971). Schütz was a philosopher and social theorist, much influenced by the phenomenology of Husserl, who was also devoted to music and an enthusiastic amateur player. 'Music', says Schütz, 'is a meaningful context which is not bound to a conceptual scheme' (1971: 159). However, it is precisely because the 'social interactions connected with the musical process' are meaningful yet 'not capable of being expressed in conceptual terms' that the study of such interactions, Schütz suggests, may prove to be illuminating for our understanding of social relationships more generally (1971: 159), since his central thesis is that such relationships are not, as is often supposed, founded on linguistic or other forms of communication. On the contrary, he wishes to argue that 'certain forms of social intercourse ... necessarily precede all communication', and in particular that the co-participants in any social interaction must establish what he terms a 'mutual tuning-in relationship' (1971: 161). The purpose of Schütz's analysis of musical communication, then, is to clarify and exemplify these ideas.

Schütz begins by offering some criticisms of an earlier discussion by the French sociologist Halbwachs. Musical ideas, Schütz argues, do not necessarily involve the intention of communication, as Halbwachs had suggested, nor do they depend on a system of notation. Moreover, even when notation is used as a guide to performances, it remains just that – a guide, not a set of explicit and exhaustive instructions, which must be interpreted on the basis of the general 'musical culture' already acquired by the performer. Even a highly skilled player who is an excellent 'sight-reader' will approach a new piece with a particular set of expectations about it; these are derived from what is accepted as typical of its style. It does not matter that some of these expectations may not be met: they provide a way of approaching the piece, a basis, as it were, on which to proceed.

Thus, 'the player's general preknowledge of its typicality becomes the scheme of reference for his interpretation of its particularity'; Schütz's point is that 'the bulk of musical knowledge – as of knowledge in general – is socially derived' (1971: 168). It is this general 'stock of knowledge' on which the performer draws in order to produce an intelligible version of a previously unseen piece, rather than attending to the notation alone. This background knowledge, however, provides only the basis for the relationship which Schütz wishes to examine: 'It is the grasping of the composer's musical thought and its interpretation by re-creation which stand in the center of the player's field of consciousness' (1971: 169).

The essence of Schütz's argument is that musical meaning arises out of performers' or listeners' ability to synchronise their own experience with that of the person or persons who created the music. Following the philosopher Bergson, Schütz makes a fundamental distinction between 'outer' time – external, 'clock' time, which is always passing at a regular rate and can be precisely measured – and 'inner' time, the realm of the subjective consciousness of the individual. As we know from experience, the two may seem inconsistent, as when we talk of time 'flying' or passing 'slowly'. The latter terms refer to our personal, 'inner' states; for Schütz, it is the achievement of a correspondence between these states of consciousness that creates the meaningful musical relationship between composer and listener:

> Although separated by hundreds of years, the latter participates with quasi-simultaneity in the former's stream of consciousness by performing with him step by step the ongoing articulation of his musical thought. The beholder, thus, is united with the composer by a time dimension common to both, which is nothing other than a derived form of the vivid present shared by the partners in a genuine face-to-face relation such as prevails between speaker and listener. (1971: 171–2)

This passage reveals some of the central elements of Schütz's perspective on music, which he defines as 'a meaningful arrangement of tones in inner time'; its occurrence in 'inner time', indeed, is 'the very form of existence of music' (1971: 170). Further, musical meaning is 'polythetic' – that is, it can be grasped only through a 'step by step' process. Unlike the meaning, for example, of a mathematical proof which can be expressed concisely and precisely in a theorem, or a whole argument summarised neatly in a conclusion, musical meaning can unfold only gradually, when the listener is immersed in 'the ongoing flux of the musical process'. Meaningful musical communication thus cannot be condensed – it becomes possible only when the stream of consciousness lived through by the listener corresponds to that of the composer, by re-creating it; for Schütz the fundamental point, and the thesis of his essay, is that the establishment of such a 'vivid present', when the subjectivities of two or more people are bought into alignment through being synchronised, is the basis of all human communication:

> this sharing of the other's flux of experiences in inner time, this living through a vivid present in common, constitutes ...the mutual tuning-in relationship, the experience of the 'We', which is at the foundation of all possible communication. (1971: 173)

For Schütz, then, making music together is only a special case – albeit an important and illuminating one – of the 'tuning-in' process that must occur for any kind of organised human communication to take place; as such his essay on music relates directly to his general, and fundamental, concern with the 'intersubjective lifeworld' as the paramount social reality (Anderson *et al.*, 1986: 91).

The general and profound implications of Schütz's work for the methodology of the social sciences cannot be pursued here; in another essay, however, he applied his analytic methods specifically to Mozart's operatic works, suggesting – as we might expect – that the composer's great achievement was to fashion his music so that 'a simultaneity between the stream of consciousness of the persons on the stage and that of the beholder is established' (1971: 198). Not only that, but Mozart is able to use the unique polyphonic resources of western music (1971: 173) to bring out in his ensemble passages the *different* perspectives and reactions of the various characters even as they are 'bound together in [the] intersubjective situation of a community, in a We'. In doing this so brilliantly, says Schütz, Mozart was 'one of the greatest philosophical minds that ever lived', his main theme nothing less than 'the metaphysical mystery of the existence of a human universe of pure sociality' (1971: 199).

It will be apparent that in this insistence that musical meaning depends on experience of, and participation in, a particular cultural community, and the consequent acquisition of a 'stock of knowledge' which enables people to 'make sense' of the sounds they hear, Schütz's analysis is consistent with that of Becker. In the latter's

terms, it is people's socially acquired knowledge and experience of
the operative conventions which enable artists to produce an 'emotional effect' in their audiences (Becker, 1974: 771). As we have seen,
this emphasis on the fact that musical knowledge is socially derived,
transmitted and approved (Schütz, 1971: 168) is a useful and necessary corrective to the ideas that musical meaning is either inherent in
the sounds or somehow 'given' in the constitution of the human
mind. Yet Schütz's account makes clear that this 'background'
knowledge, which furnishes schemes of interpretation, provides only
the 'setting' for 'the main social relationship' (1971: 169) in which
the subjectivities of the composer and listener become mutually
'tuned-in', and in this respect his discussion of musical communication has been viewed as problematic. For Tim Costelloe (1992),
Schütz's account resonantes with our everyday experience of music,
and rightly emphasises the social basis of musical knowledge, but in
an important sense does not pursue the implications of a sociological approach:

> although Schütz feels the need to provide a general criterion in terms of
> which musical intelligibility can be accounted for, he does not feel the
> same need when it comes to individual participants who move inten-
> tionally into the finite province of musical meaning. When we move
> from outer to inner time in other words, when the grasping of meaning
> becomes a purely subjective as opposed to a public matter, then the
> social character of music seems to disappear. (1992: 20)

In treating time as though it really had outer and inner dimensions,
Costelloe argues, Schütz is conflating the metaphorical with the real,
and thus reifying it: individual consciousness is not to be conceived
of as a 'subjective and private' space in which supposed 'mental'
phenomena hold sway. If musical knowledge is fundamentally social,
then so are musical understanding, appreciation and meaning:

> The only meaningful way to say this is to accept that these concepts are
> used contextually or descriptively; or to be more precise, they are terms
> of evaluation. The alternative to this is to regard them as 'things', a
> course which ... is based on and produces ... fallacious reasoning.
> (1992)

Moreover, if these concepts really did describe purely internal phenomena, then 'there could be no criteria for saying of oneself or others
that they have understood a piece of music, or appreciated it, or that
they have grasped its meaning', since 'there would be no standards

governing the use of the concepts 'understanding', 'appreciation', 'grasping meaning' (1992: 21–2).

As with the outer-inner time dichotomy, Costelloe detects reification in Schütz's notion of meaning. It is not something 'there', in the music, waiting to be 'grasped', as Schütz sometimes seems to imply (e.g. 1971: 174):

> To say something has meaning, or is meaningful is to employ the concept for specific reasons and under certain circumstances. To talk of 'meaning' in a generic sense is to talk of nothing in particular, and is certainly not to identify an object of any kind, or to characterise an inherent property. (Costelloe, 1992: 26)

Whereas Schütz's work echoes the themes of Husserl and Bergson, Costelloe's argument draws on the linguistic philosophy of the later Wittgenstein, and its 'documentation of the constitutive power of natural language' (1992: 1). The fact that we talk about musical and other experiences in terms of 'inner' and 'outer' time, or refer to them as 'meaningful' in various ways, does not mean that these terms refer to real phenomena or processes in the world; rather, these are some of the ways in which we can talk about such matters, and as such are not descriptive, but *constitutive* of the 'world of taken-for-granted reality' which Schütz saw as fundamental to any understanding of social life. In this respect, Costelloe's argument converges with that of Kingsbury, who, as we have seen, also highlights the ways in which metaphors and images used to describe music and musical experience are eventually taken as 'actual references to the essential phenomena' (1991: 205). Such musicological discourse, Kingsbury suggests, is to be understood not as descriptive of real phenomena but as constitutive, both of music (1991: 201) and of an 'interpretive community' (1991: 211).

One important implication of these ideas is that the sociologist is led away from a reliance on general characterisations of music and its social context, and from participants' accounts of these phenomena, towards a concern with the production of these accounts – what participants take for granted as the evident realities of their social worlds – as a topic in its own right. Whereas Kingsbury examined the discourse that both constitutes and sustains the 'academic music community', providing its members with concepts, images and ways of classifying things which they believe to be unproblematic – in short with an orderly world of meaning – Hatch and Watson investigated the ways in which 'the community of blues enthusiasts' routinely recognise 'authentic' rural blues as compared to, for example, 'Black rural folk songs', although the difference is not always clear to the outsider (1974: 163). Making the distinction appropriately, and being seen to do so, requires the acquisition of certain competences which, while normally taken for granted within the circle of blues listeners, can themselves be analysed and studied as topics in themselves (1974: 165). Following Garfinkel's (1967) elaboration of the 'documentary method' of interpretation, Hatch and Watson focus on the ways in which particular musical elements are heard by competent listeners as evidence of an underlying pattern (the rural blues style), and, simultaneously, how the assumption of the latter as a coherent, meaningful entity provides the grounds for the interpretation of the former. In this way, the particular 'document' and the 'underlying pattern' are mutually determining:

> Competent members in the blues hearing community have the cultural knowledge and procedures to repair, redress, i.e. make sense of, ... contextually-specific features in terms of their status as 'evidence of blues music'. Thus the identification of a 'number' as a 'country-blues number' depends on the member possessing the cultural resources to relate all these 'indexical particulars' or 'appearances' – e.g. background understanding, knowledge of lyrics and tonal distribution, rhythm, etc. – to a perceived underlying pattern. (1974: 169)

It follows, too, that through engaging in this discourse the listeners are affirming and sustaining their membership of a particular community (1974: 163), demonstrating it publicly through their ability to distinguish country, classic, urban and other black music styles, and at the same time reinforcing the assumption that such 'styles' really exist.

Hatch and Watson's focus on the rules by which competent hearers make sense of music has been complemented more recently by studies which focus on the details of performers' practices in the process of making music. In his detailed analyses of orchestra rehearsals, Peter Weeks develops two more of the topics raised by Schütz – the fact that performers (unlike listeners) must achieve synchrony in 'outer' as well as 'inner' time, and the relative openness of the musical text (in the form of published scores) to a range of possible interpretations. In the course of rehearsals, Weeks argues, 'the practices underlying collective music-making' are made explicit and observable (1994: 1), and through analysing them with resources drawn from ethnomethodology he examines the precise ways in which the musical score is 'translated into a concrete and collective course of action' (1990: 350). Weeks shows how, through using both 'verbal expressions' and 'imitative expressions', orchestra conductors display for players a preferred way of playing particular passages. In general, verbal expressions precede imitative ones – i.e. humming, singing and so on – providing for the musicians a way of hearing the latter which is to be treated as exemplary for the playing of the passage (1994: 20). Both conductor and players are seen as attending to 'correctables' – passages which the conductor wants played differently – not only in order to eliminate errors but to produce a particular interpretation or to deal with practical difficulties, such as the acoustics of the room.

In contrast to other studies of instructional sequences, however, Weeks finds that in rehearsals conductors' corrections tend to be imposed decisively rather than elicited from the players, who are often interrupted peremptorily. This may be explained in terms of the status difference between them, says Weeks, but only in part: there are arguably greater status differences between primary school children and their teachers, yet the pattern of instruction is less directive (1994: 24–5). For Weeks, the contrasting patterns have to be understood as consequences of the practical tasks being undertaken: 'while lessons are a form of instruction that aims at the cultivation of generalised skills, rehearsals are directed to achieving a concerted specific rendering of specified texts' (1994: 25). Thus Weeks is concerned to examine precisely how the talk and gestures of the co-participants in rehearsals 'are clearly oriented to a nonverbal activity of embodying a text as a concerted work process'. The musicians' talk, moreover, cannot be understood 'without taking account of the wider work process in which it is embedded' (1994: 27). Weeks thus raises two themes which have been explored in other studies of music-making as social action: the notion of musical activities as embodied, which we will consider briefly below, and the topic of music as work, which is discussed in the next section.

David Sudnow's *Ways of the Hand* (1978) is a unique account of the author's progress in becoming a capable jazz improviser on the piano: it is, therefore, 'a phenomenologically motivated enquiry into the nature of hand work from the standpoint of the performer' (1978: xiii). Sudnow describes how, step by step, he gradually learned to find right-sounding paths through the harmonic sequences of the music, at the same time negotiating the 'terrain' of the keyboard. Through time, practice and experience, the two phases of the process – planning a course of action, and carrying it through – merged into one indivisible flow of activity, in just the same way that a person sings. While in the act of playing, the distinctions between thinking and doing, and between instrument and performer, both dissolve. The tentative and awkward explorations of the novice, and the conscious formulation of plans, eventually receded from consciousness: Sudnow came to find that 'usable notes for any chord lay just at hand, that there was no need to find a path, image one up ahead to get ready in advance for a blurting out. Indeed, to conceive particular terrain places up ahead seriously undermined the singing that I sought to sustain' (1978: 94). Sudnow's reflexive account of his own learning experience leads to a more general recognition that the social world is to be understood not as a world of definite things and objects, thoughts and actions, but as processes of doing: 'there is no melody, there is only melodying ... jazz music *is* ways of moving from place to place as singing with my fingers. To *define* jazz (as to define any phenomenon of human action) is to *describe* the body's ways' (1978: 146).

Clearly, Sudnow's account anticipated a later awakening of interest in social action as fundamentally embodied; Becker, moreover, has emphasised the relevance of this concern to his view of art worlds as organised around conventions, which 'become embodied in physical routines, so that artists literally feel what it is right for them to do' (1982: 203). He also suggests that Sudnow's work echoes and illuminates his conceptualisation of artistic work as a process in which 'editorial choices' are made in the course of an 'internal dialogue'. Editorial decisions, says Becker, come to be experienced 'as acts rather than choices', as conventionally sanctioned ways of doing things are internalised, and 'in those moments of simultaneous feeling and thinking what is being thought consists of a continual dialogue with the world relevant to the choices being made. The editorial and creative moment fuse in a dialogue with an art world' (1982: 204).

Music as work

If making music is 'work', in the sense of tasks which must be accomplished in order for it to be performed, it is also 'work' in the everyday sense that people make their living by doing it. In general terms, the emergence of professional musicians as a distinct occupational group has occurred along with the division of labour, although it seems that in all historical periods many musicians combined this work with some other trade or profession. It also appears that, while music itself is often highly valued, the social position of those who perform it is rather less exalted: documents drawn from two thousand years of recorded history provide evidence of the generally low prestige accorded to musicians, and examples of their ambiguous and often dubious status. In ancient Greece, musicians were scorned as merely manual workers, while in Rome women instrumentalists were 'ranked with the courtesans'; in other times and places they have been slaves, while in Mesopotamia and ancient China 'musicians – indeed entire orchestras – were yielded up as war tribute' (Supicic, 1987: 198–201). The ambiguous and often precarious social position of the professional musician is a topic to which we will return.

The marginal position of musicians in modern industrial societies is in some respects an echo of their origins as a distinct occupational group, in the travelling players of medieval Europe, who themselves may have been descended from magicians of earlier times. Such players left few historical traces, yet their activities were 'intense and perhaps of even greater importance to the citizenry as a whole than learned musicians instructed in polyphonic art' (Supicic, 1987: 206). The latter, of course, were in the service either of the aristocracy or of the church, producing works for events at court or for religious ceremonies – works in which the unique system of western tonality began to develop. By the thirteenth century, the social roots of the distinction between popular and art music, between the scholarly music of the elite and the oral tradition of the people, are clearly evident. It is not surprising that the *jongleurs* and, later, minstrels of medieval society were regarded with suspicion, since their unusual occupation, their geographical mobility, and their 'scandalous behaviour' placed them at the outer fringes of the social order. They were, says Harman, 'a constant thorn in the sides of both civil and ecclesiastical authority' (1988: 75). But while the low prestige of these players was no more than a reflection of the humble status of the common people they entertained, the elevated social position of the courtiers was not extended to more than a handful of the musicians in their service. As late as the eighteenth century, Mozart, 'at the table of Arch-Bishop Colloredo, was seated between the valets and the cooks' (Supicic, 1987: 208).

Yet it was Mozart, too, whose decisive break with the Archbishop has been regarded as the 'paradigmatic' case of an artist no longer prepared to tolerate the constraints and servitude of patronage, and who sought to establish himself as an independent, 'freelance' professional musician (Elias, 1993: 28). 'As a bourgeois outsider in service to the court', writes Elias, 'Mozart fought with astonishing courage to free himself from his aristocratic patrons and masters' (1993: 11).

There is some debate about the extent to which Mozart succeeded. For Elias, Mozart's heroic effort was doomed, partly because it came too soon, at a time when 'the traditional power structure was virtually intact' (1993: 15), and partly because, once freed of the conventions and constraints which necessarily circumscribed his compositional work at court, his musical imagination ran 'far ahead of his listeners' habits' (1993: 31). More recent scholars have disputed this, arguing that Mozart did not die a failure, and on the contrary was beginning to establish himself as an independent professional composer (Robbins Landon, 1990). There is no doubt, however, that by Beethoven's time court and church patronage were in decline; indeed, as we have seen, he was regarded by Adorno as the very embodiment of the new rising bourgeoisie – not only because bourgeois emancipation was represented in his music but because he was himself a 'freelance' composer whose work and income no longer depended on aristocratic or ecclesiastical patronage. Increasingly, music was becoming a business like any other – and we will return to the implications of this in the next chapter. For the present, though, Mozart's case may serve to introduce the theme which has been the *Leitmotif* of most sociological studies of music as work: the problem, regularly confronted by freelance musicians, of reconciling artistic ideals with economic realities.

For all the indignities, injustices and artistic restrictions of patronage, a court musician could at least expect a measure of security and some protection from the harsh realities of the world outside. Thus Mozart's determination to break with the Archbishop Colloredo, and give up his posts as orchestra leader and court organist, was 'incomprehensible' to his father Leopold, himself an experienced musician thoroughly imbued with the values of the old order (Elias,

1993: 23). Much as Leopold expected, even as gifted a musician as his son subsequently struggled, sometimes desperately, to make a living. Moreover, and the point is amplified in studies of players and composers from Mozart's time to our own, the independent professional, while free of the traditions and routines – and the arbitrary whims – of a patron, nevertheless finds that meeting the demands of the market may be experienced in ways just as demanding and frustrating. To make things even more difficult, the security so prized in Leopold Mozart's day has been exchanged for an intensely competitive and precarious situation. Judith Adler has expressed the matter clearly and with some force:

> [The] mythology of the art occupations, which sees them as constituting a privileged realm of freedom from the constraints and alienation of industrial life, especially since it plays an important role in the recruitment of young artists, is the backdrop against which the real problems of art workers and of those who socialize them take on their ironic significance. For contrary to the original expectations of those who enter them, these occupations expose their workers to some of the hazards of the contemporary work world in their most extreme form. Rather than being a refuge from some of the alienating aspects of work in advanced industrial society (the molding of work and the worker to meet the market's shifting demand, rapid occupational change and the consequent early obsolescence of work skills), they afford particularly virulent forms of such experience. (1975: 362–3)

Not surprisingly, studies of professional musicians in a wide range of contexts have persistently reflected their experience of stress, insecurity and the need to make artistic compromises in order to survive. Of course, as in any occupation, there are a few highly successful people who may be both well rewarded and personally fulfilled; indeed, it is their achievements which often motivate the majority (Cohen, 1991: 103). There are also many musicians who are generally satisfied with their lot, and who enjoy the particular lifestyle it affords. But it is equally likely that they will experience their work (and the lack of it) as deeply frustrating; as we shall see, moreover, studies suggest that individuals' degree of satisfaction may depend to a great extent on the stage they have reached in their careers, or in the life-cycle generally.

In one sense, it is only to be expected that musicians' work produces stress and anxiety: for even the most accomplished professionals, every performance entails potential risks. Things can go wrong, for all sorts of reasons, and when they do it is immediately a public matter, evident both to an audience, and – perhaps more important – to colleagues, whose esteem is of paramount importance. In the orchestral world, doubts about a player's competence may mean the non-renewal of contracts; in the recording studios, as the saying goes, 'you're only as good as your last call,' and players who are perceived as unable, or no longer able, to cope with the considerable demands and pressures of the task may cease to be called by the 'fixers' or 'contractors' who hire players for 'sessions' (Faulkner, 1971: 107). In addition, the onset of even relatively minor ill-health, of the sort which can go unnoticed in many other occupations, can mean the end of the top player's career; there is, too, a constant surplus in the supply of capable players over the demand for their services.

The prevalence of high levels of stress and anxiety has been documented in other areas of musical activity (Wills and Cooper, 1988). Similarly, Sara Cohen has pointed to the financial and artistic pressure endured by young rock musicians struggling to 'make it': for some it is their only hope of an escape from unemployment and poverty; others have made considerable sacrifices in order to pursue their musical ambitions. Despite their marginal position in the music business, and the often inconsequential nature of their 'gigs', the aspiring players studied by Cohen therefore displayed a deep involvement with their bands, their music and their performances. As a result, their social relationships were often strained and conflict-ridden. Issues which to an outsider might seem trivial assumed enormous significance, and 'splits' and sackings were frequent (1991: 44–5). In fact, of course, only a tiny minority ever do 'make it', even as far as obtaining a recording contract, and the knowledge of this imposes a further pressure to get things right. Of those bands who do achieve a contract, the majority are 'dumped' by the record companies quite soon (1991: 126), but even those who 'make it' to the heights of the pop 'charts' regularly find that their fame is short-lived, and their fortune non-existent. Advances paid to artists on signing recording contracts must be recouped before any royalties on sales are paid; once the considerable costs of recording and promotion are added, it is clear why moderately successful artists, performing regularly and selling quite large numbers of discs and tapes, can still find themselves in debt to their recording company. From the companies' perspective, persevering with bands who are failing to 'make it' can soon become unacceptably expensive: 'Accounts released for the UK division of BMG Records in June 1990 showed that the company was £7.2 million in debt due to "advances paid to artists in respect of future royalties together with recording costs recoverable from future royalties" ' (Negus, 1992: 136). Companies therefore are under pressure to take a hard attitude when reviewing their artists' progress; the experience of being 'dropped' or 'dumped' often comes as a crushing blow, intensified by the heightened aspiration which has preceded it, and exacerbated by the fact that other companies are very unlikely to sign an artist or group who are now perceived to have failed (1992: 138). Keith Negus has described the somewhat bleak scenario: 'the majority of artists who are signed by record companies enjoy a very brief period of success. ... A large number do not achieve any form of success whatsoever ... a vast majority simply return to their day jobs in offices, banks, warehouses, factories, equipment stores and record shops' (1992: 138–9).

The turbulent world of the music business will be discussed further in the following chapter. For the present, the point to be emphasised is the insecurity and vulnerability to market pressures which are routinely reported as major factors in the lives of professional or would-be professional musicians in virtually all spheres of musical activity. As Adler suggests, work as a musician in industrial societies, far from affording an escape from commercial and financial pressure, exposes people to them in their 'most virulent' forms. There is, moreover, a second strain running through Adler's remarks, relating to the specifically artistic or aesthetic aspect of musicians' motivations. Those who seek to become professionals, in all areas of musical life, typically have to undergo a quite lengthy period of preparation or training. Usually, this is undertaken willingly, out of a sense of personal commitment to the music which may become deeper as the individual becomes increasingly involved in a particular art world and its pattern of social relationships. Musicians, therefore, are likely to have strong convictions about the value and importance of forms of music, and aspirations to perform at what they take to be the highest levels of their art; it is these ideas, however, which regularly come into conflict with the commercial realities of the musical marketplace; the old adage that 'He who pays the piper calls the tune' is not one that many professionals have found easy to accept.

This theme is developed in what is probably the best-known study

in the sociology of music, Howard Becker's account of the occupational situation and outlook of the dance band musicians he worked
with in Chicago in the late 1940s (Becker, 1963). Becker's work
belongs to the tradition of occupational studies established by
Everett Hughes at the University of Chicago (Hughes, 1958), and
develops the idea that both the culture of an occupational group and
the career patterns open to its members are shaped largely by the
specific problems faced in common as part of doing the job (Becker,
1963: 81, 102). For the musicians studied by Becker, the fundamental problem was dealing with a wider world of 'squares' – the public
who, with few exceptions, did not share or appreciate the musicians'
artistic commitments yet were in a position ultimately to control not
only their employment opportunities but often the details of what
they should play, and how. The musicians, says Becker, entered the
profession with a strong commitment to 'jazz and artistic freedom'
(1963: 110); the reality of their situation, however, is that it provides
very little opportunity for either, particularly if a player aspires to
even a moderate level of income or security. The musicians' problem, then, was whether or not to 'go commercial', and how to cope
with the situation once the decision to do 'commercial' work has
been made. The ensuing threat to the individual's sense of dignity
and integrity should not be underestimated: 'The greatest rewards of
the profession are controlled by men who have sacrificed some of the
most basic professional standards' (1963: 109–10). The musicians'
orientation to their work, therefore, can be transformed from the
'idealism' of the newcomer to the 'cynicism' of the hardened professional (Becker and Geer, 1958).

It is this fundamental problem of reconciling artistic commitments
and commercial pressures, Becker argues, which gives rise to the particular features of the musicians' occupational culture, and to the
'deviant' values which it displays. To the dedicated jazz players,
'straight' society is full of people who are unable to understand their
music and incapable of appreciating their gifts; accordingly, the conventions and routines of normal society are mocked and satirised in
the musicians' culture, and emphasis is often given to contrary values
– such as hedonism, risk-taking and a cavalier attitude to money.
Becker argues, however, that similar reactions are to be found among
the 'commercial' players as a consequence of the compromises that
they have been obliged to make. Both groups develop a strong sense
of loyalty to other musicians as 'insiders', and both display a partic-

ular resentment at the extent to which their work can be controlled by people whom they view as musically incompetent and socially contemptible. Such an outlook becomes generalised into a dislike of being 'subject to the control of outsiders in any branch of life' (Becker, 1963: 86), and to a degree of tolerance for others whose ways are not those of conventional society. As with other 'deviant' groups, then, the musicians' culture not only recognises but seeks to emphasise the differences between them and the 'squares' in the world outside.

The musicians' careers, too, are largely determined by their responses to the fundamental dilemma they face. The occupation presented a hierarchy of work opportunities, ranging from casual work playing at weddings, dances and other events, up to permanent well-paid employment in television stations, recording studios and so on. Entry to each level, and allocation of work within them, is mostly organised informally by the musicians themselves through a series of networks and cliques: players recommend each other for jobs, and may act as sponsors for others.

> Cliques made up of jazzmen offer their members nothing but the prestige of maintaining artistic integrity; commercial cliques offer security, income, mobility, and general social prestige.
>   This conflict is a major problem in the career of the individual musician, and the development of his career is contingent on his reaction to it. (1963: 110)

In general, most players 'compromise to some degree' (1963: 111) by accepting work that they consider degrading. For some this move is accompanied by a change in orientation which involves a lesser emphasis on the musician as an artist, and a greater concern with the specific technical skills of the job – developing their instrumental prowess or sight-reading abilities, for example. A commitment to craftsmanship, therefore, may replace the role-model of the creative artist in the interests of career advancement.

There can be no doubt that Becker's discussion of the dance musicians captures much of the frustration and pressure that their work engenders, as the players come into constant conflict with their employers and, indeed, other members of 'square' society, including their immediate families. Other authors, however, while accepting Becker's findings have questioned the extent to which they may be generalised to other musicians, and have sought to place them in a

broader context. For Harvey (1967), an increased level of appreciation of jazz musicians by the public was leading to a reduction in the
level of hostility they displayed towards audiences and society in general. For Faulkner, the rigid contrast which Becker draws between
artistic aspirations and commercial realities may both oversimplify
the complex pattern of musicians' orientations and 'too easily assign
rather inflexible perspectives to musicians in the commercial sector
in toto' (1971: 89). It cannot be assumed, for example, that all players in the commercial sector are frustrated or failed jazz musicians:
some regard their musical abilities primarily as a means of earning a
living, others have a 'craft' orientation from the start, rather than
develop it as a response to relative failure. For the highly skilled and
highly paid players in the Hollywood film studios who were studied
by Faulkner, this sort of 'commercial' work could be experienced as
both desirable and professionally rewarding. The ability to perform
extremely demanding music, in a whole range of styles, under
pressure and with little or no rehearsal, is clearly a matter of some
pride to many of Faulkner's interviewees. The recording schedules
were flexible enough for the jazz-oriented studio musicians to con-
tinue to play their music in clubs, or for the classical players to maintain their involvement with string quartets and so on. Both sets of
players tended to see their occupational situation positively, emphasising that the economic rewards from studio work permitted them
to enjoy a lifestyle and settled family life which are simply impossible for the majority of orchestral or freelance musicians. The last
point is of some importance to Faulkner, who argues that a concern
with the factors which 'pull' players into commercial work must be
balanced by a recognition of those which 'push' them out of other
areas (1971: 88). In short, work even in a famous band or a prestigious orchestra can be unpleasant, poorly paid, personally disruptive, and intensely boring; in contrast, work in the studios was
widely perceived as upward mobility (1971: 83).

The gulf between public perceptions and the private experiences
of orchestral musicians was brought into sharp focus by one of
Faulkner's interviewees:

> I guess I thought that being part of one of the world's great orchestras,
> I should be proud to be in it. But this is false actually. You're not going
> anywhere, you're not doing anything, and you're stuck with a small
> salary. You feel trapped. (1971: 75)

These remarks are a striking echo of Westby's earlier research (1960) into the career experiences of musicians in a major American symphony orchestra. As in most occupational fields, only a relatively small number of people can reach the very top of the profession; the rest may be regarded, and come to see themselves, as relative failures. The job that was once seen as a stepping stone to better things is now experienced as a trap, and as players grow older their commitment to, and identification with, the occupation are eroded (1960: 229). One first violinist, in his late forties, put the matter graphically: 'I'd rather play in any cabaret in the country than the symphony orchestra.' The inevitable consequence was a division within the orchestra between the younger, ambitious and committed players and those who are 'older, settled and withdrawn', with 'a widening gap of communication and values between the two groups' (1960: 229).

In terms of occupational commitment and outlook, therefore, members of prominent American orchestras have been seen to display a variety of orientations: the implications of the research by Westby and Faulkner (1973b) is that such ensembles are far from the cohesive, responsive social groups which figure in the mythology of the 'classical' music literature. Indeed, in a further paper Faulkner takes up the issue of the managerial problem facing any conductor or musical director – how can compliance and closely co-ordinated action be elicited from players whose definitions of the situation may not only differ but be antagonistic? The orchestra is far from a finely tuned machine which responds instantly to a conductor. Since they have to work with a succession of conductors, the players scrutinise the abilities of each; where a particular 'maestro' is seen to lack authority, or be inconsistent or indecisive, the players' respect and compliance may be withheld, resulting in 'open disrespect, sullenness, deliberately lowered work effort, selective inattention, sarcasm, and in general the making and taking of role distance' (Faulkner, 1973a: 151). In general, the extent of the players' efforts are largely determined by their judgement of the conductor's 'expertise and leadership skills' (1973a: 153), and performances – whether judged good or bad – must be understood as the outcome of social processes as well as purely musical expertise. The interactions among orchestra members, and between them and their conductors, are crucial in generating collective definitions of the situation, and Faulkner concludes that 'part of the sum total of recognized musical knowledge is generated in ongoing organisational action' (1973a: 156).

In general, studies of musicians as an occupational group have emphasised this interdependence of musical and social factors in the work itself, that is, in the collaborative production of performances. Above all, the responses of players – individually and collectively – depend on the way in which they 'define the situation' that they are in. In this, as with members of any other social groups, they will be influenced both by the 'reference groups' with whom they compare their own situation and prospects, and by the 'significant others' whose opinions really matter to them, whether for artistic or commercial reasons. Orchestra musicians may opt to frustrate their conductors' intentions, for reasons of their own, just as jazz musicians may choose to play for themselves, or for each other, irrespective of the reactions of their audiences. Bandleaders and their managers, on the other hand, are likely to be concerned above all with pleasing the audience. In all these, and other, situations, the participants may be regarded as engaging in the 'internal dialogue' of which Becker speaks, formulating courses of action – from general career strategies to the finest nuances of performance – in the light of the anticipated responses of others.

Two points may be made in concluding this consideration of music as social action. Firstly, as I have suggested, the 'internal dialogue' need not be thought of as a conscious, rational process; on the contrary, both G. H. Mead and Howard Becker have emphasised how ways of acting become 'internalised' by individuals so that they not only do them habitually but come to feel them as somehow right and proper, as morally correct and defensible. Later authors have begun to explore the related notion of social action as fundamentally 'embodied'. Secondly, while most actions in most situations do tend to conform to established conventions – social order would be impossible if they did not – there is always the possibility that the accepted conventions and ways of doing things may be challenged. Indeed, it has been argued that while Mead does tend to present a model of the individual as 'prosocial' – compliant and co-operative, accepting and enacting established norms – more recent interactionists, and Becker in particular, have developed a view of the self as altogether less 'innocent'; the 'generalised other' may be, and may be perceived as, 'a threatening and menacing collectivity' which may provoke the individual into acts of deviance, defiance or resistance (Katovich and and Reese, 1993: 396). The words of the pianist

Thelonious Monk may serve to make the point, as a reminder of the inner drive which motivates innovators in all fields, and of the rejection and hostility which their efforts usually engender: 'I'm not commercial. I say, play your own way. Don't play what the public wants – you play what you want and let the public pick up what *you* are doing – even if it *does* take them fifteen, twenty years' (quoted in Rosenthal, 1992: 132).

Writing of musical innovators, the jazz critic A. B. Spellman once put the matter nicely when he pointed out that 'their interest in what can be done in musical self-assertion forces them to constantly alter the rules, which is about the most commercially dangerous thing a musician can do' (quoted in Rosenthal, 1992: 157). As we have seen, the working musician often faces the dilemma created by the opposed demands of artistic aspirations and commercial realities. In commercial terms, of course, musical activities are simply labour, which can be bought and sold on the market, and music itself becomes a commodity, to be produced and marketed like any other. It is to these processes that we now turn.

6

The music business in capitalist society

The bourgeoisie ... has pitilessly torn asunder the motley feudal ties
that bound man to his 'natural superiors' and has left remaining no
other nexus between man and man than naked self-interest, than cal-
lous 'cash payment'.

Marx and Engels, *The Communist Manifesto*

The single most important development in modern music is making a
business out of it.

Frank Zappa (*Telos* 91, 125)

Music and the rise of capitalism

As I suggested at the start of this book, the vast majority of studies
in academic musicology, and many of those who have sought to
establish the sociology of music as a research area in its own right,
have been preoccupied with the composed 'classical' music tradition
of the modern West. Yet as we have seen, despite its cultural pre-
eminence this 'art' music has not been the music of the mass of the
people; a genuine sociology of music, therefore, will not set out, as
Supicic does (1987: 231), to secure a wider acceptance of 'art' music
but will investigate the full range of styles and genres which have
developed, the relationship between groups' socio-economic locations and their music, and the emergence of a hierarchy of musical
styles in modern societies. In turn, this entails something of a reorientation of research interests − paying much greater attention to
'popular' music styles (as opposed to those that legitimate themselves
as 'serious'), and viewing the production of music in industrialised
societies as a business rather than an art. It is this topic that will be

explored in the present chapter.

A sociological interest in the music business, however, immediately leads to a consideration of the historical context of its emergence and development – nothing less than the rise of what Max
Weber called modern rational capitalism, and the consequent transformation of whole societies, indeed (as Marx foresaw) the establishment of industrial capitalism on a global scale. Clearly, even a
short account of the relations between the rise of capitalism as an
economic order and music in the modern world would be a vast
undertaking, far beyond the scope of this book. Accordingly, the discussion that follows will attempt only to indicate, in the briefest of
outlines, some of the major sociological issues that arise when we
consider the ways in which the development of capitalism has influenced the production and consumption of music. Following that, the
main focus of the chapter is on the modern music business itself.

The uniqueness of western music
In contrast to many of the historians of his day, Max Weber argued
that modern capitalism, which had transformed the western world,
was neither an inevitable development nor (as Marxists held) a necessary stage in world history. On the contrary, Weber's view was
that modern capitalism was able to develop only because of a unique
configuration of circumstances in medieval Europe: in particular, the
unintended ideological effects of the Protestant reformers contributed to a significant reorientation of economic activities. Whereas
previously economic life – like all other aspects of society – was
organised according to traditional patterns, or controlled by the
established customs and practices of the guilds, Protestant theology
(and in particular the idea of dedication to work in a 'calling') both
allowed and encouraged the abandonment of traditional ways. Work
now became endowed with spiritual significance; the ideal was to
work long, hard and methodically. In the long run, Weber suggested,
the wholly unintended result was the replacement of traditional
organisation by the criteria of rationality and efficiency, and the
establishment of a new and potent form of capitalism (Weber, 1930).
For all its momentous consequences, however, this reordering of economic life was, according to Weber, only one aspect of the most fundamental characteristic of western civilisation, the gradual
rationalisation of all aspects of social life. It is in this context that
Weber examined the origins and development of western music and

its unique tonal system (Weber, 1958).

According to Paul Honigsheim, who knew him well, music was 'almost a necessity of life' for Weber (1968: 83), who particularly enjoyed the chamber works of Beethoven, Brahms and Liszt (1968: 84), and who called Wagner 'the great wizard' (Marianne Weber, 1975: 501). (Apart from his music, however, Weber expressed his 'aversion' to the nationalistic cult which developed around Wagner.) It seems that one of Weber's projects – unfortunately never completed – was to write a general study of the sociology of the arts, and around 1910 he began to assemble material on the nature and development of western music. The result was not a finished essay but a lengthy series of notes which were deciphered from Weber's handwriting and published shortly after his death by the musicologist Theodor Kroyer under the title of *The Rational and Social Foundations of Music* (Blaukopf, 1992: 123). The text itself is somewhat forbidding, presupposing a considerable knowledge of history, harmonic theory and Weber's own methodological precepts, and is thus not easily summarised for the non-specialist. However, as Blaukopf has pointed out (1992: 120), Weber did outline his general approach in a lecture delivered in 1913 and subsequently published (Weber, 1978). As we saw in Chapter 2 (pp. 58–9), Weber saw modern harmonic music much as he saw modern rational capitalism – as the unique product of a unique process of development in western civilisation; as an outcome, moreover, which was neither inevitable nor predictable.

From this point of view, the central question for Weber was this:

> why was harmonic music developed from the almost universal polyphony of folk music only in Europe and only in a particular period, while everywhere else the rationalisation of music took a different path – usually indeed precisely the opposite one, that of the development of intervals by division of distance (usually the fourth) rather than by harmonic division (the fifth)? The central problem is thus that of the origins of the third in its harmonic interpretation, as a member of a triad, and furthermore of harmonic chromatics and of modern musical rhythm in place of metronomic timekeeping – a form of rhythm without which modern instrumental music would be unthinkable.
>
> (Weber, 1978: 95)

No other musical culture has approached the complexity of western composed music, the degree of co-ordination (of both instruments

and players) attained in the symphony orchestra, or the sophistication of the string quartet. The very complexity of this music, and the
need to ensure the co-ordination of all its various elements, depends
absolutely on the development of an effective system of harmonic
relationships, which in turn presupposes 'the rationalisation of tone
relations and progressions' (Martindale and Riedel, 1958: xxiv).

Thus tonal music, like the codification of legal systems or the
development of bureaucratic organisations, was for Weber evidence
of the general tendency towards rationalisation in ever-wider areas
of western culture (Collins, 1986b: 63ff.). As the passage quoted
above indicates, it is of the greatest significance for Weber that, of
the two 'natural' ways in which octaves may be divided, western
music, unusually, employs the fifth rather than the fourth. For while
the latter cannot easily be subdivided to produce a further conso-
nance, the fifth may be split into two intervals (of a major and minor
third), thus yielding the basic triad of the western harmonic system.
Moreover, on the basis of the simple intervals of octave, fifth, and
fourth (represented since the time of Pythagoras by arithmetical
ratios derived from experiments with vibrating strings – 1:2, 2:3, and
4:3 respectively), all the steps of the diatonic scale may be derived. It
would seem as though consonances may be formed, and indeed the
whole harmonic system devised, on the basis of precise and calcula-
ble rules: a triumph of rationalisation over the 'confused kaleido-
scope of sounds' (Feher,1987: 147). However, and this is a point
which Weber is particularly concerned, the rationalisation of the
tonal materials cannot be completed. The system resists closure,
largely owing to the effects of the 'unstable' seventh:

> To be be representative of its key, the dominant seventh chord should,
> through its third or the seventh of the key, form a major seventh. How-
> ever, in the minor scale the minor seventh must be chromatically raised
> in contradiction to what is required by the triad ...
>
> Any dominant seventh chord contains the dissonant diminished triad,
> starting from the third and forming the major seventh. Both of these
> kinds of triads are real revolutionaries when compared with the har-
> monically divided fifths. Not since J. S. Bach could chordal harmony
> legitimate them with respect to the facts of music.' (Weber, 1958: 6–7)

Thus there is a limit to the process of musical rationalisation, 'an
uneliminatable logical looseness which appears at the heart of harmonic chord music ... There is almost a sense that one has touched

one of the ultimate boundaries of human reason itself' (Martindale and Riedel, 1958: xxv). It has been suggested, therefore, that, in the process of its rationalisation, western music displays the fundamental conflict between 'the requirements of expression and reason' (1958: xxvi). The logical, theoretical principles of harmony are constantly subverted by another principle, that of melody, which resists assimilation to a logical scheme. It is the irrational, dissonant elements which create the sense of tension and the need for harmonic movement, and it is the expressive requirements of melody which generate chord progressions: 'The numerous chords do not grow out of the complications of chainlike progressions alone. They also, and preferably, grow out of melodic needs' (Weber, 1958: 9).

Thus, and this is what made the study of western harmonic music so interesting for Weber, 'irrational' melodic requirements remain at the heart of things, giving the music its sense of movement and direction while combinations of notes and chords which may be theoretically correct are not necessarily heard as 'right' or even consonant. Another irrational element, however, has been confronted, and for practical purposes eliminated. As mentioned above, all the notes of the diatonic scale may be derived from the division of the octave into fifths and fourths (represented by simple arithmetic ratios). This procedure was known to the ancient Greeks, and yields what has come to be known as the Pythagorean scale (although it is unlikely that Pythagoras himself was involved in the musical discoveries); 'the scale', wrote Philolaus in the fifth century BC, 'is five tones and two semitones, a fifth is three tones and a semitone, and fourth is two tones and a semitone' (Barnes, 1987: 218). The problem that arises, however, is that the pitch-values of notes derived in this way depend on the method which is chosen to calculate them. Chanan provides a simple example:

> The note E ... is a major third from C, with the relation 4:5, and a major second from D, with the relation 8:9. But the frequency of C multiplied by 5/4 is not the same as the frequency of D multiplied by 9/8 (where the value of D is also calculated from C). If C is 512, D is 576, E, moving from C, is then 640, but calculated as a major second from D, it has the value 648. Because of this anomaly, and the way it accumulates within the system, a problem begins to emerge in the manner of tuning, or tempering, the instruments. (1981: 234)

Anomalies and discrepancies such as these don't really matter where there is a single melodic line, or where instruments are combined in simple and well-tried routines. They are, however, quite incompatible with a comprehensively rationalised harmonic system, such as is required for elaborate choral works or a large-scale orchestra. Various attempts to overcome the problem culminated in the introduction during the eighteenth century of the 'tempered scale' following the development and refinement of keyboard instruments.

In the 'equal temperament' system of tuning, which has been universally adopted in modern western music, the naturally occurring irregularities in the harmonic series are removed by slightly raising the pitch of some notes (such as the third and the sixth) and slightly lowering others. In this way the octave is divided into twelve equal semitones, and, for example, keyboard instruments can be consistently 'in tune' over their entire range. All keys have the same structural basis, all sorts of combinations of instruments are possible, and there is no barrier to music which modulates from any key to any other. For Weber, of course, the process of tempering symbolised the triumph of rational thought over the recalcitrant forces of nature: the development of equal temperament was for him 'the last word in our chordal and harmonic development' (1958: 99). Characteristically, though, Weber was also aware that the gains represented by equal temperament had to be set against certain losses. 'Temperament', he wrote, 'takes from our ears some of the delicacy which gave the decisive flavour to the melodious refinement of ancient music culture' (1958: 123), and later theorists have echoed this complaint (Wood, 1975: 193–5). However, only a small number of specialists have heeded the call for a return to 'true' tuning, or for the production of pianos with more keys in order to retain small distinctions of pitch. In general, as in other areas of social life, the comprehensive, rationalised system of equal temperament has become established as normal and often accepted as 'natural', despite its clearly cultural origins (Blaukopf, 1992: 120). The advantages and possibilities of the then-novel tuning system were demonstrated in J. S. Bach's *Well-Tempered Clavier* of 1722, but, according to Harman and Milner, Bach's purpose was more general. 'He, like many Germans of his time, found such systematic arrangements logical and intellectually satisfying. This attitude was partly the result of the scientific spirit of his age; music was regarded both as an art and a science, and therefore demonstrations of its technique ... demanded a "scientific" presentation' (Harman and Milner, 1988: 568–9). It was precisely this 'scientific spirit' which both animated and accelerated the process of rationalisation which Weber saw as fundamental to western culture, generating not only modern music but modern society itself.

As I have suggested, Weber's view of the rationalisation of western music was not elaborated in any systematic way. It is clear, though, that there are certain parallels between his interpretation of this process and his account of the relationship between religion and the rise of capitalism. Firstly, as in the case of religion, Weber sees the character of modern music not as a consequence of capitalism but as having its roots much earlier, perhaps as far back as the ninth century AD, 'long before there was capitalism, not to mention bureaucratisation, or other institutional transformations' (Collins, 1986b: 66). Secondly, just as Weber had argued in *The Protestant Ethic and the Spirit of Capitalism* that the rationalisation of economic life was in part an unanticipated consequence of theological doctrines which gave some support to the abandonment of traditional customs and practices, so the clear implication of several passages in *The Rational and Social Foundations of Music* is that musical rationalisation occurred in the West (and only there) because of particular sets of circumstances which allowed it to occur; in most historical contexts, established traditions and institutional constraints inhibited any such developments. Weber's approach here anticipates later work in the sociology of culture which has emphasised ways in which accepted conventions and constraints have the effect of blocking the innovations and new styles which musicians are always likely to explore. In pre-modern societies, for example, music was an inherent part of many ritual and ceremonial activities which by definition depend on the repetition of the same acts; in the extreme case, Weber writes, where music was an element in magical practices, deviations could be fatal: 'The wrong rendition of a tone formula was an offence which often could be atoned [sic] for only through the instantaneous murder of the offender' (1958: 40). And where music has been primarily functional – which it has been in most times and places – there are likely to be practical obstacles in the way of attempts at innovation or rationalisation.

In the history of the West, however, certain factors had the effect of opening up music to the rationalisation process. Pentatonic (five-note) scales, as we have seen, are found in many musical cultures, and were regarded by Weber as a stage in the rationalisation process, representing 'a kind of selection of rational and harmonic intervals from the abundance of melodic intervals' (1958: 22). In the West, though, the process went much further than elsewhere, and Weber points to the emergence of 'professional' musicians, particularly among the medieval monks, who were responsible for devising and organising choral works, as important contributors to a 'rationalism that was peculiar to Western monasticism' (1978: 96). It was these 'learned' musicians who not only had the opportunity to experiment but needed to innovate if the music was to become more complex. The development of notation, too, was an important factor in the standardisation of musical practices; indeed, Weber suggests that this too played a crucial role in the development of modern tonality. Just as the preconditions for economic rationalisation were evident in other (i.e., non-western) societies but failed to break through the barrier to change, so the preconditions for the modern diatonic system are observable in the music of ancient Greece and Japan. But these societies did not develop the equivalent of western notation. 'A notation of our kind', said Weber, 'is of more fundamental importance for the existence of such music as we possess than is orthography for our linguistic art formations' (1958: 83). The performance of a 'complicated modern work of music' depends utterly on the system of notation and the production of a score (1958: 84).

The relationship between 'polyvocal music and notation' was thus seen as generating a 'spiral of rationalisation' (Martindale and Riedel, 1958: xlvii). The development of the music necessitated a system of notation, but that system itself stimulated further development in the direction of rationalisation – imposing standard practices permitting greater complexity, facilitating compositional work by specialists and the development of musical theory. There is a suggestion, too, that the particular doctrines of medieval Christianity may have had specific effects: Paul Honigsheim recalled Weber's argument that the rise of European instrumental music and its characteristic forms – the suite, the sonata and the symphony – stemmed from the fact that 'Christianity was the only one, among the scriptural religions, that had never had a cult of the dance. For Christianity abhorred the body' (Honigsheim, 1968: 89). Weber also pays some attention to the various ways in which developments in Western science and the technology of manufacturing were utilised by instrument-makers; of these, as we have seen, by far the most important was the progressive refinement of keyboard instruments and the consequent development of the 'tempered' scale (1958: 99–100). All

these factors, for Weber, contributed to the rationalisation of western music; with the institutionalisation of 'professional' musicians,
and 'composers' who were expected to produce 'works' for church
or court, the process generated its own momentum. As Collins has
put it: 'Both music and capitalism could become dynamic and in a
metaphorical sense 'world transforming' once they were rationalised'
(1986: 67).

As Feher has pointed out, it is somewhat ironic that 'the net effect
of rationalisation is something eminently *antipragmatic*. It is music
as an *aesthetic* phenomenon, which having shed all traces of its mag-
ical-communical-pragmatic use, arises at the end of the rationalizing
process' (1987: 150). In the present context it is significant that
instead of presupposing the validity of the 'aesthetic' realm and the
special nature of 'art', as Adorno did, Weber displays a clear sociological indifference to such claims. For him, the form and character
of a society's music is the outcome of its particular configuration of
institutions, the nature and level of its technology, historical contingencies, the emergence of individual virtuosos and so on. It does not
necessarily represent universal values, the form of society, the ethos
of a group, or anything else, and, as a scientific analyst, it is no part
of the sociologist's task to evaluate it: 'The empirical history of
music will be able to, indeed must, analyse these factors in historical development without involving itself with the aesthetic evaluation
of musical works of art' (1978: 96). While it is true that Weber's view
of rationalisation had a deep effect on Adorno, on this point the contrast between them could hardly be clearer. Weber's broad view of
history, his knowledge of other cultures, and above all his sociological imagination allowed him to escape the intellectual limitations of
his own time and place to an extent that Adorno never managed.

From patronage to the market
Adorno's view of Bach has been echoed more recently by Susan
McClary, who rejects the widely held judgement that Bach's music
reflects either transcendental truth or the Order of Things (whether
naturally or divinely inspired), and who wishes to replace him in his
socio-historical context. The social values that are articulated in
Bach's music, writes McClary, 'are those held most dear by the
middle class: beliefs in progress, in expansion, in the ability to attain
ultimate goals through rational striving, in the ingenuity of the individual strategist operating both within and in defiance of the norm'

(1987: 22). Whether this music (or any music) does in fact 'articulate' such values is another matter; for present purposes the relevant point is that in his own career J. S. Bach (1685–1750) was not an independent professional. Like his forebears, Bach depended for his living on a succession of aristocratic or municipal patrons, and was thus 'under no urgent compulsion to tickle the public's ear' (Harman and Milner, 1988: 568–9). As we have already seen in the case of Mozart, however, things were changing, with the old order and its aristocratic elite increasingly challenged by the emergence of the new bourgeoisie, whose social position did not depend on tradition or the inheritance of land and titles but on their involvement in various forms of burgeoning commerce and industry. This was the class, as Weber saw it, which harvested the fruits of scientific and economic rationalisation, and which gradually but irrevocably undermined the institution of patronage.

As in other spheres, the change was most apparent in England, the leading industrial nation, and particularly in London, the 'most prosperous urban centre in Europe'. It has been estimated that by the middle of the eighteenth century there were around 1,500 musicians based in London, which offered 'more market opportunities, as distinct from patronage, than anywhere else, and acted as a magnet to musicians throughout Europe' (Ehrlich, 1985: 3). Elsewhere in England, there is evidence of a gradual but 'fundamental transformation, both in the pattern of demand for musicians and in their potential supply' (1985: 20); in the second half of the eighteenth century, concerts and concert societies became established in many of the rapidly growing urban centres of the North and Midlands. Today, concerts are such an accepted and well-established part of the musical world that it is easy to overlook the significance of these developments, which mark a change from a period in which music was largely produced by a 'paid servant' like Bach (Harman and Milner, 1988: 528) either on a full- or part-time basis, to the modern era in which composers and performers are largely independent professionals, and the demand for their services is market-driven. Indeed, Ehrlich quotes Max Weber in suggesting that by the nineteenth century British musicians 'were forced to abandon "privileged traditionalism" without always escaping the consequences of "irrational speculation" by impresarios' (1985: 32).

Fuelled by industrialisation and rapid economic growth, the demand for music – particularly by the new middle class –

intensified, and musical activities both expanded enormously and underwent a thoroughgoing commercialisation. Up to the end of the eighteenth century, there were probably fewer than 2,000 musicians in England and Wales, with the vast majority, as we have seen, in London. By 1841 the number had risen to 3,600 and by 1861 to 9,500; if music teachers are also counted these last two figures rise to 11,200 and 15,000 respectively (Ehrlich, 1985: 235). (The number of musicians and teachers peaked at just under 50,000 by 1931; the effects of new technologies and the development of the mass media are reflected in the decline from that time.) Clearly, an account of the ways in which musical life was affected by the emergence and development of modern capitalism is far beyond the scope of this book. In the present context, however, three points concerning the decline of patronage and the rise of the musical market may be made.

Firstly, as the discussion in the previous chapter has suggested, liberation of musicians from the requirements of their patrons did not, in the vast majority of cases, guarantee them artistic freedom: the demands of the market could be just as severe and often more volatile. Accordingly, discussions of the musical world and the careers of its members return frequently to the theme of the tension between artistic aspirations and commercial realities, and to the high degree of insecurity which has been the lot of many players and composers. The topic has been considered above, and need not be elaborated further.

Secondly, while historians and social theorists often speak of the decline of the old aristocracy and the rise of the new bourgeoisie as the new dominant class in capitalist societies, it is important to remember that the transformation was neither as rapid nor as clearcut as these terms suggest. As far as England is concerned, it is evident that something more resembling a process of accommodation between the 'old' elite and the 'new' entrepreneurs took place, and this process is emphasised by William Weber in his account of the development of concert life between 1830 and 1848. Weber, like his namesake Max, sees the process of rationalisation as crucial to an understanding of modern societies, and describes the ways in which it was manifested in the musical world, notably in the commercialisation and professionalisation of activities. But these processes, he warns, should not be regarded as disembodied, external social forces:

We must not think, however, that these changes were caused by dark, impersonal forces. The use of power and gain have been central to the process; some people have wanted new things, and many times they have gotten them. Indeed, it is astounding how smoothly the upper classes have either guided the transformation or prevented themselves from being hurt by it. (1975: 115)

The period examined by William Weber saw the consolidation of public concerts and the institutionalisation of all the practices and rituals which are now considered a routine part of a 'symphony' concert. By the middle of the nineteenth century, moreover, 'some musicians and entertainment entrepreneurs had developed much of the commercial expertise of contemporary rock stars and their agents; (1975: 118). Above all, however, Weber emphasises the ways in which concert life was an expression of the emerging pattern of social stratification, and in particular a demonstration of the 'merger of the artistocracy and the upper middle class into a single upper class' which was becoming increasingly international in its membership and orientations (1975: 118, 84). Through the organisation of, and attendance at, public concerns, Weber suggests, 'the two segments of the high-status public could visualise themselves as members of a grand new 'high society' whose size and imposing cultural leadership compensated for the loss of the clearer separate elite roles of an earlier day' (1975: 119).

A third consideration is introduced in William Weber's analysis of the 'high-status' concert scene: the gradual emergence of a clear distinction between 'art' on the one hand, and 'popular' cultural forms on the other. Once again, it is important not to oversimplify what was in fact a complex process, involving the segregation of music into several different genres. 'Classical' and 'popular' music tastes could coexist fairly peacefully among the 'low-status' public, says Weber, but among the elite matters were different, with considerable tension between members of the professions and those engaged in commerce:

> While wholesalers dramatised their affluence with a gregarious salon life and vigorous support for virtuosi and the Italian opera, lawyers, artists and civil servants capitalised upon their learning and intellectual skills with intensive involvement in symphonic and chamber-music concerts. The dispute between the two musical camps served the interests of both groups by giving them arenas in which they could show off their various assets, and it has not ended to this day. (1975: 125)

In the long run, though, it was the professionals who 'built much of the institutional and intellectual groundwork for the modern concert world' and who propelled 'classical music' to the apex of the stylistic hierarchy.

It is also evident from Weber's remarks that participation in concert life involved rather more than simply the enjoyment of music – indeed, as we shall see, the music itself was sometimes regarded as a secondary aspect of the proceedings. Musical tastes generally, and concerts in particular, were means by which different groups could 'show off their various assets'. Music had become – and to an extent remains – a way of claiming or proclaiming a particular social identity, and it is to this that we may now turn.

Music as distinction

The progressive differentiation of music, a process characteristic of the modern era, and the simultaneous availability of diverse styles, makes them available as means of establishing and displaying identities and social positions: 'nothing more clearly affirms one's "class", nothing more infallibly classifies, than tastes in music', writes Pierre Bourdieu. 'This is of course because, by virtue of the rarity of the conditions for acquiring the corresponding dispositions, there is no more "classificatory" practice than concert-going or playing a "noble" instrument' (1984: 18). While some might be inclined to doubt the closeness of the correspondence between musical taste and social position which Bourdieu claims, several studies have illuminated ways in which the now-familiar stylistic and institutional framework of modern musical life has been influenced by groups seeking to protect, assert or display their status.

In her examination of musical patronage in Vienna in the period following Beethoven's arrival in 1791, Tia DeNora describes the historical and institutional conditions in which, she suggests, the new (and ultimately pervasive) ideology of 'serious' music was established. In the second half of the eighteenth century, it had become customary for the higher members of the aristocracy to maintain their own private orchestras, or *Hauskappellen*, in emulation of the Emperor's *Hofkappelle*, which by 1740 was an orchestra of 140 players (DeNora, 1991: 327). By the last decade of the century, however, the *Hauskappellen* were a thing of the past; drawing on research by Julia Moore, DeNora explains this not in terms of the artistocrats' declining economic fortunes (this came later) but as a result of the diminishing prestige which the orchestras could generate for their patrons. In short this extensive and expensive phase of musical patronage was initiated not by any particular concern for the music itself but out of the aristocrats' desire to display their wealth and social eminence to each other and to those they sought to emulate. Accordingly, when the *Hauskappellen* ceased to produce these desired effects, they were abandoned: when the imperial orchestra could no longer outshine those of the aristocrats it was allowed to decline, and when they, in turn, saw that the royal court had lost interest they too turned to other sources of social distinction (1991: 331–2).

Following the decline of the *Hauskappellen*, however, it seems that music still remained 'a primary medium for acquiring and demonstrating prestige' (1991: 332). Performances were given – by increasingly independent musicians – at *salons* and private functions, and there was an increase in the number of public concerts. These forms of musical activity, DeNora argues, allowed the participation of lesser aristocrats and members of the upper middle classes, and therefore presented a threat to the cultural dominance of the aristo-cratic elite. Increasingly, therefore, this group sought to maintain its leading role and to distinguish itself by embracing and espousing a new and specifically musical ideology: so purely quantitative demon-strations of wealth – the 'conspicuous consumption' represented by the *Hauskappellen* – gave way to *qualitative* 'demonstrations of dis-cernment and 'good taste' and a heightened emphasis on the appre-ciation of 'greatness' according to which the notion of master composers was constituted' (1991: 337).

It was in this context that Beethoven's aspirations received a sym-pathetic hearing: in defining him as a 'great' composer of 'great' music – 'beyond the horizons of most middle-class musical experience' (1991: 342) – Beethoven's aristocratic patrons recognised themselves as connoisseurs, as possessed of 'good taste', and as cul-tural leaders. In general then, and in the case of Beethoven in par-ticular, 'the aristocratic embrace of the new idea of musical greatness may have served as an attempt to maintain status in the face of the loss of exclusive control over the traditional institutional means of authority in music affairs' (1991: 337).

DeNora's examination of Viennese musical life around the turn of the nineteenth century is thus an excellent analysis of the processes through which a particular group sought to preserve social distinction through music. It also gives fascinating insight into the social origins of the ideology of 'greatness' in music which was to become so pervasive, and influential, through the nineteenth century and into the twentieth; moreover, as Citron argues, there is a further aspect of social distinction involved here, in that the model of the 'great composer' was in reality part of the ideology of the 'great man', which served to exclude and marginalise women (Citron, 1993: 201). In the present context, however, what is even more striking about DeNora's account is its critical implications for the widely held view of Beethoven as, *par excellence*, the composer of the new bourgeoisie. In the first place, Beethoven's early patrons and sponsors, as we have seen, were aristocrats seeking to maintain their elite status, not members of the bourgeoisie attempting to challenge it. Secondly, the evidence is that Beethoven's music was programmed overwhelmingly at concerts organised by the old aristocrats, and hardly at all at the middle-class concert venues (DeNora, 1991: 318–91). Such empirical evidence is difficult to reconcile with the grand (and grandiose) theories of those who, like Adorno, saw the rise of the new class represented in 'art' by the rise of the new music. It is, however, consistent with the view developed in this book that the meaning of music is not inherent, that it is not a direct expression of group values, but is, rather, socially constructed by particular people in particular times and places.

Other recent studies have investigated the origins of the pervasive distinction between 'high' and 'popular' culture, and the contrasting connotations of the terms 'art' and 'entertainment'; in general such work has emphasised the links between the emergence of a hierarchy of musical styles and more general patterns of social stratification in the industrialising societies of the nineteenth century. Broyles has shown how 'cultivated' instrumental music was introduced into Boston in the 1830s and 1840s as part of an effort to re-establish an earlier, republican vision of social order: to bring 'the masses into the fold of the eighteenth-century hierarchy through a common shared culture' (1991: 478). The attempt was doomed. 'The new socioeconomic elite', writes Broyles, 'were politically antidemocratic, socially insular, and at times pretentious about their wealth' (1991: 478). But the concept and practice of 'cultivated' music was now established, and available to be appropriated by the new rich, who soon availed themselves of 'the notion of high musical culture' and the institution of the symphony orchestra 'as a means of distancing themselves from other segments of society' (1991: 493).

Also focusing on the important case of Boston, Paul DiMaggio has examined the ways in which the newly dominant elite created an 'organizational base for high culture in America' (1986: 194).

> The sacralisation of art, the definition of high culture and its opposite popular culture and the institutionalisation of this classification, was the work of men and women whom I refer to as *cultural capitalists.* They were capitalists in the sense that their wealth came from the management of industrial enterprises from which they extracted a profit, and cultural capitalists in that they invested some of these profits in the foundation and maintenance of distinctly cultural enterprises. They also – and this is the second sense in which I use the term – were collectors of what Bourdieu has called 'cultural capital' (1986: 196)

The so-called 'Brahmins' of nineteenth-century Boston controlled, and displayed their mastery of, those forms of culture which could be legitimated in terms of the ideology of great art and institutionalised in socially exclusive ways. In his analysis, DiMaggio shows how the Boston Symphony Orchestra – the first in America to be philanthropically supported on a permanent basis – was created through the aggressive cultural entrepreneurship of Henry Lee Higginson, a partner in a brokerage firm and a well-connected member of the 'Brahmin' elite. Within a short time after its founding in 1881, the BSO had established an ascendancy over all previously rival organisations, with its players tied to exclusive and highly restrictive contracts. The Orchestra (and the Boston Museum of Fine Arts) were, says DiMaggio, central organisations in the life of the elite, and in his conclusion he echoes themes developed by Weber and Bourdieu, and by Marx and Gramsci:

> The Brahmins were a status group, and as such they strove towards exclusivity, towards the definition of a prestigious culture that they could monopolise as their own. Yet they were also a social class, and they were concerned, as is any dominant social class, with establishing hegemony over those they dominated. (1986:209)

The effect of the cultural capitalists' activities, therefore, was not simply to exclude the masses below but to render such exclusion legitimate by establishing the validity of the hierarchy of cultural forms.

Similar events were unfolding in other centres of nineteenth-century economic transformation. In Manchester, the first and for a time 'most important industrial city in the world' (Messinger, 1985: 1), a series of 'Gentlemen's Concerts' had been established as early as the 1740s. A century later – around the time when Engels was writing of the destitution of Manchester's working people – the 'Gentlemen's Concerts' provided a forum for the city's dominant elite which was expensive and socially exclusive. As Wilfred Allis has shown, the organisers of the Concerts paid large amounts of money to engage the leading soloists and singers of the day, yet it is evident that as often as not these were not listened to with any great degree of attention when they performed. The Concerts' programmes, too, were heterogeneous and musically undemanding; overall it seems that the Concerts were patronised for social rather than musical reasons – a conclusion which is supported by some contemporary accounts (Allis, 1994). Indeed, when Charles Hallé, having been invited to Manchester by the Gentlemen's Concerts, heard their orchestra he was tempted to return to France. Events surrounding Hallé's subsequent career, though, support the view of the Gentlemen's concerts as above all a forum for the new bourgeoisie. Hallé's own commitment was to 'serious' symphonic music, performed to a high standard and open to all; once his own orchestra and concerts became established, the Gentlemen's Concerts went into a long-term decline. Even when heavily in debt, however, with new subscribers hard to find, the Gentlemen's Concerts did not respond by relaxing their membership requirements or changing their policies (Allis, 1994).

The studies of the development of orchestral concerts in the great cities of the nineteenth century have prompted authors such as Christopher Small to understand them not in terms of musical ideology, but as rituals, affirming and celebrating the values and achievements of 'the power-holding class in our society' (Small, 1987: 7). It is in this sense that music may serve as a means of social distinction. But the ability of musical practices to proclaim and affirm group values should not be thought of as restricted to the display and consolidation of social class differences. Indeed, in recent years there has been increasing interest in examining the ways in which music may serve to demarcate identities in terms of gender, age, ethnicity, nationality, religion and other fundamental status factors which may be important in processes of social differentiation. Academic concern with these factors has been much stimulated by the rise of 'postmodern' thinking and in particular by the decline of the 'grand narratives' provided by Marxism and the ideology of modernity. Much of this work is consistent with Weber's perspective on social stratification, and seems likely to develop considerably in the near future.

Music as social control

Just as music has played a part in displaying and reinforcing the patterns of social stratification in capitalist societies, so it has been seen as a means by which the consequences of such social divisions – disintegration and conflict – might be mitigated. Challenges to the status quo, in others words, might be avoided by 'gentling the masses', and to the Victorian middle classes music seemed an eminently suitable means by which the virtues of Christianity, temperance, patriotism and so on might be cultivated (Russell, 1983: 100). To many later theorists, of course, this has appeared simply as an effort to inculcate a 'false consciousness' among the working class, preventing people from coming to an understanding of their real situation, and deflecting them from effective political action. The choral societies and brass bands – many of them sponsored by employers – which proliferated in Victorian England have often been interpreted in this light, and from his examination of popular music-making in this period Dave Russell concludes that in significant ways it 'reinforced, perhaps helped generate, conservative tendencies' (1987: 250). In Russell's view, three main factors were involved. Firstly, music 'rivalled politics for the time, money, and commitment of the working classes'. Secondly, it could provide events and occasions at which members of potentially antagonistic classes met and co-operated in a common enterprise. Thirdly, 'and most importantly, music provided artistic, social, economic and emotional satisfactions which made existence under capitalism far richer than might otherwise have been the case' (1987: 251). This last point is important for Russell in that it recognises the intrinsic satisfactions which people could obtain from musical activities, and leads us to resist the application of any 'crude models of social control' in which 'the working class dance like well-schooled puppets' (1987: 251). While there is no doubt that elements of the ruling-class ideology did indeed percolate 'downwards', particularly in the case of the music halls, the situation was in reality quite complex: music could be used also to symbolise resistance and alternative values, and, above all, 'the greatest emphasis has to be on the ability of people to *discover for themselves*, upon their ability to work out their own destinies' (1987: 252).

Other authors have examined some of the ways in which popular traditions of music were themselves reshaped according to the values and conventions of the Victorian middle class and their successors. Folk songs and rituals, as Georgina Boyes has shown, were recast, formalised and refined according to the mythology of 'Merrie England' and the delicate sensitivities of contemporary sexual mores (1993: 226). Interestingly, Boyes also points out that at a later stage in the 'folk revival', bawdiness and explicit eroticism was rediscovered and presented as evidence of authenticity, providing us with an excellent example of how the same tradition can be selectively represented in contrasting ways for different political or ideological purposes (1993: 229–30).

It has been suggested also that nineteenth-century music-making was formalised in ways which not only trampled on the vernacular traditions of the people but did so in a manner which opened the door to the commercialisation of popular music:

> By marginalising, dismissing and devaluing positive elements of the old plebeian musical tradition, the mid-nineteenth-century encounter between autonomous lower-class culture and middle-class taste and reforming zeal created the conditions for both the incorporated, patronised and denigrated culture of brass bands (albeit a culture in which new and in many ways positive identity could be forged) and, ironically, in the cultural partial vacuum created, the conditions for the success of the commercial provision of popular music. (V. and S. Gammon, 1991: 140)

The 'commercial provision of popular music' has, of course, been the story of the next century and beyond, and aspects of it will be considered later in this chapter. But fear of the potentially subversive power of music has remained, and from time to time inspires 'moral panic' and media campaigns against particular styles or performers. The wave of 'publicly legitimated attacks on rock' in the 1990s, argues Grossberg, 'can be seen as part of the larger project of regulating the possibilities of pleasure and identity as the basis of political opposition by dismantling the cultural and political field constructed in the 1960s' (1993: 193–4). Such attacks may be particularly intense when, as in the case of rap, the music concerned can be identified in the media with a social group – young, urban black men – which is seen as threatening (Binder, 1993).

From private to public patronage

One further aspect of the relationship between music and modern capitalism should be mentioned, although this has not been discussed widely in the academic literature. This is the transition from the era, discussed above (pp. 225–9), when 'serious' music was financed privately, through donations from benefactors (many of them members of successful commercial or industrial families), through subscriptions to concert societies or through sales of concert tickets at the 'box office', to a period in which this source of support has in many cases proved insufficient to sustain the presentation of operas, the maintenance of symphony orchestras and so on. Perhaps inevitably, this has led to forms of patronage by the community as a whole, through grants made by the state.

In Britain, the era of state patronage of the arts in general, and music in particular, began with the establishment of the Arts Council just after the Second World War. Its origins lay in the Council for the Encouragement of Music and the Arts which was set up early in the War in response to the need for something to 'be done for the minds and spirits of the civilian population' (Baldry, 1981: 12). In the early days, among other activities, a group called the Music Travellers gave concerts in factory canteens, air-raid shelters, churches, village halls and so on, and the Sadlers Wells Opera company 'took to the road with a scratch orchestra' (1981: 14). Things began to change from 1942, however, under CEMA's new chairman, the economist J. M. Keynes, who was created a baron at the time. Keynes had long been an advocate of public support for the arts, but not of the populist, amateur sort which had characterised CEMA's early days. As his contemporary Lord Clark put it, Keynes 'was not a man for wandering minstrels and amateur theatricals. He believed in excellence' (Baldry, 1981: 15). Under Keynes, the administration of CEMA became much more professionalised, but even more significant was the move towards the support of established, professional arts bodies, notably the establishment of a permanent company at the Royal Opera House, Covent Garden (of which Keynes was also chairman). The commitment to 'serious' orchestral music, and particularly to opera, was maintained when the Arts Council of Great Britain was established in 1946: in the years that followed, these forms of music were subsidised to a far greater extent than any others, with opera alone accounting for almost a quarter of all arts expenditure (Hutchinson, 1982: 35).

Neither Keynes nor Clark (one of his successors as Chair of the Arts Council) seemed to see any conflict of interest in their persistent advocacy of the Royal Opera House. Indeed, as Hutchinson has shown, they were central members of a powerful oliogarchy which linked the Government, the Arts Council, the Royal Opera House (and the new National Theatre), with the effect that arts policy increasingly reflected the needs of the major companies. 'Vested interests were fully involved in the Arts Council's decision-making from the outset', says Hutchinson, 'not as representatives or delegates, just as vested interests' (1982: 27). In the present context, we may note, firstly, the effectiveness of Keynes's role as a cultural entrepreneur, ensuring that public funds were devoted to supporting his own vision of 'art', and, secondly, the way in which money raised from general taxation was devoted to a minority art-form which had the support of a powerful and well-connected elite. By the 1980s, however, the situation was becoming increasingly uncertain, with the costs of operatic production and orchestras escalating, new demands for more equal disbursement of subsidies among the various musical genres, and government attempts to restrain public expenditure.

A similar story can be told about the development of national ratio broadcasting. Scannell has documented the process by which the professionals in the BBC's Music Department gradually (from the 1920s to the 1940s) brought about a change of emphasis in the Corporation's music policy: 'away from trying to educate the ordinary listener in the appreciation of good music, towards winning the approbation of the knowledgeable musical world' (1981: 242). With the establishment of the Third Programme after the War, the Department's victory was complete, and its view of 'serious' music institutionalised. The new channel allowed them to broadcast their music exclusively 'without being unduly bothered by demands from the authorities to serve the multitude' (1981: 258). The ensuing statistics tell their own story. By 1952 the percentage of the BBC's music budget devoted to the three radio channels was: Light Programme (70 per cent of audience) 15 per cent; Home Service (30 per cent of audience) 39 per cent; Third Programme (less than 1 per cent of audience) 46 per cent (1981: 260). It should be remembered that the BBC was (and is) funded by licence fees paid by *all* listeners. As in the case of opera, the revision of the BBC's music policy is a further excellent example of how influential minorities can use the ideology of 'serious' music to secure general public sponsorship for their own particular genres (and to marginalise and exclude others) where market demand is either absent or insufficient to make them commercially viable. Most music in industrial societies, however, is produced in response to a perceived market demand, and it is to this that we now turn.

The music business

> I wrote about what people wanted to hear. I packaged their feelings and sold them back. They wanted to laugh, they wanted to cry, they wanted to dance. I serviced them. I met the market.
>
> Irving Berlin (quoted in Whitcomb, 1987: 12)

Most of the music which surrounds us in modern societies reflects neither the age-old traditions of the people nor the impassioned strivings of the dedicated artist. It is, rather, the product of a vast and profitable industry, multinational in scale, which like any other business needs to produce the sort of goods that its customers will buy. In what follows we will consider the nature of modern music business operations and some of their implications – not least for the music itself, and those who create and buy it.

For many people, the music business seems symbolic of modernity itself – fast-moving, competitive, concerned with style rather than substance; an industry in which the pace of events and pressure for profits are so great that agents and managers operate just within the law and, as we shall see, sometimes beyond it. It has an undeniable glamour. Novelty and innovation are at a premium, and the rate of technological change is high. Yet the roots of the modern music business are long and deep: the basic process of producing and marketing songs was established in England by the late Middle Ages (Lloyd, 1975). The story of the origins and development of the music business is fascinating, and important for an understanding of its modern forms, but is much too vast a topic to be considered here. For present purposes, the crucial developments were those which led to the establishment of the recording industry as the dominant sector in the business, following the invention of Emile Berliner's 'gramophone' in Philadelphia in 1888, and the demonstration of Thomas Edison's 'phonograph' in London in 1890. This latter event prompted the eminent Victorian composer Sir Arthur Sullivan to declare that he was 'terrified at the thought that so much hideous music may be put on record for ever' (Sanjek, 1988, vol. 2: 366). By 1910 the infant industry had established itself in most countries throughout the world, and the two biggest companies – Victor, of Camden, New Jersey, and The Gramophone Company, of Hayes, England – were multinationals from the start (in fact the latter owned half of the former) (Gronow, 1983: 56).

The record business grew steadily, and sales accelerated in the years after the First World War. But the 1920s and early 1930s brought first a decline and then a virtual collapse, from the effects of, firstly, the proliferation of domestic radio receivers, and then the onset of the catastrophic economic slump in the years after 1929. The business did revive, but in a significantly different form, with major recording companies linked to film and radio interests, and mainly concerned with the marketing of 'star' names rather than recording established musicians. The recovery was given a major boost by the repeal of Prohibition in the USA in 1933, and the installation of juke boxes in thousands of bars and saloons: by 1938 there may have been as many as half a million of these machines (Sanjek, 1988, vol. 3: 133), taking up to 40 per cent of US record production. American record sales had recovered to their 1921 level by 1945 (Gronow, 1983) and by the 1960s 'for the first time record sales surpassed the gross revenues of all other forms of entertainment' (Peterson and Berger, 1975: 167). At the start of the post-war period, then, 'the basic structure of the modern music industry was in place' (Frith, 1988: 19). Inevitably, this structure, and the industry's characteristic policies and practices, were a reflection of the sequence of techno-logical innovations which had kept the business in a dynamic state from the start, and of its particular pattern of historical develop-ment. Frith, for example, has argued that 'the British record industry was formed by the specific conditions of the 1930's recession' (1987a: 288). More generally, it is such circumstances which have governed the process by which the record business became institutionalised; once established, of course, its practices and procedures may well come to seem necessary and inevitable, particularly by those whose livelihoods depend on them.

In its pattern of development, moreover, the recording industry has been characteristic of its era, indeed in certain respects it has been prototypical. It owes its existence, and its continued develop-ment, to successive waves of technological innovation, each of which, in its time, represented the 'state of the art'. In its pattern of organisation, too, it has been in the forefront, evolving rapidly from the small companies of inventors and entrepreneurs typical of the late nineteenth century to the giant corporations which CBS, RCA and EMI had become by the late 1930s, and on into the vast multi-national, multi-media communications empires which dominate the entertainment business (and much else) in the 1990s. Almost from the start, the record business catered to a mass market (though it was some time before its orientation became dominated by considerations of mass sales). In this respect, records, radio and films together constituted a fundamental challenge to the dominant cultural conventions of the early twentieth century: they gave people the power to hear what they wanted, rather than what others thought they should have. In America, says Sanjek, the new media meant the end of the long reign enjoyed by Stephen Foster's songs and Sousa's marches: in the 1920s 'the secular-music business was the most obvious element in the general revolt against the cultural tradition that had dominated the nation for a century' (1988, vol. 3: 92). The 'bland music programmes' of classical and semi-classical material which had predominated in the early years of American radio were replaced, under pressure from advertising agencies, by popular singers, 'hot' bands, and dialect comedy; the result was huge increases in both audiences and advertising revenues (1988, vol. 3, 89). In Britain, even the BBC, established according to the 'public service' philosophy of Lord Reith, eventually had to dilute its principles once the record companies 'moved from educating the masses to servicing them' (Frith, 1987a: 287). Ultimately, the matter is one of *control* – whether the content of the media is to be decided by established authorities or by popular demand via the market. As the twentieth century progressed, the balance of power moved irrevocably from the former to the latter, in no small part owing to the influence of the new means of mass communication.

Of course it would be quite wrong to regard the market as a simple mechanism for the expression of popular tastes. Record companies and others who operate in it try s far as possible to reduce its uncertainties and their own risks – increasingly by promoting as 'popular' the sort of music which will have the widest possible appeal, and offend as few people as possible. Thus, just as in the early days of radio, the resulting 'popular' music is often an adulterated form of some more vital style, or, increasingly in recent times, is manufactured in the studio with a mass audience in mind.

For many critics, such tendencies are evidence of the vacuous nature of 'pop' music, which they see as constructed at the lowest common denominator of public taste, simply in order to yield profits. Others, however, are more impressed by the fact that the market does provide a choice for the consumers, who can then buy what they like, and interpret it in any way they choose. Naturally, most of those who have made careers in the industry incline towards the second interpretation, and Sanjek draws attention to a fascinating editorial from the *New York Times* of 18th September 1940, which celebrated the relatively new freedom that records and radio had given people – to choose what they wanted to hear, when to hear it, and how often. This, said the paper, was evidence of 'surviving individualism in a mass production age' (Sanjek, 1988, vol. 3: 145–6).

The organisation of the music business
We shall discuss these contrasting interpretations of the social role and function of popular music below. Before that, however, it will be useful to consider certain ideas about the operation and organisation of the music business, particularly since the implication of these ideas is to cast some doubt on the belief that music inevitably reflects fundamental aspects of the societies or groups in which it develops. As I argued in Chapters 3 and 4, the emergence of cultural forms is not an automatic or predetermined process, like the growth of plants from seeds or chickens from eggs. Such forms emerge and are sustained as a consequence of a perpetual process of action and interaction among individuals and groups in pursuit of their interests; thus the nature of cultural forms is neither predictable nor reducible to some supposed basic characteristics of the society, but is shaped by the specific historical circumstances of their production.

The development of the music business in America provides an abundance of examples which may serve to make the point in a less abstract way. It would be easy, and plausible, to interpret the transformation of American popular music from the sentimental songs of the Stephen Foster era to the ragtime of the twentieth century simply as a direct reflection of rapid industrialisation, the tranquility of rural life replaced by the hustle and bustle of the city, and the growing sense of American national identity. Clearly, such processes were important in reshaping the musical culture, in all sorts of ways; this conventional explanation, however, fails to account for the specific forms of music which did occur. Nothing comparable, for example,

occurred during rapid industrialisation, urbanisation and nationalism in Britain or Germany: individually or jointly, these processes *in
themselves* cannot be held to explain ragtime or the 'jazz age'. Most
authorities, of course, have rightly emphasised the importance in
America of black music traditions, consolidated in the relative isolation of the post-Civil-War period, and interacting with European
styles following the subsequent northern migration. But the presence
of black people in North America, the isolation and the migration
are all historically contingent factors, and the nature of the music
which emerged can be understood only as the unpredictable outcome
of a field of contrasting and often conflicting forces. It does not
express the soul of 'the' people, or mirror the core of a monolithic
culture but is the unplanned and unanticipated consequence of different traditions as they converge and collide.

A further essential ingredient in the mix was the equally contingent influx of immigrants from Europe, and in particular the emergence of the Jewish songsmiths and entrepreneurs who created the
music business in something like its modern form. The business was
already big and comfortable, and in the Tin Pan Alley era they made
it dynamic and very much bigger, as their new songs were sold in the
burgeoning cities. But once again it would be an over-simplification
to see this success as just a matter of giving the people what they
wanted. Without a doubt, the preferences of the new urban dwellers,
many of them only recent arrivals in America, were different from
those of the small towns and counties of the vast rural areas, and it
is clear, too, that the fashion was for novelty and innovation, not
least in music. None the less, it is also clear that the market – then
as now – was particularly volatile, with a few songs selling in vast
numbers but the majority disappearing without trace. Around 1900,
according to Sanjek, only one in two hundred songs made a substantial profit, and fewer than half broke even (1988, vol. 2: 411).
Inevitably, such uncertainties led publishers to make attempts to control their situation, and before long elaborate and extensive networks
of 'song-pluggers' had been established, and artists enlisted to perform certain material. 'Vaudeville provided the music trade for many
years with its chief means of exploitation, through forty-week
engagements of headliner music stars across the nation, who constantly performed songs they had been paid to feature.' This was not
cheap: the cost of popularising a new song could be up to $75,000
(1988, vol. 3: 33). But the persistence of such practices, both legal and

illegal, strongly suggests that promotion paid off – in other words, that demand could not only be met in rather haphazard ways but could be created in rather more systematic ones.

So while it would be absurd to deny that music becomes popular because people like it, at the same time it cannot be taken for granted that the music business simply provides them with what they want. Preferences and wants, as we have seen in Chapter 1, are themselves the results of socialisation experiences, and in modern capitalist societies it is the business of a vast army of advertisers, opinion-formers and 'public relations' professionals to manipulate such experiences. From the very earliest days, record companies have spent much time and money trying to associate their products with positive personal images, desirable life styles and so on: by 1912, Victor's advertising budget was already $1.5 million (Gelatt, 1954). Moreover, as Tin Pan Alley publishers and record company executives have always understood, the public can choose only from what it is offered. Recorded music has never been a wholly representative sample of musical activity, and in recent times, as we shall see, there has been increasing emphasis on the cultivation and promotion of 'star' names who will sell in massive quantities, to the exclusion of most other styles. The issue around which we can organise this discussion, then, is the extent to which the record companies' activities may be seen basically as *responses* to market demand, and the extent to which they can themselves *create* such demand. In any real situation, of course, both factors are likely to be involved, and we should be wary of simple arguments which emphasise one at the expense of the other. However, sociologically-minded authors have been sceptical of accounts which simply assume the freedom of the consumer to make choices in an open market, precisely because such an interpretation neglects the strenuous efforts which are made both to influence patterns of choice and to mitigate the harsher effects of the market.

It was a celebrated economist, however, who made the point most forcefully. In considering the operation of the large industrial corporations which are the dominant forces in modern economies, Galbraith argues that the classic price mechanism no longer serves to tell producers what goods they can sell, and what they ought to cost. The development of, for example, new aircraft or cars is such a complex, expensive and time-consuming business that the manufacturer cannot leave it to chance that there will be a demand for the new products and that the price will be right for intending buyers:

> in addition to deciding what the consumer will want and will pay, the
> firm must take every feasible step to see that what it decides to produce
> is wanted by the consumer at a remunerative price. And it must see that
> the labor, materials and equipment that it needs will be available at a
> cost consistent with the price it will receive. It must exercise control
> over what is sold. It must exercise control over what is supplied. It must
> replace the market with planning (Galbraith, 1967: 23–4)

Even with such planning, the risks are considerable, and it is obvious that only very large organisations can participate, given the enormous amounts of time and money which must be expended before
any income is generated, and the possibility that heavy losses may
still be the outcome. It is Galbraith's contention, then, that at the
heart of the modern economy the market must give way to planning,
and his conclusion is uncompromising: 'Much of what the firm
regards as planning consists in minimising or getting rid of market
influences' (1967: 26).

But can Galbraith's analysis be applied to the operations of the
modern music business? The developments which concern him, so
corrosive of the ideal of the free market economy, are in his view the
direct consequence of advanced and complex production technology,
and it could be argued that despite a remarkable series of technical
innovations which have transformed the recording and reproduction
of sound in the last century, the basic processes of the record business are *not* all that different from those which were established in
the days of Gaisberg and Caruso. Moreover, in the view of Denisoff,
record companies are not in a position to control their markets in
the way that the industrial giants described by Galbraith are presumed to do, since 'discs and cassettes are a discretionary item, a
product a consumer buys with leisure funds. Records are also in
competition with all of the other entertainment media' (1986: 80).
Not surprisingly, this view is favoured by most of those who work
in the industry, confronted daily by the intractable problem of knowing what a fickle public will decide to buy. Indeed, the industry's
development has been spasmodic, the history of individual companies chequered and, on the level of individual items, there are countless tales of expensively produced 'surefire' hits which went down
like the Titanic while some novelty recording notched up sales of a

million or more.

Moreover, all those involved in the record business are from time to time made uncomfortably aware of the vulnerability of even the most successful operations. A spectacular example is provided by the case of Capitol Records, which through its parent company, the British giant EMI, had the good fortune in 1963 to acquire the Beatles' records for the American market. (Significantly, Capitol, like most American companies, was initially uninterested in the English group, rejected 'She loves you', and only released 'I want to hold your hand' following personal pressure from the Beatles' manager, Brian Epstein. Within weeks the record was number one in the US chart, selling a million copies in the process (Rogan, 1989: 167–8, 173.) For the next few years, Capitol simply had to release Beatles records in order to make huge profits. It signed dozens of relatively unprofitable artists, became lazy and was then almost destroyed by the break-up of the Beatles, the Beach Boys' move to Warners and a slump in country music sales. So the company which could do no wrong in the mid-1960s suffered a rapid decline. 'By 1972', says Denisoff, 'Warner was the king of the mountain and Capitol was $8m in the red. Its stock had dropped over the years from 63 to 6 points on the American Stock Exchange' (1986: 94). Capitol survived, but it was a close thing, and a painful reminder that, for all their imposing offices, established names and extravagant ways, the profits of the record companies ultimately depended on the whims and foibles of millions of temperamental adolescents. This is not a very secure source of finance for the multi-million dollar corporations which, ever since income from record sales exceeded that from sheet music in the early 1950s, have been the 'power centre' of the music business (Garofalo, 1987: 78).

Given the turbulent conditions in which they have to operate, then, it is not surprising that much of the discussion of the operation of modern record companies is concerned with the strategies they have evolved to cope with the uncertainties of the market, by attempting either to control it, in Galbraith's sense, or to minimise its risks. The theme is a general one – indeed it seems that many of the activities of organisations, as of individuals, can be understood as attempts to protect themselves from the unpredictability of their environment: stability and security are sought in the face of constant and inevitable change.

There is something of a paradox here, since, in order to survive, organisations need to change, adapting themselves to new circumstances and protecting themselves against new threats. In the earliest phases of industrialisation, this was not such a problem – enterprises were generally small, and could open up and close down causing a minimum of social disruption, particularly during periods of economic growth. In the era of the large corporation, however, this is much harder. As Tom Burns has put it: 'Firms employing many thousands of people cannot close down without wrecking large areas of social organisation. Such concerns must keep alive, and in order to keep alive they must become adaptive; change must occur within the organisation and not through its extinction and replacement, if it is to occur' (Burns and Stalker, 1961: 35). For Burns, there is an important implication for the organisation of industrial and commercial activities – the classic formal model of bureaucracy, elaborated by Weber as the maximally rational form of organisation, is only so under certain conditions: 'the effective organisation of industrial resources ... does not approximate to one ideal type of management system, but alters in important respects in conformity with changes in extrinsic factors. These extrinsic factors are all ... identifiable as different rates of technical or market change' (1962: 96). Where both market and technology are relatively stable and predictable, then the classic formal bureaucracy ('mechanistic' organisation in Burns's terms) may be perfectly appropriate and efficient. But where, as in the music business, both technology and market are subject to rapid change, less rigid and more adaptable forms of management ('organic' organisation) must be evolved. As we shall see, there are indications that this is exactly what has occurred as a means of coping with the perpetual uncertainities of the record business. Moreover, it appears that the major sources of uncertainty derive, as Burns suggests, from the market and from technology. We may consider these in turn.

The volatile market

Peterson and Berger develop the idea that, in conditions of extreme market turbulence, organisations must rely on a strategy which, following Joseph Schumpeter, they term entrepreneurship: 'the use of a novel combination of the available means of production' (1971: 98). In contrast to the routine procedures of the bureaucratic organisation, the 'exercise of entrepreneurship requires the freedom to work outside normal channels ... so that the entrepreneur is likely to find the organisation stultifying, while the organisation may find the entrepreneur disruptive' (1971: 98). For this reason, Peterson and Berger suggest that significantly different organisational patterns are to be found within the three main divisions of a major record company. In an analysis consistent with that of Burns, they observe that, because of the routine nature of its tasks, 'the manufacturing division of the company is fully segregated from environmental turbulence, and ... this division is quite bureaucratic in organisation'. Similarly, the sales and promotion division, while not entirely unaffected by market uncertainties, 'operates as if it were unaffected by turbulent aspects of the environment'. On the other hand, the production division 'is expected to create a succession of hit records and thus is more directly in contact with the turbulent environment ... The production division is loosely organised so that it can adapt to the continuous changes in the turbulent market.' And within the production department, 'the entrepreneurial function is isolated as far as possible into one specific role ... In the record industry, this is the producer – sometimes called an artist and repertoire man or A and R man' (1971: 99). The producer's job is to find suitable artists and, if necessary, material for them to perform, and to arrange for them to record it. Potentially, this gives producers great power *vis-à-vis* both artists and record company, but it also makes them extremely vulnerable if the records fail to sell in the necessary quantities. Moreover, although producers are given a budget and, in principle, a free hand to pursue their projects, record companies have evolved effective strategies to limit their risks, as Peterson and Berger point out. Firstly, the freedom of each producer is limited: 'the degree of entrepreneurial discretion given to a producer is a function of his recent track record' (1971: 101). Secondly, companies try to maximise the number of entrepreneurial decisions while minimising their investment in each. There may be a number of producers, each with a roster of artists, all releasing records: the theory is that, if costs are kept as low as possible, the few records which sell in large quantities will generate sufficient profit to more than compensate for the many that do not. Thirdly, the success of each producer is rapidly monitored, using the all-important 'charts' of sales and radio plays. Finally, producers are hired, rewarded and fired in ways which closely reflect the success – or otherwise – of their efforts. A string of 'chart' successes may bring a lucrative long-term contract, but failure to make an impression on the 'charts' will lead to a producer being 'let go' fairly swiftly.

Since the publication of Peterson and Berger's paper in the early 1970s, and confirming their general analysis, there has been a clear tendency for producers and record companies to become even more independent of each other, with most producers in the popular music field now 'freelance' contractors, who lease or sell the recordings they make to the companies for marketing, manufacture and distribution (Fink, 1989: 59–61; Lopes, 1992).

Through this separation of the 'creative' from the 'routine' aspects of record production, then, the companies aim to be able to cope with the inevitable fluctuations of their market. In Peterson and Berger's terms, the greater the 'degree of turbulence' in the environment, the more scope for 'entrepreneurship' there is likely to be (1971: 102), just as Burns argued that an 'organic' form of organisation would be more effective in a turbulent environment. Inevitably, however, business organisations will make efforts not only to adapt to market uncertainties but to reduce them, and this theme is developed in a later paper by Peterson and Berger. In this, they examine the cycles of concentration and dispersion which seem to characterise the history of the record business, as the gradually increasing size and power of an ever-decreasing number of companies is interrupted by a sudden outbreak of competition sparked by many new, small entrants to the market. Thus the 'degree of turbulence' is itself variable: during periods of concentration, the big companies will establish some degree of control over the market, but in periods of competition they will be less able to succeed in this. These ideas are examined through a consideration of the pattern suggested by the post-war development of the business. Peterson and Berger (1975) divide the period from 1948 to 1973 into five phases:

(1) *1948–55: Corporate concentration.* The American record industry was dominated by four companies – RCA Victor, Columbia, Decca and Capitol – who shared 75 per cent of the total market in 1948, while the top eight companies accounted for 'virtually all of the hit singles during the period'. This 'oligopolistic' control extended across 'the total production flow from raw materials to wholesale sales' (1975: 161–2). The big four firms were linked to songwriting and publishing interests and to radio and movie companies; through their domination of distribution networks, moreover, they could squeeze out small independent firms and apply pressure to retailers. Even the 'star' names were treated much as any other

item of company property (Denisoff, 1986: 83). The system seemed to work well: Mitch Miller's 'sexy, simple and sad' formula produced eighty million sales for Columbia between 1950 and 1956 (1975: 83).

(2) *1956–9: Competition.* 'I'm all shook up', sang Elvis Presley in 1957. So was the record business: the big four companies, which two years earlier had still produced 74 per cent of American 'hit' singles, were down to 40 per cent and still slipping. Whereas in 1949 all US 'hits' had been produced by eight companies, forty-two had top ten 'hits' in 1959. New independent companies were mushrooming, and sales boomed. For Peterson and Berger, this eruption of activity was in many ways a direct result of the major companies' earlier oligopoly: their efforts to market bland, innocuous music with maximum mass appeal left many tastes uncatered for. Moreover, the steady growth of record sales is not so impressive if cost-of-living and other economic indicators are taken into account – the absolute increases in sales concealed a relative decline in the industry's performance. In short, the explosion of demand from 1955 to 1959 (when sales grew by 261 per cent) is evidence of 'a great reservoir of unsated demand' (1986: 164). As early as 1951 the disc jockey Alan Freed had considerable success by playing black 'rhythm and blues' tracks to mainly white audiences (Gillett, 1983: 13).

Other factors combined to undermine the majors' position, notably the growing availability of portable 'transistor' radios, and in particular the response of American radio to the advent of network national television, which was to become local, and specialised. As a result, a diverse range of music received unprecedented airplay around the country (Peterson and Berger, 1975: 165), stimulating demand for many of the black music styles which the majors had marginalised. Before long it was evident that rock 'n' roll was not a passing fashion (as the industry had hoped), but was here to stay and the big companies were trying to follow the example of Decca, who had signed Bill Haley from the independent Essex in 1954. (Haley's 'Rock around the clock' was in the US top ten for nineteen weeks from May 1955; of equal significance is the fact that the song was an ordinary twelve-bar blues whose initial melody bears more than a passing resemblance to a theme copyrighted by the black composer Richard M. Jones many years earlier (Morgan, n.d.).) RCA managed to remain in the top four only by its acquisition of Elvis Presley (for $30,000 and a Cadillac) from Sun Records of Memphis. Presley, too, especially in his early days, sang black music in a way that could be sold to white audiences of the time, but in the view of many rock critics his career exemplifies a typical pattern by which the raw and vital talent of an artist is rendered smooth and lifeless in the interests of mass consumption (Gillett, 1983: 54). In George Melly's phrase, it is the process that turns 'revolt into style' (1972). Undoubtedly Presley and others were turned into nice guys with mass sales potential, but, as Gillett's account indicates, it is too simple to view the major companies as 'baddies' and the independents as 'goodies'. Once the latter had made the initial breakthrough into the national big time, they made every effort to stay there, and both major companies and independents attempted with some success to 'knock the rough edges off rock 'n' roll' (Gillett, 1983: 41). So by the end of the 1950s, there was a much reduced level of concentration in the industry, but already there were signs that the familiar logic of the business was reasserting itself.

(3) *1959–63: Secondary consolidation.* In comparison with the previous period, the increase in record sales was sluggish. But the major companies continued to buy the contracts of established (white) artists, and to develop some of their own, notably the Beach Boys (Capitol) and Bob Dylan (Columbia). Typically, the latter, championed by the veteran producer John Hammond, met with great resistance inside the company. Before long, 'Hammond's folly' had transformed the company (Hammond, 1981: 351–8), and by 1963 three of the old big four held the top three positions for number of 'hits' in the top ten. The trend towards concentration had been reestablished.

(4) *1964–9: Renewed growth.* Fuelled by Dylan and the Beatles, US record sales leapt ahead once again. The value of sales almost doubled in the period, and, for the first time, 'record sales surpassed the gross revenues of all other forms of entertainment' (Peterson and Berger, 1975: 167). The trend towards renewed concentration continued – yet this was a time in which artists were given a much greater amount of freedom by their record companies. The situation is not easily reconciled with Peterson and Berger's hypothesis that there is an inverse relationship between artistic innovation and the degree of industrial concentration, and they speculate that there may be a time-lag before it becomes effective.

(5) *1970–73: Reconcentration.* Growth of record sales was again modest, but the trend to concentration accelerated. By 1973, only

two real independents – Motown and A & M – remained in the top eight companies; moreover the big companies themselves were by now divisions of large multinational corporations. As we have seen, the emergence of the latter has been regarded with suspicion by economists like Galbraith, since they seek to overwhelm the market, and by Marxist thinkers who argue that, in an era of monopoly capitalism, such companies will produce only what is profitable, rather than what people want, and will do all they can to manipulate demand.

On the other hand, according to Peterson and Berger, each phase of concentration in the music business has been followed by sudden outbreaks of 'competition and diversity', driven by the accumulation of unsatisfied demand. In the very process of attempting to pacify the market, the big companies sow the seeds of an inevitable revolt against their dominance. Thus for Peterson the crucial factor necessary to explain the eruption of rock 'n' roll around 1955, and neglected in most accounts of the period, is the way that the constraints which the industry had successfully applied to the production and marketing of music were, for a variety of technological, legal and economic reasons, considerably loosened. The momentous stylistic transformation came about not as a response to changes in youth culture (post-war 'baby boomers' were still children in 1955) but because the industry's ability to control the market was weakened. The result was that both artists and record-buyers had greater freedom to make and hear the music they wanted. More generally, Peterson's argument once again emphasises the inadequacy of viewing a change in musical styles as reflecting more general social changes: as he puts it, 'the times were not changing, but the constraints were' (1990: 98).

It would be too simple, however, to see the development of the music business only in terms of a recurring cycle of concentration and dispersion. As we have seen, the late 1960s saw both corporate concentration and increased autonomy for recording artists. And when the 'punk' revolt did occur following the reconcentration of the early 1970s, its nature and outcome were different from that of 1955. By the mid-1970s, three companies in Britain (EMI, CBS and Polygram) had half the singles market and 44 per cent of album sales; six companies had two-thirds of the market (Laing, 1985: 1). In the USA, the majors were 'the only game in town' (Eliot, 1990: 172). Highly expensive recording and marketing procedures were standard, and there is evidence that sales were beginning to stagnate. Developing out of 'alternative' pubs and clubs, however, and using 'garage' rather than state-of-the-art technology, the punk bands could make and distribute records at a small fraction of the majors' costs. As Dave Laing puts it, they had begun to open up '... a *space* for both performing and recording which lay outside the constraints of the mainstream music industry' (1985: 9). In 1974–5 EMI released 145 singles, of which a mere ten were 'hits', with the result that the break-even point for any single was above twenty thousand sales. In contrast, the punk labels which proliferated from 1977 could break even at sales of two thousand by producing the records themselves, establishing alternative distribution channels, knowing their market and hence avoiding the need for expensive promotional activities (1985: 10). In Laing's words: 'If punk rock's concern with political and social topics took its cue from general ideological trends, *its achievement was nevertheless to introduce such themes into songs*, something which the mainstream of popular music had successfully resisted for a decade' (1985: 31, emphasis added). Once again the point is that the radical messages of punk were not a simple reflection of 'general ideological trends'; what was distinctive, and significant, about the movement was that the young rebels were in a position to produce their own records without the need to deal with established companies and their market-orientation. The constraints were off.

In retrospect, of course, it is clear that punk did not become the Next Big Thing for the music business; as an essentially oppositional movement, beset by internal contradictions, its disintegration was inevitable (1985: 109). But while the 'revolt' did indeed soon turn into 'style', the more enduring consequence for the music business was that: 'Independent label economics had been born' (1985: 9) and the independent sector continued to provide 'a base for a range of radical music unimaginable a decade earlier' (1985: 128).

Others have argued that the 'new' independent sector has changed the relationship between the big companies and the smaller ones: where earlier there was competition, and conflict, there is now complementarity, with small labels now being used by the majors to develop and market new talent. For Frith, Peterson and Berger's pattern of cyclical concentration and dispersion should now be replaced with a model of the record business as a large corporate centre surrounded by 'a periphery of local music scenes' established on both a geographical and a stylistic basis; these reflect not only long-established 'minority' interests but also the 'fragmentation of pop taste' which new technology has made possible (Frith, 1990: 110). In an important up-dating of Peterson and Berger's work, Lopes concluded that the industry in the years up to 1990 displayed both high levels of corporate concentration *and* increasing innovation and diversity in its products. Within the major companies, a new strategy has been developed: 'an "open" system that incorporates or establishes a number of semiautonomous label divisions within each company, which then establish links with smaller independent labels and record producers' (Lopes, 1992: 57). To cope effectively with their turbulent environment, these organisations have had to become more flexible and decentralised, in other words to abandon the 'mechanistic' form of bureaucracy – as Burns said they should – and develop 'organic' patterns of management and control.

Increasingly, then, the aim of the major companies is to concentrate on the production and marketing of a selected handful of actual or potential superstars, with results that can produce spectacular profits. Almost by definition, such rewards are unlikely to be achieved by the independents, but – as I have suggested – the quest of the majors for market domination no longer means that the independents have to be squeezed out or eliminated. Some things, however, have changed little. It is generally accepted that the predominance of the big four in the 1950s was secured by various illegal means, notably the payment of bribes – payola – for the performance of records on radio. In one account of these years, it is suggested that the successful prosecution of DJ Alan Freed, and his subsequent downfall, was inspired above all by the desire of the major companies, in the form of the ASCAP publishing house, to eliminate a threatening independent operator (Eliot, 1990: 75ff.). Though illegal, some form of payola seems to have been widespread whenever there has been intensive competition in the business – from the promotion of 'After the ball' in 1892 (Toll, 1982: 102) to the dubious activities of 'promoters' in more recent times. It was alleged to Eliot that 'as standard practice upwards of $100,000 is normally factored into the budget of any potential hit record. In reality this is payola designated under a variety of promotional headings' (1990: 218). Interestingly, an identical sum is mentioned by Frederic Dannen as the price of hiring a top 'promoter' of a pop record in the late 1970s. What these people do is ensure – by whatever means they

think fit – that the record gets radio airplay, without which it is
almost certain to fail (Dannen, 1991: 7, 9). Despite the exposure of
an informal syndicate of American 'promoters' – the 'Network' – in
the 1980s, Dannen concludes that the industry is still permeated by
corrupt practices:

> the 'new' record business of today, with its sophisticated multination-
> als, is no different from the 'old' record business of the buccaneering
> fifties. ... If the early rock and roll labels were unspeakably crooked, at
> least they did not spend tens of millions in protection money. It would
> take the big, lawyerly corporations of the eighties to bring that about.
> (1991: 27)

The apparent persistence of payola and the occasional scandals over
the question of corruption in the record business may be used to
illustrate two general sociological themes. Firstly, activities often
become defined as deviant only when it is in the interests of some
dominant group to treat them as such (Lemert, 1972: 23). As one
record executive put it: 'Only in the music industry did it become a
crime to take a client out to lunch. The payola scandal [of the 1950s]
had nothing to do with payola. It was a very successful attempt on
ASCAP's part to regain control of the music industry ... it was a
question of corporate politics, with morality the vehicle used to sell
the public' (Eliot, 1990: 79). Secondly, and of central concern to this
chapter, the resort to illegal activities may be regarded as a further
means by which individuals and groups attempt to reduce or eliminate the competition they face in a highly volatile market. As we
have seen, companies have engaged in all sorts of expensive ploys in
their efforts to influence radio DJs and programmers, and have similarly adopted various methods to induce retailers to stock their
products (and not others). The pages of the books by Garfield (1986),
Rogan (1989) and Eliot (1989) are full of the names of major stars
(and also-rans) who have been held to exploitative contracts, or who
have sought redress in the courts.

The music business, then, may be regarded as a 'game', in the
sense that Norton Long (1958) used the term: one of the many areas
of social organisation which constitute the reality of urban-industrial
life. Yet in comparison with other 'games' it is disordered and unreg-
ulated, governed neither by traditional ways of doing things nor by
the culture of what Weber called a 'status group', whose members
share a common outlook, lifestyle and a sense of 'fair play'. Indeed,

it was Weber's view that the development of such a consensus on the ethics of business was an important means by which order and stability was maintained in market transactions (Bendix, 1962: 27, 29). A similar theme is developed by Durkheim in his classic demonstration of the 'non-contractual' element in contracts, the prior framework of moral regulation upon which even the most apparently straightforward economic transactions are based (Durkheim, 1964). Rogan refers to Paul McCartney's belief that the relationship between the Beatles and their manager 'was infinitely more important than a signature on a contract' (1989: 173). You have to be able to trust people: but where there is no sense of shared attachment to a moral order or a status culture, social relations may be problematic, unpredictable and stressful.

For Durkheim, the absence of shared ethics governing economic life was a pathological social condition which 'throws the door wide open to every sort of adventure' (1952: 257). Durkheim's critics, however, suggest that such a condition of *anomie* is normal rather than pathological in a capitalist economic order where there is a low degree of regulation and a strong belief in competitive individualism (Lukes, 1975: 174–8). Interviewed in 1971, Allen Klein, the former business manager of both the Beatles and the Rolling Stones, outlined his view of the music 'game':

> The music business is about 99% no-talent losers who can't stand a winner in their midst. I'm a winner, and if they want to sour-grape my success by calling me names, let them. I don't give a shit.
>
> Q. Would you lie?
>
> A. Oh, sure.
>
> Q. Would you steal?
>
> A. Probably. Look, you have to survive, you do whatever it takes, because if you don't stay alive in this business you can't help anybody. ... It's really like chess, knowing all the moves. It's a game, for Chrissakes, and winning is everything. It's a shame it has to get nasty sometimes. (Quoted in Garfield, 1986, 257)

More usually, the conflicts, chaos and confusion which seem to characterise the record business must be understood, as Keith Negus puts it, 'as an active response – on the part of individuals and groups – to the imperative of commercial success' (Negus, 1992: 151).

Changing technology

Just as the record industry has been shaped by the need to cope with its volatile market, so its established practices and institutions have been constantly undermined by technological innovations which not only offer new and better ways of doing things but – as we shall see – have generally had the effect of increasing consumers' choice at the expense of the industry's ability to control its market. Indeed, the music business began to assume its modern form as an unanticipated consequence of the development of recording in the 1880s, and the threat which this posed was soon apparent to piano-makers and retailers, music teachers, sheet music publishers, music hall and vaudeville artists, proprietors and so on. The new gramophones and phonographs were important, too, in creating a mass market for music and entertainment (Toll, 1982).

Somewhat paradoxically, however, the new mass market was different in character: music was no longer a necessarily public, communal experience, but could be heard at home, divorced from the settings in which it was originally produced. Sound recording, then, gave a powerful boost to the 'privatisation' of experience which many have held to be a fundamental aspect of twentieth-century culture. Moreover, the chance to buy recordings gave individuals, in principle, an unprecedented degree of control over their own musical environment: this ability to choose from a range of cultural options has also been seen as an important component of modernity. According to Schafer:

> The three most revolutionary sound mechanisms of the Electric Revolution were the telephone, the phonograph, and the radio. With the telephone and the radio, sound was no longer tied to its original point in space; with the phonograph it was released from its original point in time. The dazzling removal of these restrictions has given modern man an exciting new power which modern technology has continually sought to render more effective. (Schafer, 1977: 89)

Nor should this power be thought of as confined to the sphere of domestic entertainment. 'We should have not have captured Germany', wrote Adolf Hitler, 'without ... the loudspeaker' (Schafer, 1977: 91).

The development of recording techniques threatened the structure of the nineteenth-century entertainment business, but the new record companies were themselves challenged in turn by the rise of cinema and then radio. Later upheavals were brought about by television and tape-recorders, with the latter giving people an unprecedented ability to make their own recordings. Nor is there any likelihood that the pace of change will slacken: in recent years, the 'compact disc' has brought to an end the forty-year reign of the twelve-inch LP (with considerable consequences for production, distribution and marketing). Within studios, the advent of synthesisers has blurred the established distinctions between musicians, composers, engineers and producers – to the point where they may well disappear. And recording technology has advanced well beyond the point where the main purpose is to 'record' a 'performance'. According to Brian Eno: 'There's been a break between the traditional idea of music ... and what we now do on records ... It's now possible to make records that have music that was never performed or never *could* be performed and in fact doesn't exist outside of that record' (Eno, 1983: 16). Beyond that, of course, it is now apparent that the recording studio itself is no longer necessary for the production of good-quality recordings.

The list of possible innovations, many simply using already existing technology, could be extended; indeed, the development of the music business provides countless illustrations of Marx's insight into the ways in which changes in the 'forces of production' ultimately act to undermine existing 'social relations of production' (Marx, 1976). In the present context, however, the point to be emphasised is the idea that this constant stream of technical innovations has been a perpetual source of disruption and disturbance in the music industry, posing a persistent threat to the established ways of exploiting musical materials to yield a profit. In fact, composers, publishers and record companies have waged a never-ending war in order to protect or establish copyrights on their material and collect royalties from its use.

For present purposes, the essential points are, firstly, that new technology has presented a constant threat to established interests in the music business, and, secondly, that the outcomes of the ensuing struggles for control have had a major effect on the nature of the music which becomes available to the public. Two examples must suffice. The first concerns the American Society of Composers, Artists and Publishers, formed in 1914 as a means of actually collecting the royalties from public performances which had been legally established in 1909. By the 1930s, the combined effects of recession and the rise of network radio had resulted in sharp falls in the sales of records and sheet music; to ASCAP members, radio was 'the business that killed music through repeated use' (Sanjek, 1988, vol. 3: 188). Naturally, radio stations did not see things that way, and indeed were reluctant to pay ASCAP any royalties at all, on the grounds that their use of ASCAP music was valuable free publicity. Moreover, a substantial number of musicians and songwriters, operating in fields such as country music, blues and jazz, had always been excluded from ASCAP membership by the publishing, theatre, and movie interests which had come to dominate the Society. In 1939 the National Association of Broadcasters organised a rival society, Broadcast Music Incorporated, to publish alternative, non-ASCAP, music.

Matters came to a head early in 1941, when the radio stations refused to accept a doubling of ASCAP royalties; from then on, only non-copyright and BMI music was broadcast. To the chagrin of ASCAP, the listening public got along without them very well. 'The ASCAP-BMI dispute', writes Shepherd, 'sowed the seeds for the decline of Tin Pan Alley as the major force in the production and marketing of white popular music ... the way for rock 'n' roll was undoubtedly prepared through broadcasts of country music and 'cover' versions of rhythm and blues' (Shepherd, 1982: 134–5). By October of 1941, ASCAP conceded defeat, and a transformation in the power structure of the music business was under way (Sanjek, 1988, vol. 3: 207; Hatch and Millward, 1987: 85). Thus a technological innovation – in this case national network radio – first can be seen to have presented a threat to established interests, then generated a tremendous upheaval in the industry, the outcome of which was a radical transformation of the character of the music made available through the media. In this case, too, it is evident that, as Peterson has argued, the emergence of rock 'n' roll is better understood as a result of specific alterations in the structure and power relations of the music business than as a reflection of more nebulous social or cultural changes (Peterson, 1990).

A second example of the disruption which can follow the introduction of new technology is provided by the case of the portable cassette player. It would be difficult to exaggerate the contribution which cassette technology has made to the proliferation of music as an aspect of social life in the late twentieth century. But the popularity of cassette players was viewed with great suspicion by the record companies, and when their sales started to slump in the late 1970s it was 'home taping' which was blamed. By this time, writes Sanjek in a telling phrase, the music industry was 'preoccupied' with 'public larceny and its cure' (1988, vol. 3: 593). Moreover, it is apparent that in countries with weak copyright laws (or none at all) 'pirated' cassettes constitute a major sector of the music business (Wallis and Malm, 1984). Record company interests have tried, in general with little success, to strengthen the copyright laws, or to have a levy imposed on sales of 'blank' tapes. As Frith puts it: 'if copyright laws express the tension between the need to spread culture and the need to reward authors than each new invention this century has increased the possibilities of public access while threatening authors' rewards' (1987c: 71).

However, and this is the thrust of Frith's argument, the relentless process of technological innovation has *again* transformed the situation, with the effect that:

> record companies' primary interest is no longer selling records to domestic consumers, but packaging multi-media entertainment, servicing programme-greedy satellite and cable companies, providing Hollywood soundtracks, seeking sponsorship deals, coming to terms with advertising agencies. (1987c: 72)

It is evident that these sorts of business activities are likely to be more attractive to record company executives than pandering to the whims of fourteen-year-olds; exploiting the rights they already hold, rather than trying to cope with a hugely unpredictable market and constantly changing technology. Frith's conclusion is uncompromising: 'For the music industry, the age of manufacture is now over. Companies (and company profits) are no longer organised around making *things*, but depend on the creation of *rights*' (1987c: 57).

Despite the new freedom of choice provided by cassette technology, then, it has been argued – just as by Adorno – that such freedom is essentially illusory: the bombardment of electronic messages to which we are all subject is not a response to genuine human needs and values but is rather determined by the interests of huge multinational media corporations in their endless quest for profits and market share. Interpretations of popular music have thus tended to reflect either an optimistic view, which sees in new technology the means of democratisation and empowerment, or a pessimistic one, regarding the individual in 'mass' society as little more than a docile consumer. It is possible, of course, that these contrasting views may reflect different aspects of the same situation. As we have seen, the modern music business exhibits certain characteristics of a 'dual economy' in which dominant, high-tech, mass production can coexist with small-scale, specialised and participatory projects. Indeed, as Lopes (1992) has suggested, such contrasting modes of organisation may coexist within the same company. It may be, then, that the worst fears of the 'mass society' theorists will not be realised, just as it may be too optimistic to suppose that technology will lead to an era of human emancipation. As Richard Middleton has put it, in contrasting the views of Adorno and Walter Benjamin: 'The main types of development taking place in the 1930's, and extended much further since, are *both* an immense strengthening of the possibilities of uniformity and control, *and* a broadening and democratising of opportunities' (1990: 67). So, by way of conclusion, it seems appropriate to consider some of the ways in which both the threats and the opportunities presented by the modern music business have been interpreted.

Interpretations
Until quite recently, critics and theorists of culture have – in so far as they have bothered with it at all – tended to be dismissive of modern popular music. For Adorno, as we have seen in Chapter 3, it was nothing but the repugnant commodity manufactured by one of the most pervasive branches of the 'culture industry', an effective means of inculcating an acceptance of the 'administered society'. Thus Jay has argued that Adorno's famous and intense dislike of what he took to be popular music stems not so much from intellectual or aesthetic elitism as his profound hostility to the perversion of human qualities which he regarded as inherent in such societies: 'the culture of the masses', in Adorno's view, 'was a wholly synthetic concoction cynically imposed on them from above' (Jay, 1984a: 119). In any case, there are plenty of other authors who have actively defended the distinction between 'high' and 'low' cultural forms, and who have then consigned popular music to the latter. An influential strand of critical writings, echoing the views of F. R. Leavis and often identified with the political right, deplores the brutalising effects of industrial society – splintering the main cultural traditions, trivialising forms of expression and fostering a destructive ideology of egalitarianism. Just as Leavis was concerned to defend what he

took to be the 'great tradition' of English literature, a similar great tradition of western (classical, composed) music is venerated and perpetuated in educational institutions and concert halls. From this perspective, popular music appears the very antithesis of 'art' – incapable by its very simplicity and standardisation of expressing anything other than trivial adolescent sentiments.

Such a conclusion is not confined, however, to thinkers of a conservative inclination. There are many on the left who echo, though not usually so vehemently, Adorno's strictures. Dave Harker, for example, noting that Irving Berlin's 'White Christmas' 'is the most popular song ever recorded in the English language' (135 million sales of various versions up to 1975 (1980: 42), goes on to argue that the song 'operates at the level of wish fulfilling fantasy' (1980: 46). Similarly, the effect of 'Rudolph the red nosed reindeer' may be 'the inculcation of servility' (1980: 48), and 'Winter wonderland' is seen to be 'articulating elements of the dominant ideology' (1980: 50). Such songs, from this point of view, are neither innocent nor neutral, acting – with a host of other inescapable cultural messages – to encourage an acceptance of the political and economic status quo, or to facilitate an escape into fantasies which may obliterate our consciousness of the harsh realities of competitive capitalism. As Harker points out, however, a simple 'conspiracy theory' in which workers are 'bamboozled' into an uncritical acceptance of capitalist ideology will not provide an adequate explanation for the complex ways in which such music has its effects, and he points to the ways in which elements of the 'dominant ideology' – in this case the bizarre cultural constellation revolving around 'Christmas' – may be 'appropriated, and transformed' by working-class people themselves (1980: 44–5). The idea is an important one, alerting us to the danger of assuming that the 'message' of songs is simply received and assimilated passively, and hinting at the ways in which meanings are actively, and collectively, constructed. This is a point to which we will return.

For the most part, however, early analyses of popular music by American sociologists tended to reinforce the views of the pessimistic critics, whether conservative or radical. In reviewing the situation in the 1950s, for example, Hirsch refers to 'the sociological consensus that mass entertainment and mass media programming serve to reinforce conventional morality, play a small role in motivating individuals towards organised social action, and present their audiences with a continuous flow of standardised trivia' (1971: 373). But, as we have seen, the conditions in which the endless succession of 'moon in June' love songs was created were disrupted with the rise of rock 'n' roll, and it was not long before pop songs and their singers came under attack precisely because they *did not* support conventional morality.

Rock 'n' roll songs and their singers were widely portrayed in the late 1950s as a threat to the values of civilised society, just as, twenty years later, the British tabloid press ran a series of stories emphasising the antisocial elements in the punk movement. The greatest reaction, however, was provoked by the emergence of 'progressive' rock as perhaps the main unifying strand in the youth counter-culture of the 1960s, when two particular political issues – civil rights for blacks and the involvement of America in the Vietnam war – were the basis of a more general cultural critique of capitalist industrial society. Rock 'n' roll, punk and progressive rock, then, are three instances of movements in popular music which have been generally understood as expressing explicit opposition to the 'dominant ideology'; moreover, in the last case, the very depth and commitment of the music has been used to justify the claims that it has approached the status of 'art'. Within the world of popular music, as Vulliamy has argued, musicians, critics, producers and fans routinely make distinctions – unlike the critics of 'mass culture' – among a wide range of styles and genres, and in particular between purely commercial 'pop' (musically often based on simplified aspects of the European classical tradition) and serious creative 'rock' (largely derived from African-American sources). Indeed, the latter is seen as the 'exact antithesis' of the former (1977: 187). 'Rock' music, then, while it is indubitably a part of popular culture, has been seen as both politically radical and serious, in the sense that 'art' is serious. The two aspects of this claim are apparent in the following description of Jimi Hendrix's famous version of the 'Star spangled banner' at the Woodstock Festival in 1969, during the Vietnam war:

> The ironies were murderous: a black man with a white guitar; a massive, almost exclusively white audience wallowing in a paddy field of its own making; the clear, pure, trumpet-like notes of the familiar melody struggling to pierce through clouds of tear-gas, the explosions of cluster-bombs, the screams of the dying, the crackle of the flames, the heavy palls of smoke stinking with human grease, the hovering chatter of helicopters ... One man with a guitar said more in three and a half minutes about that peculiarly disgusting war and its reverberations than all

the novels, memoirs and movies put together. (Murray, 1989: 24)

It is clear, too, that the claims that rock music should be accorded the status of 'art' have been widely accepted (though seldom within the classical music establishment). As Vulliamy argues, the extent and level of rock's acceptance may have much to do with the educational and social class status of its audience, and he echoes Bourdieu's point that dominant social groups have the power and the opportunity to legitimise cultural forms and practices (Bourdieu, 1971: 174–5). Thus Vulliamy suggests that 'those types of pop music which appeal to the more educated and high status groups (for example, progressive rock) will have the highest legitimation, whilst those that appeal to the lowest status groups (for example, reggae) will have the lowest' (Vulliamy, 1977: 193). Once again, then, we are led to see the stratification of music styles as the outcome of competition and conflict among social groups with widely differing resources – both material and symbolic – available to them. A further example is provided by Negus's analysis of the ways in which 'a particular faction of college-educated white males from the rock generation of the late 1960's and 1970s' have decisively influenced the artistic ideology and working practices of the music industry in Britain (1992: 155). The marginalisation of women, and of new, unfamiliar styles and artists, is the most obvious result; commercial difficulties, brought about by the failure to identify and respond to changing trends, may follow.

It is also apparent from these examples, once again, that the meanings of musical genres cannot be taken as inherent, but emerge out of the claims and counter-claims which are perpetually made by interested parties. For some, who have considerable influence on the educational and political elites, rock music is, at best, the noisy accompaniment to youthful immaturity; for others, who have many friends in the media, it aspires to the condition of art. Similarly, there are contradictory views, as we have seen, of the political significance of popular music, with some regarding it as an important means by which young people, in particular, are imbued with the values of the dominant ideology, and others emphasising its potentially radical effects.

What is important in the present context is not to elaborate on the infinite number of possible interpretations, nor to attempt to evaluate them, but to point out that they typically rest on certain assumptions about the nature of music and its effects. As we have already seen, such assumptions are often open to question. Indeed, in general, both the supporters and the opponents of popular music have tended to assume rather than demonstrate that it is effective in the ways they suggest. Early efforts to establish that pop songs reflected dominant social values often used the methods of 'content analysis', an apparently objective procedure in which the topics of song lyrics and the messages they conveyed were coded, and the results tabulated to show the distribution of topics and meanings and the pattern of changes in these. However, the method of content analysis presupposes, among other things, that songs have inherent meanings which can be objectively identified, that the meaning of lyrics can be defined independently of their music, and that such cultural messages are effectively transmitted and received. None of these assumptions is easy to defend. As a result of their studies in the late 1960s, Robinson and Hirsch concluded that teenage record-buyers 'may not impute the same meanings to a song's words as do social researchers and critics' (Hirsch, 1971: 377). Moreover, 'the vast majority of teenage listeners are unaware of what the lyrics of hit protest songs are about' (Robinson and Hirsch, 1972: 231). It is clear, too, that any analysis which neglects the *sound* of the records risks losing the essence of the phenomenon. It would be hard to explain why one record or singer is popular, while others flop, without taking some account of the kinds of sounds that they make. Thus, as Denzin has argued, song meanings cannot simply be inferred from the lyrics – after all, in popular music, 'frequently listeners focus on the beat and not the words' (1969: 1036).

Above all, as I have suggested at various points, people do not simply receive cultural messages in an unthinking way, but actively interpret what they see and hear. A properly sociological analysis, then, will focus not just on the 'art object', but on the meanings which people bring to it, and the interaction between the two. 'There may be little correspondence', writes Denzin, 'between the intended and the inputed meanings' of such objects: thus 'an art object, because it may not invoke the intended response in the audience, cannot be taken as *a priori* valid indicator of a group's perspective' (1969: 1036). Nor can it be assumed, as the cultural critics often have done, that pop songs, whether viewed as trivial schmalz or subversive propaganda, will have the powerful effects so frequently ascribed to them.

A similar conclusion emerges when we consider the fate of the 'alternative' culture of the 1960s and the 'progressive' rock music which provided its heartbeat. Murray makes the point concisely: 'while political establishments regarded sixties counterculture as a threat, the music industry simply treated it as a market, and even when the perceived threat evaporated, the market remained' (1989: 24). Despite the idealism of many musicians and fans, the endless succession of songs which denounced the 'military-industrial complex' and the evils of capitalism while exhorting people to adopt alternative lifestyles, subversive and revolutionary activities, the one indisputable effect of progressive rock was to enlarge the market and inflate record company profits. Clive Davis, boss of CBS at the time, talked of 'a tidal wave of new music and, by no coincidence ... a happy explosion on Columbia's bottom line, jumping sales profits from five to more than fifty million dollars a year by ... 1973' (quoted in Denisoff, 1986: 92). And, as we have seen, sales did rise dramatically – from $862 million in the USA in 1965 to $2,016 million in 1973 (Gronow, 1983: 66). The big music festivals such as Woodstock, and Monterey two years earlier, have often been regarded as ritual celebrations of the new counter-culture, and their significance much debated. For the record companies, they were confirmation of a new and lucrative trend, and Eliot captures the irony of the situation in his account of Monterey: 'Between sets of social relevance and political protest, musicians eagerly signed six-figure deals with recording industry reps as they sipped the finest champagne and smoked as much dope as was available' (Eliot, 1989: 140).

For some, the story is the familiar one in which a new, innovative and raw musical style, often identified with youthful protest, is inevitably 'co-opted' by the music business, which adulterates it and packages it in ways suitable for mass-market consumption: the transformation of 'revolt into style'. For others, however, the process has an even deeper and more sinister significance, representing the ability, and necessity, of industrial capitalism to turn virtually *anything* into a commodity, whose only value is its price-ticket. Even before the counter-cultural movement had developed very far, Herbert Marcuse, an early member of the Frankfurt school and then a professor of philosophy in the University of California, had warned of what he saw as the totalitarian nature of modern industrial society, in which, often through manipulation in the 'entertainment and information industry' (1964: 12) even radical ideas and activities were defused and rendered acceptable. 'In the realm of culture', wrote Marcuse, the new totalitarianism manifests itself precisely in a harmonising pluralism, where the most contradictory works and truths peacefully coexist in indifference (1964: 61). There could be few better examples of such coexistence than the aggressive marketing of records by bands whose music was supposed to be part of a revolutionary critique of society in general, the state and its capitalist institutions in particular (Harker, 1980: 104)

Marcuse, then, was led to talk of 'repressive tolerance' – the way in which apparent freedom of expression for critical and oppositional ideas was, in reality, a means not only of containing protest but profiting from it: 'what is proclaimed and practised as tolerance today, is in many of its most effective manifestations serving the cause of oppression' (1976: 301). The media, in particular, do not simply convey cultural messages, they 'carry with them prescribed attitudes and habits, certain intellectual and emotional reactions which bind the consumers more or less pleasantly to the producers, and, through the latter, to the whole' (1964: 12). And the freedom of choice allegedly exercised by these consumers is also a myth: they must choose from alternatives over which they have no control, and even before making their choices they are 'preconditioned' by 'the indoctrinating power of the media' (1964: 8). It is for this reason that Marcuse sees modern man as 'one-dimensional' – the ability to engage in genuinely critical, oppositional thought and action is progressively being undermined.

Theoretically, Marcuse's notion of 'repressive tolerance' can thus be used to explain the failure of the 1960s counter-culture to produce any fundamental social change, and its success in generating large profits for the record companies. It is, of course, a bleak diagnosis. Like Adorno, Marcuse argued that science and rationality have freed humanity from domination by the forces of nature, and from the irrational tyranny of church and monarchy, but only at the cost of establishing rationality and its consequence, the technological society, as themselves the new dominating powers. The means have become the ends, human values have been supplanted by technical ones, and there is a consequent need for a change 'from false to true consciousness' (1964: xiii). However, like other critical theorists, and unlike most Marxists, Marcuse did not have any great faith in the inevitability of revolutionary change or in the liberating potential of the proletariat. It seems, as various commentators have noted, that there is little hope of release from the totally alienated condition which Marcuse diagnosed, and his belief in the political potential of a coalition of radical students, racial minorities and Third World peasants is no longer shared by many.

But are members of modern societies alienated in the way Marcuse suggests, and, returning to our theme, does music play a major part in their subordination? Randall Collins bluntly denies it, arguing that it is the concept of alienation itself which is ideological (1986: 262), and that its use and appeal stem largely from 'upper class intellectuals' disdain for working class culture' (1986: 253). From a sociological perspective, Collins argues, we must recognise that there has never been a pre-capitalist or pre-industrial society where individuals lived and worked in an 'idyllically unexploited situation' (1986: 252). Such a notion is a Romantic myth, as is the assumption that there is some kind of pre-social, essential self which we can recover (1986: 259–60); moreover, as Durkheim suggested, it is impossible to envisage any kind or organised society in which individuals are not constrained by established structures, whether these are institutional, linguistic, or ideological (Collins, 1986: 260). It follows, then, that, from a strictly sociological point of view, it makes little sense to distinguish between 'false' and 'true' consciousness, as Marcuse, the critical theorists and many Marxists have done.

Indeed, Collins clearly identifies himself with those who emphasise the liberating, rather than the alienating, potential of technology, since, for perhaps the first time, individuals have the capacity to choose and produce aspects of their own symbolic environment:

> People who carry around cassette recorders or radios blaring out popular music are literally wrapping themselves in a cocoon of self-chosen meaning almost every moment of the day; in a premodern society they were subject to authoritarian scheduling of religious ceremonial, at which attendance was not free but enforced. (1986: 254).

Thus, in Collins's terms, the 'means of ritual production' are available to ordinary people to an unprecedented extent, though the significance of this is seldom noticed by intellectuals dismissive of 'popular culture', and committed to the bourgeois concept of 'the so-called high arts'.

It should be evident that the contrasting positions of Marcuse and Collins in respect of technology and popular culture echo many of the themes raised in the debate between Adorno and Walter Benjamin. For one, technology is dominant, beyond human control, and popular music is only one of the ways in which a docile labour force can be kept in mindless contentment. For the other, technological innovations have given ordinary people the potential to exert some control over their cultural environment, and choosing their own music is one of the ways in which they can affirm and celebrate their new-found sense of identity.

In turn, these positions are themselves reflected in recent interpretations of the popular music business. For Harker, as we have seen, the business can be understood only in terms of the operations of large industrial corporations and their hunger for profits: 'Under capitalism, it will remain the case that most artists (if not most of the audience) will have to be content to succumb to the commercial sausage-machine, and be compensated with cash' (1980: 111). Harker stresses the ways in which the market can be manipulated by the big companies (1980: 92); the music conveys elements of the 'dominant ideology', and the system can negate and defuse challenges to it (1980: 104). Similarly, in their book on the American music business, Chapple and Garofalo emphasise that its 'alternative' image masks a harsh reality:

> At the same time that the music itself, or the musicians, or the lifestyles they embrace may be, or appear to be, critical of the current system, they are in fact tied into that system in a material way. Through its operation they make their living and provide profits to numbers of corporations, many only vaguely linked to the music itself. (1977: 219).

In a later paper, Garofalo expressed some doubts about the 'classical' Marxist perspective evident in their earlier argument (1987: 77), but none the less was concerned to reiterate some of the ways in which the producers of popular music attempt – with some degree of success – to exert control over the consumers, by saturating the market with proven-formula records, fragmenting the audience, making only certain sorts of music available in certain formats and so on. In short, in response to the idea that consumers can invest cultural objects with their own meanings and thus 'reappropriate' them, Garofalo argues that 'the fragmented audience cannot reappropriate that to which it has no access (1987: 82). For Garofalo, the situation is best comprehended theoretically by utilising Gramsci's concept of hegemony, which, while emphasising the ways in which the ideas and values of the dominant class become seen as legitimate and even natural, still allows that these processes are unstable, never totally successful, never concluded and hence always open to challenge.

Garofalo's reservations about his earlier perspective, and the modifications in his position, were largely stimulated by the work of Simon Frith, specifically Frith's emphasis ' on the power of the consumer to reappropriate the music in unintended ways, to 'resignify' its meaning' (Garofalo, 1987: 77). As we have seen, musical communication, like all forms of human symbolic exchange, is indeterminate in the sense that it cannot be understood simply as the passage of an unambiguous message from a transmitter to a receiver. Between the 'stimulus' and the 'response' is a complex, though usually unnoticed, process of interpretation in which meaning is constructed on the basis of prior knowledge, commitments, experience and so on. It has long been known that even material which is deliberately designed to convey information clearly, or to act as propaganda, may be subject to a variety of interpretations rather than eliciting a uniform response (Merton, 1957: 510–12). Such interpretations are not random, as Durant points out (1984: 206), being subject to prevailing conventions and institutional arrangements; none the less, within the range of possible responses to rock songs,

> specific interpretations are created in connections and disconnections across the lyric, and in surrounding elements of fantasy and memory. In this way (and since there cannot be for any song a singular or exhaustive listening relation), responses engage and construct pleasures and desires as much in displacement and disconnection as they do in perceptions of coherence. (1984: 209)

Even the words, let alone the music, are 'polysemic' in that they both permit and generate a variety of meanings.

Moreover, it is evident that once we recognise the heterogeneity of the consumers of popular music, rather than treating them – as in theories of 'mass culture' – as an undifferentiated mass, different groups of people will be seen to respond in different ways; further, once it is acknowledged that the process of meaning-construction is above all a collective, rather than an individual, one, it is clear how various styles or genres of music may be redefined, reappropriated or in other words invested with meanings which reflect the interests and experiences of the consumers rather than the producers. Studies of subcultures, then, are in Frith's terms 'descriptions of the struggle for the sign: youth subcultures are said to make their own meanings, to *create* cultures in their acts of consumption' (1983: 57).

Moreover, as Frith points out, the general context in which all this takes place is that of leisure, as a distinct set of understandings and social practices, in capitalist industrial societies (1983: 250). Thus the rock music with which Frith is concerned must be understood not simply as a commodity but specifically as a leisure commodity (1983: 261). In this sphere of activity, there are certain particular tensions and contradictions which have the effect of reducing the ability of cultural producers to control the ways in which their works are used. Most obviously, it is the sphere in which people seek to recover their sense of identity and autonomy, sometimes in ways which represent a direct contrast to the norms and values of disciplined work: it is exactly in this context that rock can be thought of as 'the magic that can set you free' (quoted in Frith, 1983: 169). Moreover, it is in the nature of competitive capitalism that products will be marketed which have the effect of subverting the authorities' wish for disciplined work and orderly consumption. Drink, as Frith points out, has long been a contentious issue, and in general: 'There are capitalists ready to market anything that is potentially profitable, whatever its effects on morality, law and order, or everyone else's profits. If pornography, drugs, weapons, or revolution will sell, then they will be sold' (1983: 253–4)

Moreover, as we have seen, the unyielding logic of the market has meant that record companies have had to swallow and digest all sorts of material which they regarded as unpalatable, or subversive or both, and some of this – suitably repackaged – has achieved mass popularity. But, as Frith points out in a later paper, it is too simple just to see this process as one in which the original authenticity of the music is dissolved: 'The industrialisation of music cannot be understood as something which happens *to* music, since it describes a process in which music itself is made – a process, that is, which fuses (and confuses) capital, technical, and musical arguments (1988: 12). The cultural product is the record, not some prior song, or singer, or musical ideal, and it is this product which may be invested with meanings quite independently of the intentions or ambitions of composers, performers, producers and so on. Besides, as long as they are getting paid, why should they as professionals worry about its meaning, or the uses to which it may be put?

For all these reasons then – the apparently irrational nature of many leisure activities, the market compulsion to turn anything saleable into a commodity, and the 'industrial' process by which popular music is produced – the meaning of the music cannot be 'fixed' in any lasting way, whether by those who regard their songs as a celebration of the American Way of Life, or by those who wrote them in the hope of subverting it. (Just as Hendrix tore the 'Star spangled banner' to shreds, so several of the oppositional anthems of the progressive rock era are now oiling the wheels of the 'consumer society' through their use in mass-market advertising.) Such considerations highlight the ways in which the establishment of musical meaning must be understood as an active process of negotiation among parties who, however, have grossly unequal resources: few people, as the mass culture theorists constantly point out, can offer much resistance to the ideological bombardment they receive from the modern electronic media. As Marx put it in one of his most celebrated aphorisms, 'men make their own history, but they do not make it just as they please'. Thus for several authors the very significance of popular music is its power to release people from the grip of taken-for-granted realities, in Chambers's words to generate 'those innumerable points of individual affirmation that prick the routines we inherit' (1985: 206). More generally, innovations in popular music

> represent a real intrusion upon an earlier organisation of the music and its surrounding culture. Whenever a sound powerful enough to threaten existing arrangements emerges, previous interpretations, choices and tastes are put in question. In the successive cultural struggle, the powers of the record companies, radio and television, and the music press to shape the situation briefly surface from their daily and subconsciously administered obscurity. Aesthetic criteria and judgements that were once taken for granted have suddenly to be justified and defended. (1985: xi–xii)

For Chambers, then, popular music is a site upon which 'cultural struggle' can take place, and resistance to the dominant ideology collectively articulated. Similarly, Garofalo concludes that it is 'on this ever-changing terrain that the possibilities for counter-hegemonic practice arise' (1987: 89). And Frith's position, despite Garofalo's dissent, is not too far removed: 'Cultural politics are about situation and intention, and rock matters because it can change the situation

...rock *is* a form of capitalist culture, but that capitalist culture is what we're trying to understand and use, to subvert and enjoy' (1983: 269).

It is, as Frith recognises, an ambivalent conclusion, perhaps inevitably so given what he sees as the 'central tension' of the music – 'it is a source of pleasure that is both disturbing and relaxing' (1983: 268), thus generating a range of consequent 'contradictions'. Moreover, it is hardly surprising that thoughtful efforts to comprehend the popular music business should display some degree of ambiguity, given the tendency for it to develop the contrasting primary and secondary sectors discussed above (pp. 259–60). Nevertheless, from a sociological point of view, such conclusions are unsatisfactory. After all, as I have argued, the idea that cultural products and patterns must be understood as, above all, the outcome of constantly dynamic processes of conflict and competition should be the starting point rather than the end of analysis. And if this analysis is to be undertaken in a thoroughly sociological way, then it is the processes of conflict, competition, negotiation, compromise and so on – the 'struggle' – which must be the centre of attention. We will not, ever, uncover the 'real' meaning of rock or any other kind of music, whether by speculation or detailed examination of it as a cultural object, but we can hope to establish why and how some sorts of musical forms were established in particular places at particular times, how they were regarded by various contemporaries and by posterity, what consequences they had, and so on.

The point may serve to return us to some of the themes raised at the start of this book. In contrast to the assumptions of conventional western musicology, it was argued that the meaning and significance of music in other cultures has been found by anthropologists to be inseparable from the context of conventions and social practices in which it is embedded. It now appears that the same point must also be made in relation to popular music – the music of the vast majority of the people – in modern, industrial, capitalist societies. 'Is the individual song the only, or even the basic unit of meaning', asks Richard Middleton, 'rather than larger discursive categories (genre, style, performers, album, radio programme, and so on) and the context provided by social practices (dancing, driving, partying, discussing)?' (1990: 114).

In short, the meaning of popular music is to be found in, and only in, the uses to which it is put. (This conclusion may be uncongenial to most critics, theorists of and commentators on the music, but it is at least consistent with a powerful current of philosophical opinion: 'the meaning of a word', says Wittgenstein, 'is its use in the language' (1958: 20.) The sociological implications of such a view have been spelled out by Denzin: 'The study of artistic productions must be returned to those situations where meaning is given [to] those objects termed 'art' ... It is here in the status and political battles between individuals that art takes on meaning' (1969: 1037). In the sphere of 'popular' culture, Denzin draws attention to the activities of powerful groups and influential people in attempting to confer prestige and favourable images on certain individuals and products, often in competition with the claims of others. Similarly, as we have seen, other authors have pointed to the ways in which 'official' meanings may be subverted, ironicised or reappropriated.

While the uses to which popular music can be put are indeterminate, there has been some agreement about its potent role in contemporary culture. Once cultural products, or artists, have been legitimised, says Denzin, they provide for individuals 'a point around which social relationships and images of self can be built' (1969: 1037), and Richard Peterson refers to a tradition of studies which examine the ways in which 'popular culture helps to build or manipulate the master-symbols through which the world is viewed and in terms of which people act (in Denisoff and Peterson, 1972: 6). Echoes of this view are also apparent in Simon Frith's answer to the question 'Why do songs have words?'. Recognition that music has no inherent meaning, that people rarely appreciate the intended 'message' of a song, and that the words themselves may be trivial and unrealistic, does not, according to Frith, therefore make them insignificant. After all, in terms of sales and general popularity, vocal music is much preferred to instrumental. It is lyrics which give songs their social *use*, in the sense of 'access to songs' (1987b: 101). 'Pop love songs don't "reflect" emotions ... but give people the romantic terms in which to articulate and so experience their emotions' (1987b: 102). This, Frith argues, is the use which pop songs have for people – and in their use, I have suggested, is their meaning.

This, however, is to raise a further issue, and one which once again returns us to the discussion in Chapter 1, in which I mentioned the enormous and unprecedented demand for music in the industrialised countries of the twentieth century. Why should this remarkable cultural phenomenon have occurred? After all, in such societies, music is generally considered to belong to the emotional, irrational sphere of human experience, in marked contrast to the scientific and rational principles which have come to dominate. Other areas of 'irrational' thought – religion and magical beliefs for example – have withered in this ideological climate. So why is there such a demand for music? Or, in other words, why do people find it so useful?

An important part of the answer may lie in the diagnoses of the condition of modern society offered by the classical sociological theorists. For Marx, as we have seen, industrial capitalism had produced nothing less than the total alienation of human beings from their real essence, reducing the relationships between them to little more than the 'cash nexus'. Similarly, Durkheim saw that the relentless division of labour and the modern 'cult of the individual' could lead to a society so fragmented that the result was *anomie* – the pathological social condition in which people no longer feel any sense of attachment to the community, its values or its norms. And it was Max Weber's bleak fear that the combined forces of technical and economic rationality would come to dominate human life, trapping people in an 'iron cage' of bureaucratic regulation, and producing an incapacity to think in any ways other than the scientific, the logical and the impersonal. Echoes of such views are evident, as we have seen, in the work of Adorno, among many others, and in general one of the fundamental themes of both social theory and modern literature has been the idea of the loss of community, leading to the isolation and powerlessness of individuals in modern society, and their consequent search for meaning, identity and a sense of belonging.

It is perhaps in this context that modern popular music is best understood, offering above all an affirmation of personal identity and a sense of membership in a larger collectivity. From this point of view, the phenomenon is more sociological than musical, and the pedantic objections of the cultural critics that pop music is trivial and escapist are not so much reactionary and elitist as irrelevant. As Iain Chambers puts it, 'it is not changes in popular culture that threaten to reduce us to an undifferentiated mass, but the structure and organisation of work. At this point, modern leisure is transformed into the very fabric of personal life, the most significant context in which we have the chance to affirm our "selves" ' (1985: 17). Thus, although the modern music business can be understood only as the outcome of a lengthy process of historical development, its position and significance in contemporary culture are unprecedented. In the modern world, it provides one of the ways in which people can live in communities, however amorphous, illusory or fantastic they turn out to be. The close-knit communities of Romantic mythology have given way to the quest for a sense of belonging, which is satisfied less and less by locally-based networks of family and friends. Instead, individuals may seek to identify themselves with symbolic entities – the organisations which employ them, for example, or football teams or cultural heroes and the trappings of fashionable lifestyles. It is in this context that popular music becomes a useful commodity, and we can begin to understand something of the unprecedented demand for it. We can also begin to understand the otherwise perplexing fact that people tend to remain loyal to the music which involved them during their formative years – why the Rolling Stones, once regarded as the embodiment of rebellion, still draw audiences who have grown up (and grown comfortable) with them, and why other wizened, grey-haired old rockers can still evoke powerful feelings of youthful liberation. What they, and the dominant figures in other genres, have to offer, above all, is a sense of who you are and where you belong.

An adequate understanding of music in modern culture, then, must go beyond the music itself, seeing it as a part – perhaps an essential one – of a much wider cultural configuration. Indeed, those very aspects of popular music which have so irritated its critics – its repetitiveness, simple structures, predictable resolutions, 'warm' major chords and so on – may be precisely what give it its power and popularity, providing a sense of security, of involvement, of experiences easily shared. Significantly, a similar conclusion emerged from John Blacking's study of music in a very different culture: the Venda make music, he noted, when their material needs have been met: their music-making occurs 'when their stomachs are full because, consciously or unconsciously, they sense the forces of separation inherent in the satisfaction of self-preservation, and they are driven to restore the balance with exceptionally cooperative and exploratory behaviour' (1977: 101). In both simple and complex societies, it seems, there is an awareness that the satisfaction of material needs tends to pull people apart from each other, and it is often in music that they seek to repair the social damage.

Bibliography

Abercrombie, N., Hill, S. and Turner, B. (1980) *The Dominant Ideology Thesis*. London: Allen & Unwin.

Adler, J. (1975) 'Innovative art and obsolescent artists', in *Social Research*, 42.

Adorno, Theodor W (1967) *Prisms*. London: Neville Spearman.

—— (1973a) *Philosophy of Modern Music*. London: Sheed & Ward (First published 1948.)

—— (1973b) *Negative Dialectics*. London: Routledge.

—— (1976a) *Introduction to the Sociology of Music*. New York: Seabury Press. (First published 1962.)

—— (1976b) 'Alienated masterpiece: the Missa Solemnis', *Telos*, 28. (first published 1959.)

—— (1978) 'On the social situation of music', in *Telos*, 35 (First published 1932.)

—— (1988) 'The ageing of the new music', *Telos*, 77 (First published 1973.)

—— (1990) 'On popular music', in S. Frith and A. Goodwin, eds, *On Record*. London: Routledge. (First published 1941.)

—— (1991a) 'On the fetish character in music and the regression of listening', in T. W. Adorno, *The Culture Industry* ed. J. M. Bernstein. London: Routledge. (first published 1938.)

—— (1991b) 'Marginalia on Mahler', *Telos*, 87. (First published 1936.)

—— (1992) *Quasi Una Fantasia: Essays on Modern Music*. London: Verso. (First published 1963.)

Adorno, T. W. and Horkheimer, M. (1979) *Dialectic of Enlightenment*. London: Verso. (First published 1944.)

Albertson, C. (1975) *Bessie: Empress of the Blues*. London: Abacus.

Allis, W. (1994) 'The Manchester Gentlemen's Concerts', research in progress, Department of Sociology, University of Manchester.

Althusser, L. 'Ideology and ideological state apparatuses (1972)'; in B. Cosin, ed., *Education: Structure and Society*. London: Penguin.

Anderson, B. (1983) *Imagined Communities*. London: Verso.

Anderson, R. J. Hughes, J. A. and Sharrock, W. W. (1986) *Philosophy and the Human Sciences*. London: Croom Helm.

Arts Council of Great Britain (1991) *Arts and Cultural Activities in Great Britain*. London: Arts Council.

Backus, J. (1970) *The Acoustical Foundations of Music*. London: John Murray.

Bailey, P., ed. (1986) *Music Hall: The Business of Pleasure*. Milton Keynes: Open University Press.

Baldry, H. (1981) *The Case for the Arts*. London: Secker & Warburg.

Baldwin, J. D. (1986) *George Herbert Mead: A Unifying Theory for Sociology*. Beverly Hills: Sage.

Ballantine, C. (1994) *Music and its Social Meanings*. New York: Gordon & Breach.

Barnes, J. (1987) *Early Greek Philosophy*. Harmondsworth: Penguin.

Basie, Count (W.) (1986) *Good Morning Blues* (as told to Albert Murray). London: Heinemann.

Becker, H. S. (1963) *Outsiders*. New York: Free Press.

—— (1974) 'Art as collective action', *American Sociological Review*, 39.

—— (1976) 'Art worlds and social types' *American Behavioural Scientist*, 19.

—— (1978) 'Arts and crafts', *American Journal of Sociology*, 83.

—— (1982) *Art Worlds*. Berkeley: University of California Press.

—— (1989) 'Ethnomusicology and sociology: a letter to Charles Seeger', *Ethnomusicology*, 33.

—— (1992) Review of Shepherd, *Music as Social Text*, *Contemporary Sociology*, 21.

Becker, H. S. and Geer, B. (1958) 'The fate of idealism in medical school', *American Sociological Review*, 23.

Becker, H. S. and McCall, M. M., eds (1990) *Symbolic Interactionism and Cultural Studies*. Chicago: Chicago University Press.

Bendix, R. (1962) *Max Weber: An Intellectual Portrait*. New York: Anchor Books.

Benjamin, W. (1973) 'The work of art in the age of mechanical reproduction', in *Illuminations*, ed. H. Arendt. London: Fontana.

Bennett, T., Frith, S., Grossberg, L., Shepherd, J. and Turner, G. eds (1993) *Rock and Popular Music: Politics, Policies, Institutions*. London: Routledge.

Berger, P. and Luckmann, T. (1971) *The Social Construction of Reality*. Harmondsworth: Penguin. (First published 1966).

Berlioz, H. (1970) *The Memoirs of Hector Berlioz*. St Albans: Panther Books.

Berman, R. A. and D'Amico, R. (1991) 'Popular music from Adorno to Zappa', *Telos*, 87.

Binder, A. (1993) 'Constructing racial rhetoric: media depictions of harm in heavy metal and rap music', *American Sociological Review*, 58.

Biocca, F. A. (1988) 'The pursuit of sound: radio, perception and utopia in the early 20th century', *Media, Culture and Society*, 10.

Black, M. (1961) *The Sociological Theories of Talcott Persons*. Englewood Cliffs: Prentice-Hall.

Blacking, J. (1976) *How musical Is Man?* London: Faber.

Blaukopf, K. (1992) *Musical life in a Changing Society*. Portland: Amadeus Press. (First published 1982.)

Bloch, E. (1985) *Essays on the Philosophy of Music*, Cambridge: Cambridge University Press.

Blumenfeld, H. (1984) 'Ad vocem Adorno', *Musical Quarterly*, 70.

Blumer, H. (1969) *Symbolic Interactionism: Perspective and Method*. Berkeley: University of California Press.

Boehmer, K. (1980) 'Sociology of music', in S. Sadie, ed., *The New Grove Dictionary of Music and Musicians*. London: Macmillan.

Booth, M. W. (1978) 'Popular music', in M. T. Inge, ed., *Handbook of American Popular Culture (vol. I)*. Westport, Conn. Greenwood Press.

Bourdieu, P. (1971) 'Intellectual field and creative project', in M. F. D. Young, ed., *Knowledge and Control*. London: Collier-Macmillan.

—— (1977) *Outline of a Theory of Practice*. Cambridge: Cambridge University Press. (First published 1972.)

—— (1984) *Distinction: A Social Critique of the Judgement of Taste*. London: Routledge. (First published 1979.)

—— (1990) *In Other Words: Essays Towards a Reflexive Sociology*. Cambridge: Polity.

Bourdieu, P. and Passeron, J.-C. (1990) *Reproduction: In Education, Society and Culture*. London: Sage: (First published 1970.)

Boyes, G. (1993) *The Imagined Village: Culture, Ideology and the English Folk Revival*. Manchester: Manchester University Press.

Bradley, D. (1992) *Understanding Rock 'n' Roll: Popular Music in Britain 1955–1964*. Buckingham: Open University Press.

Brogan, H. (1985) *The Longmans History of the United States of America*. London: Longman.

Broyles, M. (1991) 'Music and class structure in antebellum Boston', *Journal of the American Musicological Society*, 44.

Bucher, R. and Strauss, A. L. (1961) 'Professions in process', *American Journal of Sociology*, 66.

Büchmann-Møller, F. (1990) *You Just Fight for your Life: The Story of Lester Young*. New York: Praeger.

Buck-Morss, S. (1972) 'The dialectic of T. W. Adorno', *Telos*, 14.

—— (1977) *The Origin of Negative Dialectics*. Hassocks: Harvester Press.

Burns, T. and Stalker, G. M. (1961) *The Management of Innovation*. London: Tavistock.

Cairns, D. (1990) *Berlioz, vol. I: The Making of an Artist*. London: Sphere.
Cerulo, K. A. (1984) 'Social disruption and its effects on music – an empirical analysis', *Social Forces*, 62.
Chambers, I. (1985) *Urban Rhythms – Pop Music and Popular Culture*. London: Macmillan.
Chanan, M. (1981) 'The trajectory of Western music or, as Mahler said, the music is not in the notes', *Media, Culture and Society*, 3.
Chapple, S. and Garofalo, R. (1977) *Rock 'n' Roll is Here To Pay*. Chicago: Nelson Hall.
Chomsky, N. (1971) 'Recent contributions to the theory of innate ideas', in J. R. Searle, ed. *The Philosophy of Language*. Oxford: Oxford University Press.
—— (1972) *Language and Mind*. New York: Harcourt, Brace, Jovanovich.
Citron, M. J. (1993) *Gender and the Musical Canon*. Cambridge: Cambridge University Press.
Cohen, S. (1991) *Rock Culture in Liverpool*. Oxford: Oxford University Press.
Coker, W. (1973) *Music and Meaning*. London: Collier-Macmillan.
Collier, J. L. (1981) *The Making of Jazz: A Comprehensive History*. London: Macmillan.
—— (1987) *Duke Ellington*. London: Michael Joseph.
Collins, J. and Richards, P. (1989) 'Popular music in West Africa', in S. Frith, ed. *World Music, Politics, and Social Change*. Manchester: Manchester University Press.
Collins, R. (1975) *Conflict Sociology*. New York: Academic Press.
—— (1980) *The Credential Society*. New York: Academic Press.
—— (1986a) *Weberian Social Theory*. Cambridge: Cambridge University Press.
—— (1986b) *Max Weber: A Skeleton Key*. Beverly Hills: Sage.
Cooke, D. (1959) *The Language of Music*. Oxford: Oxford University Press.
Coulter, J. (1979) *The Social Construction of Mind*. London: Macmillan.
Cressey, P. G. (1932) *The Taxi Dance Hall: A Sociological Study in Commercialised Recreation and City Life*. Chicago. University of Chicago Press.
Dahlhaus, C. (1982) *Aesthetics of Music*. Cambridge: Cambridge University Press (First Published 1967.)
—— (1983) *Foundations of Music History*. Cambridge: Cambridge University Press. (First published 1967.)
—— (1989) *Nineteenth Century Music:* Berkeley: University of California Press.
Dannen, F. (1991) *Hit Men: Power Brokers and Fast Money Inside the Music Business*. London: Vintage.
Davies, J. B. (1978) *The Psychology of Music*. London: Hutchinson.

Dearling, R. and C. (with B. Rust) (1984) *The Guinness Book of Recorded Sound*. Enfield: Guinness.

Denisoff, R. S. (1986) *Tarnished Gold: The Record Industry Revisited*. New Brunswick: Transaction Books.

Denisoff, R. S. and Peterson, R. A. eds (1972) *The Sounds of Social Change: Studies in Popular Culture*. Chicago: Rand-McNally.

DeNora, T. (1986) 'How is extra-musical meaning possible? Music as a place and space for "work" ', *Sociological Theory*, 4.

—— (1991) 'Musical patronage and social change in Beethoven's Vienna', *American Journal of Sociology*, 92.

—— (1992) Review of Shepherd, *Music as Social Text*, *Sociological Review*, 40.

Denzin, N. K. (1969) 'Problems in analysing elements of mass culture: notes on the popular song and other artistic productions', *American Journal of Sociology*, 75.

—— (1992) *Symbolic Interactionism and Cultural Studies*. Cambridge, Mass.: Blackwell.

DiMaggio, P (1986) 'Cultural entrepreneurship in 19th century Boston: the creation of an organisational base for high culture in America', in R. Collins, J. Curran, N. Garnham, P. Scannell and C. Sparks, eds, *Media, Culture, and Society: A Critical Reader*. London: Sage.

Durant, A. (1984) *Conditions of Music*. London: Macmillan.

Durkheim, E. (1915) *The Elementary Forms of Religious Life*. London: Allen & Unwin. (First published 1912.)

—— (1952) *Suicide*. London: Routledge. (First published 1897.)

—— (1964) *The Division of Labour in Society*. New York: Free Press. (First published 1893.)

—— (1965) *Montesquieu and Rousseau*. Ann Abor: University of Michigan Press. (Written in 1892.)

Ehrlich, C. (1976) *The Piano: A History*. Oxford: Oxford University Press

—— (1985) *The Music Profession in Britain since the Eighteenth Century*. Oxford: Oxford University Press.

Elias, N. (1993) *Mozart: Portrait of a Genius*. Cambridge: Polity.

Eliot, M. (1990) *Rockonomics: The Money Behind the Music*. London: Omnibus Press.

Ellis, A. J. (1885) 'On the musical scales of various nations', *Journal of the Society of Arts*, 33.

Eno, B. (1983) 'Excursions in the electronic environment', *Downbeat*, June.

Etzkorn, K. P. (1964) 'Georg Simmel and the sociology of music', *Social Forces*, 43.

Faulkner, R. R. (1971) *Hollywood Studio Musicians*. Chicago: Aldine.

—— (1973a) 'Orchestra interaction: some features of communication and authority in an artistic organisation', *Sociological Quarterly* 14.

—— (1973b) 'Career concerns and mobility motivations of orchestra musicians', *Sociological Quarterly*, 14.

—— (1983) *Music on Demand: Composers and Careers in the Hollywood Film Industry*. New Brunswick: Transaction Books.

Feather, L. (1988) *The Jazz Years: Earwitness to an Era*. London: Picador.

Featherstone, M., Hepworth, M. and Turner, B. S. (1991) *The Body: Social Process and Cultural Theory*. London: Sage.

Feher, F. 'Weber and the rationalisation of music', *International Journal of Politics, Culture and Society*, 1/2, winter.

Feld, S. (1984) 'Sound structure as social structure', *Enthnomusicology*, September.

Fink, M. (1989) *Inside the Music Business – Music in Contemporary Life*. New York: Schirmer Books.

Finkelstein, S. (1948) *Jazz: A People's Music*. New York: Citadel Press.

Fraser, W. H. (1981) *The Coming of the Mass Market, 1850–1914*. London: Macmillan.

Freund, J. (1968) *The Sociology of Max Weber*. London: Allen Lane.

Frith, S. (1983) *Sound Effects: Youth, Leisure and the Politics of Rock 'n' Roll*. London: Constable.

—— (1986) 'Art versus technology – the strange case of popular music', *Media, Culture and Society*, 8.

—— (1987a) 'The making of the British record industry, 1920–64', in J. Curran, J. Smith and P. Wingate, eds, *Impacts and Influences*. London: Methuen.

—— (1987b) 'Why do songs have words?' in A. L. White, ed., *Lost in Music: Culture, Style and the Musical Event*, London: Routledge.

—— (1987c) 'Copyright and the music business', *Popular Music*, 7/1.

—— (1988) *Music for Pleasure: Essays in the Sociology of Pop*. Cambridge: Polity.

—— (1990) 'Picking up the pieces' in Frith, ed., *Facing the Music*. London: Mandarin.

Firth, S., ed. (1990) *Facing the Music*. London: Mandarin.

Frith, S. and Goodwin, A., eds (1990) *On Record*. London: Routledge.

Galbraith, J. K. (1967) *The New Industrial State*. London: Hamish Hamilton.

Gammon, V. and S. (1991) 'From "Repeat and Twiddle" to "Precision and Snap": the musical revolution of the mid-nineteenth century', in T. Herbert, ed., *Bands: The Brass Band Movement in the Nineteenth Centuries*. Buckingham: Open University Press.

Garfield, S. (1986) *Expensive Habits: The Dark Side of the Music Industry*. London: Faber.

Garfinkel, H. (1967) *Studies in Ethnomethodology*. Englewood Cliffs: Prentice-Hall.

Garofalo, R. (1987) 'How autonomous is relative: Popular music, the social formation, and cultural struggle', *Popular Music*, 6(1).

Gelatt, R. (1954) *The Fabulous Phonograph*. London: Cassell (2nd edn 1977).

Gerth, H. H. and Mills, C. W. (1948) *From Max Weber* London: Routledge.

Giddens, A. (1987) 'Structuralism, post-structuralism, and the production of culture', in A. Giddens and J. H. Turner, eds, *Social Theory Today*. Cambridge: Polity.

Gillett, C. (1983) *The Sound of the City: The Rise of Rock 'n' Roll*. London: Souvenir Press. (Revised ed.)

Gilmore, S. (1988) 'Schools of activity and innovation', *Sociological Quarterly* 29.

—— (1990) 'Art worlds: developing the interactionist approach to social organisation', in H. S. Becker and M. M. McCall, eds, *Symbolic Interaction and Cultural Studies*. Chicago: University of Chicago Press.

—— (1992) 'Tradition and novelty in concert programming: bringing the artist back into cultural analysis', paper presented to the American Musicological Society Conference, Pittsburgh, November.

Gould, S. J. (1984) *The Mismeasure of Man*. London: Pelican.

—— (1990) *Wonderful Life: The Burgess Shale and the Nature of History*. London: Hutchinson Radius.

Granzotto, G. (1986) *Christopher Columbus: The Dream and the Obsession*. London: Collins.

Green, L. (1988) *Music on Deaf Ears: Musical Meaning, Ideology and Education*. Manchester: Manchester University Press.

Gronow, P. (1983) 'The record industry: the growth of a mass medium', *Popular Music*, 3.

Grossberg, L. (1993) 'Rock and the new conservatism', in T. Bennett, S. Firth, L. Grossberg, J. Shepherd and G. Turner, eds, *Rock and Popular Music: Politics, Policies, Institutions*. London: Routledge.

Hall, S. and Jefferson, T., eds (1976) *Resistance Through Rituals: Youth Subcultures in Post-War Britain*. London: Hutchinson.

Hamm, C. (1983) *Music in the New World*. New York: Norton.

Hammond, J. (1981) *John Hammond on Record*. Harmondsworth: Penguin.

Hanslick, E. (1891) *The Beautiful in Music*. London: Novello, Ewer & Co. (First published 1854.)

Harker, D. (1980) *One For the Money*. London: Hutchinson

—— (1985) *Fakesong: The Manufacture of British 'Folksong', 1700 to the Present Day*. Milton Keynes: Open University Press.

Harman, A. (1988) *Mediaeval and Early Renaissance Music*. London: Barrie & Jenkins.

Harman, A. and Milner, A. (1988) *Late Renaissance and Baroque Music*. London: Barrie & Jenkins.

Harvey, E. (1967) 'Social change and the jazz musician', *Social Forces*, 46.

Hatch, D. and Millward, S. (1987) *From Blues to Rock: An Analytical History of Pop Music*. Manchester: Manchester University Press.

Hatch, D. and Watson, D. R. (1974) 'Hearing the blues: an essay in the sociology of music', *Acta Sociologica*, 17.

Headington, C. (1977) *A History of Western Music*. St Albans: Paladin.

Held, D. (1980) *Introduction to Critical Theory*. Berkeley: University of California Press.

Heritage, J. (1984) *Garfinkel and Ethnomethodology*. Cambridge: Polity.

Hesse, H. (1972) *The Glass Bead Game*. Harmondsworth: Penguin. (First published 1943.)

Hildebrandt, P. (1988) *Pianoforte: A Social History of the Piano*. London: Hutchinson.

Hirsch, P. M. (1971) 'Sociological approaches to the pop music phenomenon', *American Behavioural Scientist*, 14.

Hobsbawm, E. J. (1987) *The Age of Empire*. London: Weidenfeld & Nicolson.

Hobsbawm, E. J. and Ranger, T. (1983) *The Invention of Tradition*. Cambridge: Cambridge University Press.

Honigsheim, P. (1968) *On Max Weber* New York: Free Press.

Horkheimer, M. and Adorno, T. (1973) *Aspects of Sociology*. London, Heinemann.

Horwood, W. (1983) *Adolphe Sax, 1814–1894: His Life and Legacy*. Baldock: EPL.

Hughes, E. C. (1958) *Men and Their Work*. New York: Free Press.

Hughes, M. (1989) 'The Duc d'Elgar: making a composer a gentleman', in C. Norris, ed., *Music and the Politics of Culture*. London: Lawrence & Wishart.

Hullot-Kentor, R. (1988) 'Popular music and Adorno's "The aging of the new music" ', *Telos*, 77.

—— (1991) 'The impossibility of music: Adorno, popular and other music', *Telos*, 87.

Hutchinson, R. (1982) *The Politics of the Arts Council*. London: Sinclair Browne.

Jameson, F. (1971) *Marxism and Form*. Princeton: Princeton University Press.

—— (1990) *Late Marxism: Adorno, or the Persistence of the Dialectic*. London: Verso.

Janik, A. and Toulmin, S. (1973) *Wittgenstein's Vienna*. New York: Simon & Schuster.

Jay, M. (1973) *The Dialectical Imagination*.

—— (1984a) *Adorno*. London: Fontana.

—— (1984b) *Marxism and Totality*. Cambridge: Polity.

Katovich, M. A. and Reese, W. A. (1993) 'Postmodern thought in symbolic interaction: reconstructing social enquiry in light of late-modern concerns', *Sociological Quarterly*, 34.

Keil, T. (1969) *Tiv Song*. Chicago: Chicago University Press.

Kingsbury, H. (1991) 'Sociological factors in musicological poetics', *Ethnomusicology* 35.

Kofsky, F. (1970) *Black Nationalism and the Revolution in Music*. New York: Pathfinder.

Korner, S. (1971) *Fundamental Questions of Philosophy*. Harmondsworth: Penguin.

Laing, D. (1985) *One Chord Wonders*. Milton Keynes: Open University Press.

Lang, G. E. and K. (1988) 'Recognition and renown: the survival of artistic reputation', *American Journal of Sociology*, 94.

Langer, S. (1969) *Philosophy in a New Key*. Cambridge, Mass.: Harvard University Press. (First published 1942.)

Lemert, E. M. (1972) *Human Deviance, Social Problems, and Social Control*. Englewood Cliffs: Prentice-Hall.

Leppert, R. and McClary, S. (1987) *Music and Society: The Politics of Composition, Performance and Reception*. Cambridge: Cambridge University Press.

Lerdahl, F. and Jackendoff, R. (1983) *A Generative Theory of Tonal Music*. Cambridge, Mass.: MIT Press.

Litweiler, J. (1985) *The Freedom Principle: Jazz after 1958*. Poole: Blandford Press.

Lloyd, A. L. (1975) *Folk Song in England*. St Albans: Paladin.

Lomax, A. (1968) *Folk Song Style and Culture*. New Brunswick: Transaction Books.

—— (1970) 'Song structure and social structure', in M. C. Albrecht, J. H. Barnett and M. Griff, eds, *The Sociology of Art and Literature*. New York: Praeger.

Long, N. (1958) 'The local community as an ecology of games', *American Journal of Sociology*, 64.

Lopes, P. D. (1992) 'Innovation and diversity in the popular music industry, 1969–1990', *American Sociological Review*, 57.

Lukes, S. (1975) *Emile Durkheim: His Life and Work*. Harmondsworth: Penguin.

McCarthy, A. (1974) *The Dance Band Era*. London: Spring Books.

McClary, S. (1987) 'The blasphemy of talking politics in Bach year', in R. Leppert and S. McClary, eds. *Music and Society: the Politics of Composition, Performance and Reception*. Cambridge: Cambridge University Press.

—— (1991) *Feminine Endings: Music, Gender and Sexuality*. Minneapolis: University of Minnesota Press.

MacDonald, M. (1976) *Schoenberg*. London: J. M. Dent.

MacIntyre, A. C. (1958) *The Unconscious: A Conceptual Analysis*. London: Routledge.

McLuhan, M. (1967) *Understanding Media: The Extensions of Man*. London: Sphere Books.

Magee, B. (1988) *Aspects of Wagner*. Oxford: Oxford University Press. 2nd ed.

Manicas, P. T. (1987) *A History and Philosophy of the Social Sciences*. Oxford: Blackwell.

Manuel, P. (1988) *Popular Music of the Non-Western World*. Oxford: Oxford University Press.

Marcuse, H. (1964) *One Dimensional Man:* London: Routledge.

—— (1976) 'Repressive Tolerance', in P. Connerton, ed. *Critical Sociology*. Harmondsworth: Penguin.

Martindale, D. and Riedel, J. (1958) 'Max Weber's sociology of music', introduction to M. Weber, *The Rational and Social Foundations of Music*: South Illinois University Press.

Marx, K. (1959) *Economic and Philosophical Manuscripts of 1844*. Moscow: Progress Publishers.

—— (1976) Preface to *A Contribution to the Critique of Political Economy*. Peking: Foreign Languages Press. (Written 1857–8.)

Marx, K. and Engels, F. (1974) *The German Ideology*. London: Lawrence & Wishart. (Written 1845–6.)

Matthews, D. (1985) *Beethoven*. London: Dent.

Mead, G. H. (1934) *Mind, Self, and Society*. Chicago: University of Chicago Press.

Mellers, W. (1988) *The Sonata Principle*. London: Barrie & Jenkins.

Melly, G. (1972) *Revolt Into Style*. Harmondsworth: Penguin.

Merquior, J. G. (1986) *Western Marxism*. London: Paladin.

Merriam, A. P. (1964) *The Anthropology of Music*. Evanston: Northwestern University Press.

Merriam, A. P. and Mack, R. W. (1960) 'The jazz community', *Social Forces*, 38.

Merton, R. K. (1957) *Social Theory and Social Structure*. New York: Free Press. (2nd ed.)

Messinger, G. S. (1985) *Manchester in the Victorian Age*. Manchester: Manchester University Press.

Meyer, L. (1970) *Emotion and Meaning in Music*. Chicago: Chicago University Press. (First published 1956.)

Middles, M. (1993) *Red Mick: The Biography of Muck Hucknall of Simply Red*. London: Headline.

Middleton, R. (1990) *Studying Popular Music*. Milton Keynes: Open University Press.

Mills, C. W. (1959) *The Sociological Imagination*. New York: Oxford University Press.

Mitzman, A. (1985) *The Iron Cage*. New York: Knopf.

Monk, R. (1991) *Ludwig Wittgenstein: The Duty of Genius*. London: Vintage.

Moore, J. (1992) 'The social construction of a feminist musical aesthetic', paper presented at the American Musicological Society Conference, Pittsburgh, November.

Morgan, A. (n.d.) Sleeve note for MCA LP 0052.045 (The Count Basie Quartet).

Murray, A. (1978) *Stomping the Blues*. London: Quartet Books.

Murray, C. S. (1989) *Crosstown Traffic: Jimi Hendrix and Post-War Pop*. London: Faber.

Murrells, J. (1984) *Million Selling Records from the 1900's to the 1980's*. London: Batsford.

Negus, K. (1992) *Producing Pop: Culture and Conflict in the Popular Music Industry*. London: Edward Arnold.

Nettl, B. (1973) *Folk and Traditional Music of the Western Continents*. Englewood Cliffs: Prentice-Hall.

Norris, C., ed. (1989) *Music and the Politics of Culture*. London: Lawrence & Wishart.

Oakes, G. (1980) Introduction to Georg Simmel, *Essays on Interpretation in Social Science*. Totowa: Rowman & Littlefield.

Orlov, (1981) 'Towards a semiotics of music', in W. Steiner *The Sign in Music and Literature*. Austin: University of Texas Press.

Ostransky, L. (1978) *Jazz City: The Impact of Our Cities on the Development of Jazz*. Englewood Cliffs: Prentice-Hall.

Paddison, M. (1982) 'The critique criticised: Adorno and popular music', *Popular Music*, 2.

Parsons, T. (1961) 'The point of view of the author', in M, Black ed. *The Social Theories of Talcott Parsons*. Englewood Cliffs: Prentice-Hall.

Pearsall, R. (1976) *Popular Music of the 20's*. Newton Abbot: David & Charles.

Peterson, R. A. (1976) 'The production of culture: a prolegomenon', *American Behavioural Scientist*, 19.

—— (1990) 'Why 1955? Explaining the advent of rock music', *Popular Music*, 9.

Peterson, R. A. and Berger, D. G. (1971) 'Entrepreneurship in organisations: evidence from the popular music industry' *Administrative Science Quarterly*, 16.

—— (1975) 'Cycles in symbol production: the case of popular music', *American Sociological Review*, 40.

Piston, W. (with DeVoto, M.) (1978) *Harmony*. London: Gollancz. (Revised ed.) (First published 1941.)

Poggi, G. (1988) 'Max Weber's conceptual portrait of feudalism', *British Journal of Sociology*,

Pratt, R. (1990) *Rhythm and Resistance: Explorations in the Political Uses of Popular Music*. New York: Praeger.

Read, O. and Welch, W. L. (1976) *From Tin Foil to Stereo*. Indianapolis: Howard W. Sams (2nd ed.)

Regev, M. (1994) 'Producing artistic value: the case of rock music', *Sociological Quarterly*, 35.

Riesman, D. (1950) *The Lonely Crowd*. New Haven: Yale University Press.

Robbins Landon, H. C. (1990) *1791: Mozart's Last Year*. London: Flamingo.

Robinson, J. and Hirsch, P. M. (1972) 'Teenage response to rock and roll protest songs in R. S. Denisoff and R. A. Peterson, eds., *The Sounds of Social Change: Studies in Popular culture*. Chicago: Rand-McNally.

Rochberg-Halton, E. (1982) 'Situation, structure and the context of meaning', *Sociological Quarterly*, 23.

Rocher, G. (1974) *Talcott Parsons and American Sociology*. London: Nelson.

Rock, P. (1979) *The Making of Symbolic Interactionism*. London: Macmillan.

Rogan, J. (1989) *Starmarkers and Svengalis*. London: Futura.

Rose, G. (1978) *The Melancholy Science: An Introduction to the Thought of T. W. Adorno*. London: Macmillan.

Rosen, C. (1972) *The Classical Style*. London: Faber.

—— (1976) *Schoenberg*. Glasgow: Fontana.

Rosenthal, D. H. (1992) *Hard Bop: Jazz and Black Music 1955–1965*. New York: Oxford University Press.

Russell, D. (1983) 'Popular musical culture and popular politics in the Yorkshire textile districts, 1880–1914' in J. K. Walton and J. Walvin, eds, *Leisure in Britain, 1780–1939*. Manchester: Manchester University Press.

—— (1987) *Popular Music in England 1840–1914: A Social History*. Manchester: Manchester University Press.

Said, E. (1992) *Musical Elaborations*. London: Vintage.

Sanjek, R. (1988) *American Popular Music and its Business*, 3 vols. New York: Oxford University Press.

Scannell, P. (1981) 'Music for the multitude? The dilemmas of the BBC's music policy, 1923–1946', *Media, Culture and Society*, 3.

Schafer, R. M. (1977) *The Tuning of the World*. Bancroft: Arcana Editions.

Schoenherr, U. (1991) 'Adorno and jazz: reflections on a failed encounter', *Telos* 87.

Schuller, G. (1968) *Early Jazz: Its Roots and Musical Development*. New York: Oxford University Press.

Schütz, A. (1964) 'Making music together', in *Collected Papers, vol. 2*. The Hague: Martinus Nijhoff.

—— (1972) *The Phenomenology of the Social World*. London: Heinemann.

(First published 1932.)

Scott, D. B. (1990) 'Music and sociology for the 1990's: a changing critical perspective,' *Musical Quarterly* 74.

Scruton, R. (1983) *The Aesthetic Understanding*. Manchester: Carcanet Press.

Shepherd, J. (1982) *Tin Pan Alley*. London: Routledge.

—— (1987) 'Towards a sociology of musical styles' in A. L. White, ed., *Lost in Music: Culture, Style and the Musical Event*. London: Routledge.

—— (1991) *Music as Social Text*. Cambridge: Polity.

Shepherd, J. and Vulliamy, G. (1994) 'The struggle for culture: a sociological case study of a national music curriculum', *British Journal of the Sociology of Education*, 15.

Shepherd, J., Virden, P., Vulliamy, G. and Wishart, T. (1977) *Whose Music? A Sociology of Musical Languages*. London: Latimer.

Sheppard, A. (1987) *Aesthetics: An Introduction to the Philosophy of Art*. Oxford: Oxford University Press.

Shibutani, T. (1962) 'Reference groups and social control' in A. M. Rose ed. *Human Behaviour and Social Processes*. London: Routledge.

Silbermann, A. (1963) *The Sociology of Music*. London: Routledge. (First published 1957.)

Sloboda, J. (1985) *The Musical Mind: the Cognitive Psychology of Music*. Oxford: Clarendon Press.

Small, C. (1980) *Music–Society–Education*. London: John Calder. (2nd ed.)

—— (1987) 'Performance as ritual: sketch for an enquiry into the true nature of a symphony concert', in A. L. White ed., *Lost in Music: Culture, Style and Musical Event*. London: Routledge.

Solie, R. A. (1991) 'What do feminists want? A reply to Peter van den Toorn', *Journal of Musicology*, IX.

Solie, R. A., ed. (1993) *Music and Difference: Gender and Sexuality in Music Scholarship*. Berkeley: University of California Press.

Southern, E. (1983) *The Music of Black Americans*. New York: Norton. (2nd ed.)

Steiner, W., ed. (1981) *The Sign in Music and Literature*. Austin: University of Texas Press.

Stewart, R. (1991) *Boy Meets Horn*. Oxford: Bayou Press.

Storr, A. (1993) *Music and the Mind*. London: Harper Collins.

Stradling, R. (1989) 'On shearing the black sheep in Spring: the repatriation of Frederick Delius' in C. Norris ed., *Music and the Politics of Culture*. London: Lawrence & Wishart.

Strauss, A. L. (1959) *Mirrors and Masks*. Glencoe: Free Press.

—— (1978) *Negotiations: Varieties, Contexts, Processes and Social Order*. San Francisco: Jossey-Bass.

Stravinsky, I. (1942) *Poetics of Music: In the Form of Six Lessons*. Cambridge,

Mass.: Harvard University Press.

Sturrock, J. (1986) *Structuralism*. London: Paladin.

Subotnik, R. R. (1976) 'Adorno's diagnosis of Beethoven's late style', *Journal of the American Musicological Society*, 29.

—— (1991) *Developing Variations*. Minneapolis: University of Minnesota Press.

Sudnow, D. (1978) *Ways of the Hand*. London: Routledge.

Supicic, I. (1987) *Music in Society: A Guide to the Sociology of Music*. New York: Pendragon Press.

Tar, Z. (1985) *The Frankfurt School: The Critical Theories of Max Horkheimer and T. W. Adorno*. New York: Schoken Books.

Taylor, R. (1983) *Richard Wagner: His Life, Art, and Thought*: London: Panther Books.

Temperley, N. (1987) 'Tonality and the bourgeoisie', *Musical Times*, December.

Toll, R. C. (1982) *The Entertainment Machine: American Show Business In The Twentieth Century*. New York: Oxford University Press.

Turner, G. (1992) *British Cultural Studies: An Introduction* London: Routledge.

Turner, J. H. and Beeghley, L. (1981) *The Emergence of Sociological Theory*. Homewood: Dorsey Press.

UMI (1983) *Catalogue of Doctoral Dissertations on Music*, 1861–1983 and (1987) 1983–1986.

van den Toorn, P. C. (1991) 'Politics, feminism, and contemporary music theory', *Journal of Musicology*, IX.

van der Merwe, P. (1989) *Origins of the Popular Style*. Oxford: Oxford University Press.

Volpacchio, F. (1991) 'The unhappy marriage of music and emancipation', *Telos*, 87.

Vulliamy, G. (1977) 'Music and the mass culture debate' in J. Shepherd, P. Virden, G. Vulliamy and T. Wishart, eds, *Whose Music? A Sociology of Musical Languages*. London: Latimer.

Vulliamy, G. and Shepherd, J. (1984) 'Sociology and music education: a response to Swanwick', *British Journal of the Sociology of Education*, 5.

—— (1984b) 'The application of a critical sociology to music education', *British Journal of Music Education*, 1.

—— (1985) 'Sociology and music education: a further response to Swanwick', *British Journal of the Sociology of Education*, 6.

Weber, Marianne (1975) *Max Weber: A Biography*. New York, John Wiley. (First Published 1926.)

Weber, Max (1930) *The Protestant Ethic and the Spirit of Capitalism*. London: Allen & Unwin. (First published 1904–5.)

—— (1948a) 'Class, status party', in H. H. Gerth and C. W. Mills, eds, *From*

Max Weber. London: Routledge.

—— (1948b) 'Science as a vocation' in H. H. Gerth and C. W. Mills, *From Max Weber*. London: Routledge.

—— (1958) *The Rational and Social Foundations of Music*. Carbondale: Southern Illinois University Press. (First published 1921.)

—— (1978) *Economy and Society*, ed. G. Roth and C. Wittich. Berkeley: University of California Press.

—— (1978b) 'Value judgements in social science' in W. G. Runciman, ed. *Weber: Selections in Translation*. Cambridge: Cambridge University Press.

Weber, W. (1975) *Music and the Middle Class*. London: Croom Helm.

—— (1977) 'Mass culture and the reshaping of European musical taste, 1770–1870', *International Review of the Aesthetics and Sociology of Music*, 8.

Weeks, P. A. D. (1990) 'Musical time as a practical accomplishment: a change in tempo', *Human Studies*, 13.

—— (1994) 'A rehearsal of a Beethoven passage: an analysis of its constituent talk', unpublished paper, Dept of Sociology, St Thomas University, Canada.

Westby, D. L. (1960) 'The career experience of the symphony musician', *Social Forces* 38.

Whitcomb, I. (1972) *After the Ball: Pop Music from Rag to Rock*. Harmondsworth: Penguin.

—— (1987) *Irving Berlin and Ragtime America*. London: Century.

White, A. L., ed. (1987) *Lost in Music: Culture, Style, and the Musical Event*. London: Routledge.

Williams, A. (1989) 'Music as immanent critique: stasis and development in the music of Ligeti', in C. Norris ed., *Music and the Politics of Culture*. London: Lawrence & Wishart.

Williams, B. (1978) *Descartes: The Project of Pure Enquiry*. Harmondsworth: Penguin.

Williams, R. (1983) 'Culture' in D. McLellan, ed. *Marx: The First Hundred Years*. London: Fontana.

Wills, G. and Cooper, C. L. (1988) *Pressure Sensitive: Popular Musicians Under Stress*. London: Sage.

Wilmer, V. (1977) *As Serious As Your Life*. London: Quartet.

Wittgenstein, L. *Philosophical Investigations*. Oxford: Blackwell. (2nd ed.)

Wood, A. (1975) *The Physics of Music*, revised by J. M. Bowsher. London: Chapman & Hall. (First published 1944.)

Wright, D. F. (1975) 'Musical meaning and its social determinants', *Sociology* 9.

Wrong, D. (1961) 'The oversocialised conception of man in modern sociology', *American Sociological Review*, 26.

Zimmerman, D. and Pollner, M. (1971) 'The everyday world as a phenomenon', in J. D. Douglas ed *Understanding Everyday Life*. *London:* Routledge.

Index